# Hot Metal

*Hot Metal*

Published by The Conrad Press in the United Kingdom 2020

Tel: +44(0)1227 472 874
www.theconradpress.com
info@theconradpress.com

ISBN 978-1-913567-05-7

Typesetting and Cover Design by: Charlotte Mouncey, www.bookstyle.co.uk
Cover image created with authors own images

The Conrad Press logo was designed by Maria Priestley.

Printed and bound in Great Britain by Clays Ltd, Elcograf S.p.A.

# Hot Metal

a motorcycle adventure ride
like no other

# JIM TAYLOR

# ALSO BY JIM TAYLOR:

*Wheels of Steel –*
a rollercoaster ride of adventures by road and by rail

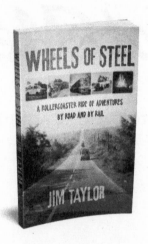

Published by The Conrad Press.
ISBN 978-1-911546-60-3
£9.99 Also available as an ebook

# INTRODUCTION

*Hot Metal* is the first of my works: originally written as a biographical project with the title *Years of the Horse*, it was intended as a tribute to the thirty-six motorcycles I've owned and worked on during my lifetime.

Presented in three parts (or books) researched from diaries and journals I had written, over a thirty-year-period, each book aims to lead the reader through a progression of incidents and adventures ranging from the mundane to the insane.

It is about youth culture in the 1980s motorcycle scene, discovering the world on two wheels in the 1990s and putting it all into perspective post millennium.

As well as the fantastic, perhaps even lunatic, experiences I am sharing here, the many notable characters that made the early years as mad as they were, become as important to the story as the motorcycles themselves.

Jim Taylor March 2020

# CONTENTS

# PREFACE

It's July 2018...

The XT 660 pulled out of the driveway, exhaust popping, and we were off. A few twists of the throttle and the farm was behind me, I'd made the 200 yards straight, and was breaking heavily for the blind junction that slips around the corner bank of the pub beer garden.

Downhill now, trees meeting overhead in a tunnel of green, as I lean it one side to the other; eyeballs trained on the emerging curve of tarmac – and there's the straight, a hundred yards clear and open for the taking. Wrist back and neck forward for the sunshine ride.

The car is halfway out of that hidden driveway before the woman even looks and I know I'm going to hit it; there's no time to think, stuff just happens.

My front wheel is through as the gap closes, and I touch the rear brake to whip the back around, skipping the tyre off the kerbstone and I've made it! Loose gravel, bollards and more kerbstones. I can't brake, I can't lean, and I'm heading for the ditch; nothing for it but to lay her down and hope for the best.

This book is dedicated to every young greaser who grew up in the 1970s and 80s, lived and breathed motorcycles, couldn't afford the one they dreamed of, so went with whatever was out there and they could afford to keep on the road.

It's for all those kids who started out with a screwdriver and a pair of mole grips, stripped every thread, snapped a few spark plugs and did their own spray jobs with a can they'd nicked from the local garage. But most of all it's about a bunch of teenagers from a small village, getting around and having fun. It's about rivalries and camaraderie, denim and leather.

# BOOK ONE
## *Genesis*

<sup>4</sup> *And the Serpent Said Unto the Woman, Ye shall not Surely die.*

<sup>5</sup> *For God doth know that in the day ye eat thereof, then your eyes shall be opened, and ye shall be as gods, Knowing good and evil.*

*Chapter III verses 4-5*

# CHAPTER ONE

## *Milk and alcohol*

My earliest recollections and involvements with motor-cycles include: my dad taking me up the main field of our little farm on the back of a Lambretta he had bought in the early seventies, when I was about seven years old. The scooter slid from under us and we hit the pasture. I remember we were wearing brand new Stadium open-faced crash helmets with peaks and chinstraps. I still have the original blue one.

Then there was Dad's old BSA A10 sidecar rusting away amongst a pile of junk and stinging nettles in the back yard with just its tyre showing. Dad's old mates turning up on different bikes over the years and Uncle Chris' motorbike shop in Tontine street (just off Folkestone sea-front) with the smell of petrol, rubber tyres and oil changes.

For us in the day it was Evel Knievel, Eddy Kidd, Steve McQueen, Kickstart, the Fonz and CHIPS, and of course Marlon Brando in *The Wild One*.

I learned to ride on Sam Lillywhite's bright red ex-post office Puch, which actually looked like a motorbike, as it had a proper petrol tank unlike the later Maxi step-through. It had pedals and a throttle cable that stuck, causing the engine to race, every time I tried to slow up on the slopes at the old Brabourne chalk quarry where we rode it as thirteen-year-olds. I had at least two terrifying crashes before I learned to keep calm and use the brakes rather than panic at the noise and lay it down amongst the brambles and scrap metal.

I was fifteen years old and the year was 1982. I had been working Saturday mornings for several months and saving up, so that when I was sixteen, I would be able to go out and buy a motorcycle. Dad had taken me to a small bike shop in Tontine street, which was the main drag for the seaside town of Folkestone in Kent. I had set my heart on a beautiful white Yamaha TY50 Enduro; that was my dream, but the price was beyond the scope of my savings and would still be out of reach until the following summer at best.

As it happened, I got the opportunity to buy, for twenty quid from a local nutter, a Suzuki B120, P reg. as I remember. It was badly neglected and not fit for the road. Dad was keen on the idea, as I would be able to get used to controlling a bike within the safety of our six-acre smallholding. This place included woods, ponds and fields, dotted with sheep and cows and discarded equipment amongst the stinging nettles like ploughs, rollers and disc harrows.

I thought I would have this motorbike all ready and brought back to road worthiness, so that once I was seventeen, I could take my test on it. It was a maroon colour with white side panels, looked and smelt like a real bike and it was mine.

The very next day I found I couldn't start it due to a fuel problem. The day after that it did start and ran, until I stalled it, but then no amount of kicking would raise a splutter. I discovered that if I left it for four or five hours it would start again and run fine for a short time, then stop and refuse to start again. Dad did help me by opening and cleaning the carburettor and the suspicion was that it must be flooding due to wrong adjustments, or some other mystery reason.

The following day we cleaned the petrol tap filter and this confirmed that it had not been flooding but starving, as once the filter inside the tank became clogged again, with a decade of tank rust, the engine would stop, due to the petrol in the float chamber being used up and it would take hours for more to seep through and re-fill the chamber. This discovery had been made after we removed the sediment bowl from the petrol tap and found it to be absolutely full of silted rust particles. No matter what position the tap lever was in, no fuel would flow. We had emptied this sediment bowl out, but it would keep filling with sediment until we had the tank off and shook that out with gravel from our driveway.

I had been completely ignorant of the mechanisms of a petrol engine at age fifteen. My only experience having been draining the carburettor on my Dad's Ferguson tractor prior to starting, to flush the tractor vaporising oil mix from the system until it filled back up with neat petrol. Then it would start and as long as we could get the engine warm enough before the small petrol tank ran dry, we could switch over to TVO, which was four parts central heating oil, to one part petrol, before getting down to business. We used to use an old trench coat draped across the front grill to deprive the radiator of cold air and bring the switching temperature up quicker.

I had bought the bike on Tuesday October 26th and spent three days sorting out the fuel system. Below are the subsequent diary entries I made verbatim, during the week following on.

### Monday 1st November

*I cleaned out the air filter and recharged the battery. Put two bolts in the seat, two in the petrol tank but one sheared. Put some air in front tyre and a dust cap on.*

### Tuesday 2nd November

*Dad and I inspected the points and I bought a new oil cap to replace the plastic bag jammed in the hole and a screw for the points cover panel.*

### Wednesday 3rd November

*I lost the screw I bought yesterday and broke the choke cable.*

### Thursday 4th November

*I took the front mudguard off but sheared two nuts in the process. I polished up the points side cover and the clutch side cover.*

### Friday 5th November

*I bought another screw (for points cover) and a choke cable.*

To put things into comparison; Saturday 6th's entry reads:

*Found some burnt-out firework cylinders for re-filling with gunpowder, fell in the pond. Down in Cheriton, three girls wolf whistled at me and I waved.*

I had lived quite a sheltered life up to about this time. I was quite shy and had not worked out how to chat up, or be chatted up by, the fairer sex. I did know lots about playing in the woods with guns, hunting rabbits with ferrets and making explosives though. I used to mix my own gunpowder in the loft of our decaying old bungalow; the space up there had become my bedroom. Saltpetre, charcoal and sulphur, a recipe given me by one of my dad's old mates, a brilliant but casually unreliable back street mechanic called Martin. I rarely got the mixture right but did occasionally manage to fire marbles from the musket I made out of a length of gas pipe. In metalwork at school they had allowed me to make a model cannon, using the metal lathe. I never got to test it, as whilst drilling out the barrel, I managed to snap the school's extra-long drill bit before it reached the powder hole where the fuse would go. I hid the broken bit rather than own up. It had been agreed the cannon could only have a superficial muzzle hole, as of course it was only supposed to be an ornament.

At the beginning of the year 1983, those of us in the fifth year who were hoping to soon be riding motorcycles on the road were able to do *The Star Rider* course during school hours. This was conducted by Mr Rutt, I think he might have taught physics. He rode a bike into school every day and walked around in big motorcycle boots and leathers with a big moustache.

Mrs Rutt was a teacher there too, at Brockhill & St Leonards Secondary Modern in Saltwood; she had nice legs. I thought it odd that, although the course was open to all 5th years (about 150 teenagers), it got you out of lessons and was free, there were only a handful of us who took up the opportunity. I learned two things in particular: firstly, when approaching a T-junction with lose grit on the road surface: don't pull the front brake. I did and the bike slid away from me to the great amusement of all, except Mr Rutt. Neither the Fizzy nor I were damaged, but it was embarassing and I didn't forget the technique. Secondly, we were shown that if you bump-started a two-stroke engine by getting a group of teenagers to push it backwards in gear, once you dumped the clutch, you could actually ride the thing in reverse. They don't teach kids useful things like that anymore, I'm sure.

On the 1st of August, '83, following a tip from my mate Dave Bishopp, I bought my first road legal bike: a bright green Honda CB50 for £170, including a full face black crash helmet. The bike was late seventies, with a four-stroke engine, cable disc front brake and a tool-box incorporated into the stylish seat moulding at the back: more useful as a sandwich box actually, which is what it resembled. It cost me all the money I had in savings from my Saturday jobs and I had to raid my piggy bank for the last eight or ten quid it cost for road tax, then wait another week before I could fill it up with petrol.

I was mobile at last and all I wanted to do was go places – any places – and be seen to have arrived. I was acknowledged by the older lads in the village and respected by the younger ones and I was pretty sure that some of the girls were impressed too. One way of getting noticed, I discovered, was to follow the school bus, the infamous no. 68 double-decker, back into Sellindge, and pull clutch wheelies right up against the back of it when it stopped to let people off along Swan lane. I was hanging around with a half-caste kid (that was how we said it then) called Aggi at the time, who had just got himself a Fizzy. The FS1-E was an unrestricted super-light 50cc bike with pedals; people who had these were always leaning flat down on the skinny tank and claiming they could get 50 mph out of them. It was odd looking with an air-filter drum bigger than the cylinder head. Aggi, had the metal side panels custom sprayed with a palm tree design which wasn't quite right.

We would hang out down at the brook, which was a swampy wooded common land area, where the Sellindge village kids gathered before we looked old enough to get into the local pubs. If we went in one at a time with Dave Bish, or Craig Gammon, and kept a low profile we were all right; they were close to eighteen and quite tall.

Dave rode a red TS100 Suzuki trail bike, he called it 'The goddess of evil' and painted BESS on the exhaust silencer, he would ride it up the park in his moccasins.

Craig was one of those kids who always had something fast and cheap and spent time tuning his bikes to get an extra five mph out, before he wrecked them.

We would turn up at the Dukes head, put our crash hats on the bar and order – 'half a mild please Ron.' I didn't quite have enough that first time I went in, so Ron counted out my coins and said 'You want thirty two pence worth of beer do you?' and I was in; Joan Jet and the Blackhearts was playing on the juke box, *I love Rock and Roll.*

# CHAPTER TWO

## *Juvenile years*

It wasn't long before I started having little scrapes out there on the road. I remember Mr Rutt telling us that a learner bike was 'fast enough to get you into trouble but not fast enough to get you out of it.' I hadn't perfected the leaning technique – at 32 mph downhill, (40, free-wheeling with the clutch in) it was hardly worth while trying; I'd just open it up, steer it and brake hard at the last minute.

I mostly only used the back brake: due to fear of another front wheel skid, and of course the fact that skidding to a halt beside a group of people made an impression. I remember racing around the loop of the Greenfields council estate, where you could usually find an audience, and coming so close to smashing into the back of a parked car down at the bottom, that the top of my left foot caught the end of the car's exhaust pipe, bending it round against itself and leaving a C shaped gouge in the leather of my ten-hole Doctor Martens boot. That really did hurt but I never showed it of course.

My first Motorcycle accident (that I count) occurred on 15th November, on the way back from Hythe after school. I took the narrow, winding back road of Kennet lane, between Stanford and Sellindge. There are some small hills and sharp bends, hemmed in by high hedges the whole way through and they are all blind. I was taking the lane like a private road, not anticipating that I might meet anything coming round the bends – like a big blue flat-back transit, taking up three quarters of the road width, as it swung round a bend at the foot of a steep rise. I can't have been doing more than 25 mph, but there was no room to lean into the bend and offer my head to the blue beast. No hope of braking either (downhill on the gravely edge), so I let the bike take a jump over the grass verge that fell away to a field opening and I followed it.

The damage was a snapped front brake lever housing. I was a bit un-nerved by this incident, but it was a good lesson: there were to be many more over the following few years, to the point that I came to expect such events and expect to keep surviving them virtually unscathed.

The effort and expense of repairing crash damage proved more of a deterrent than the prospect of incurring minor injuries. A visit to Cat Motorcycles in Ashford evidenced that my pocket money and clothing allowance, plus the forty-five pence a day I was getting from selling on my school dinner token, would not allow me to have the broken bit replaced with a brand new Honda part. So, I was bike-less for a while until Chris Carey, Dad's old school friend who ran the bike shop in Tontine Street, repaired it for me with some aluminium welding. I had to grind and file the piece down so that it would take the lever, but I was back on the road again quicker than it seemed.

Living in the Stowting area in Kent as a teenager, with no public transport and few neighbours, it was essential to at least have a bicycle, which to avoid ridicule had to be a racing bike (ten gears) with cow horns (three foot wide trials handlebars). My push-bike had a good set of cow-horns with motorbike grips. I had also covered my racing saddle with horrid 1970s fake brown fur, which had a texture more like matted Jacob sheep 'daggings' than actual fur. I thought it looked good though and it was more comfortable than the original hard plastic saddle, except for when the bike had been out in the rain. The custom of removing any mudguard longer than seven to ten inches in its entirety, coupled with the habit of speeding deliberately through any muddy patches at the side of the road, ensured the consistent presence of soil particles towards the back of my seat covering, which didn't look so good and obviously transferred this matter to the back of my jeans. It was also good street-cred to spray-can parts of your bike frame. Mine was multi-coloured with some crimson, yellow and black, which merged unattractively into a not excessive, but uniformly rebellious, non-pattern. So, for the short while that my Honda was laid up, the old youth club wheels came out.

The 49cc motorcycle, ideally a Suzuki ER50 Trail or Yamaha RD50, depending on the biking style you wanted to follow, with the image completed by either a Belstaff wax jacket or leather with tassels, propelled a boy into that adolescent age-of-discovery stage in one fell swoop. You could park up outside the door of a pub in the next village where they didn't already know your age, go in and order a half of whatever you knew the name of, or just go for larger, bitter or cider. If the barman seemed to be studying you, there was the safety option of requesting 'Just a 'shandy', please, I'm driving.' That was less embarrassing than being refused service and doing the walk of shame.

The gang that would meet up down at the bit of common land we called 'the brook' comprised of me, Aggi, Dave Bish,

Craig Gammon, John Read and Darren Gandhi, who all rode together at that time. There were a few others who had bikes and would turn up sometimes, but their contribution was limited. We only had three channels on the TV then and video players were relatively new. Dave had one in his household and my parents had recently bought a Betamax. We would have group viewings, at either house and I used to ride down into Hythe on a Friday, after school, to hire a couple of films (usually certificate 18), which I could keep all weekend and bring back on Monday after school. Titles like *Texas Chainsaw Massacre, American Werewolf in London, the Wanderers* and *Mad Max*. I've watched that brilliant road warrior film a dozen times or more and I'm not finished with it yet.

There were drawbacks to this new mobility though, without anything I could really call an income. Other than alcohol, petrol was a vital commodity and I remember my shame when I decided to go sneaking round the back of the council houses on Brook lane one evening, and siphoned a tank of petrol from one of the cars parked out in the dark – John, Aggi and Gammon were doing it all the time, but they didn't seem to feel guilt like I did. It was easy and generally cars didn't have locking fuel caps. I was only desperate enough to do this on three occasions and I learnt my lesson on the last one the following summer when, out of ignorance, I siphoned a gallon or so of diesel and put it in my Yamaha DT100 (which I loved) and destroyed the top end. That was poetic justice. Anyway, a mouthful of three-star is easier to get over than a mouthful of diesel.

By January '84, my Honda had been neglected to the point that it was almost un-rideable, with the exhaust down-pipe separating from the silencer, to surprisingly rapid corrosion and me not checking nuts and bolts. I quite liked this to start with as it sounded like a tank. The chain and sprockets were on the way out due to clutch abuse and lack of oil and adjustment. The brakes were inefficient and the battery failing, as well as the rear tyre wearing out in patches from me keep skidding it.

The front brake lever was bent into a J shape from an incident where I had attempted to make a right turn off the A20 at Sandling junction without looking properly. I'd turned right into the side of a van that was overtaking me at speed just on the middle line. I had struck the side of the van with the ball of my brake lever, amazingly just bending it and leaving me stopped in the middle of the road. The bloke said I hadn't indicated, well I don't know, but this second potentially fatal incident taught me two things: I was obviously not supposed to die, and the fact of whoever has the right of way is an irrelevance, because it is the motorcyclist's personal responsibility to avoid accidents and stay alive.

So, the rules of the road didn't matter unless the police were present. Getting pulled up by the cops was a common occurrence and it was often only through their interference that I would get around to bringing my bike back into roadworthy condition. Displaying L plates was the thing I most resented and we were always cutting them down or fixing them in such a way that they could not easily be seen. We resented 'the bronze' and always strived to have one or two illegal points to our machines, boasting about how many times we'd got pulled over.

One Sunday evening in late January '84, I was riding home

from Folkestone wrapped up in a scarf, wartime dispatch rider's coat and gauntlets that had belonged to my grandad. Back then they didn't salt all town roads at the hint of a snowflake and a heavy frost had settled. It was my first time out on the ice, and I didn't realise that riding safely at normal speed, then braking before a junction was not the way to do it. I only touched the rear brake and the bike went from under me. And it did hurt, I had no padding and a fall on the ice is a slam, no matter what speed you are doing. I classed this as my second bona-fide accident, as it had me and machine sliding on down the road independent of each other. There would be plenty more of that before I got old enough to think I might be vulnerable. I sold that first Honda as soon as it was fit, as at seventeen I could move up to the next level.

# CHAPTER THREE

## *Mean streets*

Diary entries from June '84 read:

**Tuesday 12th June**
*I bought Marilyn's Yamaha 100cc Enduro for £198.00, I am poor now.*

**Wednesday 13th June**
*I rode my bike to school & rode it to Folkestone & around. I took it up to 60 mph on the A20. I bought my first gallon of petrol for many months & filled her up with 2 stroke oil.*

**Friday 15th June**
*I managed to break the speedo cable on my bike. I have fitted a two-tone back mud flap on my bike.*

**Saturday 16th June**
*I rode down Folkestone & met the boys.*

So began a short lived and dangerous period of freedom and mobility, made available to me after the purchase of my cherished metallic green DT100 Enduro. It wasn't very fast but was quite rugged, with only a small tank. My almost daily trips to Folkestone town to hang out and doss about with my new set of ne'er-do-well mates required almost constant topping up of that tank.

I was doing seasonal farm work in between final O-level exams and school study work, but my mind was not on good results and career options, but rather on that petrol tank that was getting me to all the irresponsible summer parties and must-be-seen-at rebel hangouts. I was into a mixture of early punk rock, two-tone and reggae and our gang were predominantly skinheads, rude boys and rude girls. Me and Aggi lead the way (I like to think) with Gammon, Finny, Moth, Roget`-Rat and little Gerry as the main players. We rarely had more than two bikes between us, but that got four of us out there for starters, in skintight jeans, twelve-hole, Doc Martens, and flight jackets. We raised hell everywhere we went that summer and got pretty well known in Folkestone, although by autumn it was over; we all went our separate ways and never met up as a group again. That was just as well really, as half of them ended up in prison for various reasons, as I surely would have done too, if it hadn't all ended in a puff of smoke.

Moth got a steady girlfriend and left first, (I heard years later that he got 'roids rage', a Tyson style tattoo on his face and some time to think about it). Gerry was moved to a children's home in Dover, then some kind of secure accommodation, but it didn't end there. Gammon melted away and Finny moved to Blackpool, while Roget` got a job working with young offenders.

Aggi, went to court over a series of stupid crimes he had racked up and was shipped off back to Lewisham, his social worker had told him he wouldn't be known there and could make a fresh start – he did that alright, but it wasn't such a good one. So, within a month of that summer ending and me and Aggi taking a kicking at the Leas Cliff Hall disco, it was all over.

Being outnumbered four to one and getting kicked all round a dance floor by a gang of National Front supporters changes a seventeen-year-old. I ended the fight blooded and battered and missing a front tooth, but miraculously back on my feet and swinging – that was what counted to me.

While the sun had shone though on that careless period, it was all about getting pissed-up, acting tough and trying to pass first base with any girls about town who might be impressed by mean haircuts, sunburn and Brut 33.

I thought I had solved my petrol supply problems and invented the art of bilking (police terminology) by riding into the few, newly created, self-service stations in town, filling up and screaming off at top speed. No one had cameras then, but the real risk was crashing in panic while getting away.

It seemed to me to be an irresponsible way to run a business, trusting in the honesty of the customer. Although I did have a moral code, which some of the gang didn't understand, it didn't extend to the acquisition of petrol. I remember getting myself that couple of gallons from a VW camper, parked on the village through-road one night. This was quite risky, as it was right under the streetlights and there were houses either side of the road. The filler cap was on the road side and my piece of rubber siphoning tube, nicked from the school science lab, was so narrow, it must have taken ten minutes to fill the can I had sitting out in the road whilst I lay up in the shadows. I quite like VW campers now and wish I hadn't done that.

My first brush with the law that summer came when four of us, on two trail bikes, went to Dover and rode along the White Cliffs Trail, then down a coast guard track cut into the side of the escarpment above the docks. There was a police building, at the bottom, so we took a pathway we found leading back up the side of the graded cliff, too narrow for four wheels. It wasn't that what we were doing was criminal, but with no tax etc. we didn't want to get stopped. We found the Capel road again and then back into Folkestone in high spirits.

We always assumed that police would follow us anytime they spotted us and as often as not that would be the case.

It started raining as we came into town and we were racing each other to the sea front, then we shot out of the T-junction at the top of Sandgate road and I slid my DT on its side right across the road in front of a parked police car. I ended up with a £45 fine for careless driving, carrying an unqualified pillion passenger and no L plates. I stupidly elected to go to court so had to pay £10 costs too.

That was my second spill on an Enduro, as I had laid a TY50 down in the wet at the bottom of Sandling hill when we were still at school and trying out each other's bikes. Knobbly tyres do look good, but they're lethal on wet tarmac if you don't respect the bends, which I didn't. I didn't respect much at that time and was heading for a fall faster than I thought.

I never started trouble, but I wouldn't turn my back on it and my image tended to provoke a challenge. Along with some petty criminality, I also had a bravado which was beyond common sense. I nearly came a cropper when three drunken yobs jeered me as I rode down Dover hill after a party at Finny's place. I did a U-turn and rode back up, giving them the finger as I passed. This enraged them and they gave chase while I rode just fast enough to keep ahead, laughing back at them. If I'd had Aggi on the back, we'd have stopped for sure.

When they gave up, I turned around and came back down

towards them. They rushed out into the road in front of me, cutting off the downhill and I almost didn't make it. I managed to swing up into a side road and lost a couple of badges from my flight jacket in the process. It didn't need to be that close.

One morning, leaving Aggi's DHSS bedsit, in a shitty part of town near the train station, my bike refused to run. I soon discovered that my petrol pipe had been pulled off and my tank was empty. I was outraged.

I borrowed enough money from a pal for half a tank to get me home and later that night I went out looking for a siphoning target, away from the streetlights. I found an old works van parked up in a yard. I wasn't sure about this fuel as the mouthfull I got left a toxic residue I couldn't get rid of all night, no matter what I did. I'd already topped the tank up whilst the engine was hot and taken the remaining half a can home, the bike had run OK.

The next morning, it wouldn't start and I had to bump it several times down a nearby hill to get the barrel warm enough to help the petrol/diesel mix to fire. It coughed and spluttered and smoked like hell but once warm, the engine would run on the mix. I just needed either a hill or a couple of mates to push me to get it started.

I knew a petrol engine could run on a TVO mix like the old Ferguson tractor, so I wasn't worried, and kept topping her up with either petrol or diesel to keep it about 50/50. I thought I had stumbled upon a more economical way to run a bike, but no one else wanted to test it in their tanks. I suppose a two-stroke dirt bike engine revs a bit higher than a 1950s four-stroke tractor will and that may have been why within a couple of weeks I was pushing my bike home. It had come to a smoky, burned out stop on the way back from Folkestone.

I didn't have the money for a top end rebuild or the skills then to do the work myself. So, the poor machine sat in our derelict garage partly dismantled for six months before a mechanic took it off my hands.

So, then I was back to cycling to the bus stop or local train station to get me into town. My four-mile uphill trips to the farms where I did casual work turned into a real task, as far as I was concerned. That was the only way I could get beer money to spend in the Sellindge social club though, which was where I gravitated to after our Folkestone gang split up. It was a good development though for me, as I started hanging out with Dave again and the teenage pals I had left behind in the village.

# CHAPTER FOUR

## *Grebos*

There was almost no youth unemployment in the village thanks to the Ital Foods cake factory, just down the road. Me and Anthony Keeble, 'Keebs', had been sacked from our Saturday jobs there the previous autumn and we had set fire to the skip just before leaving, so I didn't think they would be keen to take me back, but I needed work.

I managed to get myself a landscape gardening job up on Farthing Common, in October that year. The three-mile cycle ride in the rain, before spending the day working in the rain, prompted me into looking out for a cheap motorbike. I bought a Suzuki A100, similar to my old B120 but not as good. It was very tatty and only just running, a non-descript sort of mauve colour. It got me to work and back, and out in the evenings too, but I never went back to 'towning' it. I felt comfortable in the village, but was always tooled up when I went into town for my own protection, usually carrying a lock-knife and a small cosh. I wasn't a vicious kid, but some people out there didn't want to fight fair and I'd be no-one's victim.

We were at home with the social club. There was a concrete shelter outside by the edge of the playing fields where the youth of the village would congregate – this quickly became our bike shelter as well as a meeting and courting place. We would go into the club, drink mild and be a harmless nuisance to the older generation, who thought the place was theirs. To be honest, they did kind of found it, so they had a right to feel that way.

The parties held at that place were some of the greatest nights out I remember, where everyone knew each other, even if they didn't much like each other. There was often friction between us young louts and the longer-term members in their twenties and thirties, who resented our presence. It was all harmless fun though and even when things got physical, there were always plenty of people around to keep the peace, it rarely came to punches being thrown amongst us.

That first job didn't last long and bad weather before Christmas shut the operation down. But due to contacts made as a local working man, I was back on my feet in the new year as part of a potato riddling gang at Walkers farm. Little Willie Missing from the school year below me was the foreman. That was a good little job and kept me busy and warm that freezing January in 1985.

The snow came down at the beginning of the year. It wasn't deep but it didn't thaw either and the country roads were packed and icy. Dad and I used my Suzuki to pull a sledge we had made, which was a bit of fun, and I learned how to keep a bike upright on the road in these conditions. One Sunday afternoon of watching videos round Dave's house ended in me riding home on the compacted ice, and coming off, three times, along the half mile stretch of Broad Street. The third time was quite spectacular, with me and the bike sliding down the road independently. It's hard on the hip and elbow joints, but other than that, great fun and that kind of bike could take it: there was not much on it to damage anyhow.

Broad Street was a dangerous road at any time, straight enough to open a machine up briefly, but you couldn't see what was coming the other way because of the hawthorn hedges. This road traps rainwater, black ice and snow like no other and ends in a blind bend that I would regularly take at fifty or sixty on the way home after dark.

By the first week of March my chain was slipping round the front sprocket, like a ratchet under any load, and when it would no longer get me up the hill to the potato barns I was forced to act.

I removed the fifty-pence shaped Suzuki sprocket and fitted a spare Yamaha DT one. The change in gearing altered my riding style, as the smaller diameter cog enabled me to pull power wheelies. The engine had no power, but if I stood on the pegs and yanked the bars up with all my body weight, at the same time as winding the throttle twist grip right back, the result would be a badly controlled wheelie that could only be attempted successfully if there was a bit of a bump in the road to get a lift started. The morning after fitting the imposter sprocket I came off the bike on the bend leading up to the farm, pulling just this trick.

Extracts from my diary at the time read:

**Friday 8ᵗʰ March**
*I have taped up the ripped end of my bike saddle with that silver aluminium tape & put a strip on the top of the tank & knocked the dent out, cleaned up my spark plug, taped up my exhaust & Dad welded the stand on the frame & we bolted the number plate on and the mud flap.*

## Saturday 9ᵗʰ March

*I went mucking out with Simon at Hastingleigh all day, then in the evening went to Georges party at the club, I had about 10 pints (of mild) & came off my bike on the way home (about 3 am) at the top of Broadstreet & my left hand is swollen up & I got a headache 'cause my helmet whacked onto the road.*

## Sunday 10ᵗʰ March

*I felt pretty bad in the morning, then Simon & I did 3 ½ hrs (mucking out) & I had a bath. I have had 9 proper accidents now, two on the CB50, one on Gavin's TY50, two on my DT100, Then four on my Susi A100.*

George was a character. He was from Nigeria originally, and he looked after me when I first turned up at Stowting primary school with no mates. He was two school years above me, which meant his biker mates, the 'Sellindge Warriors', that was Will's older brother Wilf, Tony Newport, Carlton Chislett and Steve Arnett, recognised us but were not overly pally, as we were merely whippersnappers.

I always remember the awe I felt a few years earlier, standing outside Stowting youth club when the Warriors turned up on their bikes for a planned fight with an Ashford Grebo gang that had started coming down to the area. Both groups postured for a bit, there was no actual confrontation, but honour had been satisfied and the Grebos moved on. The Warriors had their names spelled out in studs on the backs of their cut off denims; the eighties was certainly the time to be in a youth sub-cult. It was never the same after hip hop.

A month or so later, when I was up at the farm at Hastingleigh, mucking out the calves, I left my bike with a 'back-shed' mechanic called Neil Smith. He lived at one of the farm workers' cottages with his parents, who had got me the work up there. Neil was older than me and a bit of a greaser, but a steady bloke. He went on to run A1 Bike Breakers with a business partner. A few years later we worked together, fixing up engines and supervising kids on an alternative to custody program.

Neil took parts of my Suzuki to bits to diagnose the problems I had with starting and the lack of power, as I could barely get it up the hill to the farm by this time. I think I had to pay £5 for his time and he said he couldn't understand how I'd got the bike up to him for starters, as by rights it should not have been producing a spark at all. For one, it had a hole burned right out of the coil, plus all the other imaginable common faults for a small bike built in the seventies, at the tail end of a life of abuse and complete lack of maintenance.

Basically, it needed a whole new electrical system: points, plug, condenser, coil, leads and battery. Since the bike was pretty much a mechanical wreck, these new parts would have cost more than the machine was actually worth. Neil didn't want to charge me to put it back together, as he thought it probably wouldn't start again having disturbed the coil. So that was the end of the Suzuki.

Neil gave me a lift home on the back of his mean black Kawasaki KH250, a two-stroke triple.

That was my first ride on a bike that my dad consequently bought, and I was later to buy from him. The vibrations, the smell and the whirring, rattling engine/exhaust noise, struck a chord in me. I didn't know where it was leading at the time. I know I felt a touch of fear though, on account of the power harnessed in that oily black and chromed metal beast, and it felt good.

This was the second year that I remember the Kent Custom bike show being held on the hill at Stowting Common. At the time, I knew very little about the outlaw motorcycle scene, especially those gangs synonymous with hell raising and mindless violence. I was to appreciate the fuller picture later on down the trail. But at that time, to see those grizzly back-patch clubs pass by with their menacing colours sewn onto filthy rotting denim cut-offs, it had a kind of fatal attraction as strong as any revulsion I felt.

I didn't have any prejudices about the different types of machine out there; British, Japanese, American or Italian. Trail, custom or even scooters, they all had style, except BMW of course, which we thought of along a par with the CZ and MZ mutants; these marques appeared ugly, clumsy and box-like. I'd like to have a 1980s BMW now if it came to it, not an MZ though.

I went up the bike show with Dad that year on the back of the KH, as he wanted to have a look at the British bikes. Dad was into classic British machinery – not custom choppers, filthy hair and body odour. He had a low opinion of motorcycle gangs, or any kind of thug for that matter, describing outlaw bikers as 'out and out animals.'

He had the greatest respect though, for self-taught back shed mechanics who could lovingly restore old British racing steel, beards and greasy clothing notwithstanding.

I felt proud to ride pillion to my father on that day; a mutual interest in motorcycles brought us closer and helped to repair some of the damage done when I was running wild with the Skinheads that last summer. I still dressed like a yob but there was no real danger anymore and my parents approved of my recently formed conglomerate of mates from our local area, who all actually had jobs.

There was Dave (Goober) the butcher, Phil (Duck) the cow man, Demon Denis (Derek) who worked at the local garage and pumped petrol on the forecourt. He had a number of names: Dopey, Denzo, Delroy, anything beginning with a D really. And then there was Little Willie from the potato farm, who looked like the Milky bar Kid. We had all been at school together so knew and trusted each other. 1985 sealed the deal; we were the gang that was never going to break up, cemented together by the camaraderie that seemed to come from surviving a massive punch up at a Brabourne village hall disco the first time we all went out as a group.

That set us together as the originals and there were no late joiners, it was just us. We needed a name to put on our backs and came up with the 'Sellindge Magnums.' I still have my original cut-off denim. We dropped the name a year later and I replaced it with a flame design on my jacket but kept 'Sellindge.'

# CHAPTER FIVE

## Petrol

I had gone a short period without a bike of my own and had decided that I wasn't averse to getting myself a scooter. It went with the type of music I was still into at the time. Ska and Reggae rather than Rock and Heavy metal like most of the two-wheelers out there. Dave Bish phoned me up and told me of a Vespa for sale for £250 just down the road from him, in perfect nick, owned by a sensible lady in the village. I jogged over to Dave's house and twenty-five minutes after his call we were admiring the lovely compact form of the 1980 Piaggio Douglas 100, in a glossy crimson colour. It had cute little wheels and an engine like a hair drier. The engine gearbox unit made up the rear swinging arm and when you revved up the throttle the back seemed to crouch down like a dog being stroked. It wasn't a manly machine, more like a shiny toy but I liked it and so did the local girlies. It was as good as new, without a scratch on it.

I started riding my Vespa everywhere, and loved polishing the few chrome and aluminium bits on show. I fixed a small Union Jack flag to the back and used silver 'Airfix' paint to sign write 'The Whisper' above the right-hand side panel vent. I did this in the writing style of the second 'Selecter' album (after the title of one of their tracks) and it was quite tastefully done. I also fitted a new straight through exhaust system: matt black with a little chrome tail pipe. This item in itself actually looked exactly like a hairdryer.

Two days after buying it, I took my prize to a party over Rhodes Minnis way and crashed it into a hedge on the way back after I overshot a T-junction, miraculously causing no discernible damage. Two days after that, Will Missing was sitting on it outside the club and, not familiar with the clutch twist gear mechanism, he accidentally pulled a vertical clutch wheelie that tipped him straight off. It was a worrying, but amusing sight, to see him running along the tarmac, trying to bring it back down without flipping it over.

As My number plate was now snapped in half, I took the opportunity to buy myself a new half sized aluminium plate and a red and white 2-Tone mud-flap for good measure. This was a really good machine and there were no other accidents after that.

I quickly learned how to control The Whisper and to show off, pulling wheelies in a 360' turn, as well as riding the whole way from Broad Street down Swan Lane and into the Sellindge service station yard, standing up with both arms crossed over my chest. I'd be wearing that old open-faced Stadium helmet, army lightweights, green flight jacket, Fred Perry T-shirt (skintight) and braces either up or down, depending on the mood.

There was never any conflict in our village regarding youth fashion, but it was noticeable that the late teens were Biker oriented and the mid-teens were all Mods and Scooter boys, albeit waiting till they were old enough to get a scooter. When they *were* old enough, they all just went casual and bought Ford Escorts. Ours was the last of the Rocker generation.

In October I bought an ex-police Honda CB200 in pale metallic green, with a big white full fairing and panniers. It was perfect, and the fairing gave it some sophistication. Not 'super-fast', but it would be a suitable step up once I got the test over with, which I had to take on The Whisper.

The Honda cost me £120 and pretty much cleaned me out again, but it was a real bike and I rode it with style…to begin with.

We were still just a small gang of fools, hanging around the shelter of an evening and riding around on an eclectic collection of motorcycles; Dave had his TS100 that was his pride and joy and I don't think he let anyone else ride it ever. Phil had an old air cooled RD125, a good bike in its day. Will was on a dirty reddish Kawasaki KC100 and Del had just bought a Honda CM125 Custom, on HP, that he spent as much time cleaning as riding.

Del's dad, Brian, had recently left the army and ran his household in the fashion he was used to. This meant that Del was often being curfewed for minor insubordination and we had to spend regular evenings up in Del's bedroom, listening to heavy metal and planning our tactics for a return to Brabourne village hall the next time we heard of a party there.

There were some satellite members of the group by now, who were hanging around up the shelter and riding 50cc bikes, as they were a bit younger than us; Heapo, Dave Keeble, Rob (handyman), Greeny and Triton. They were good for a laugh, but none of them ever took their tests or rode proper bikes. There were regular parties/discos held at the club, which were always memorable, and these were some of the happiest times of my life.

That autumn was like a second summer and I had a girl-friend, Sarah, who I adored. She was delicate and lovely. I had a bunch of mates who could always be found, and I didn't want anything to change.

All of a sudden, things changed: winter came in quick, work dried up, Sarah didn't love me anymore, and she wouldn't even look at me.

I had this great plan to win her back, which involved staging a motorcycle crash, as I thought that would break the ice. I really didn't want to ruin my new Honda, or my scooter, but Rob inexplicably offered his bright yellow moped we called 'the Banana Bike' for my use on this mission. Anyway, we all thought it was fair for the entertainment value of the group as a whole.

I used the old front brake trick whilst turning into a junction where there was plenty of gravel to start the slide. I timed the operation perfectly, so that I had a 150-yard run up, starting on a slope. Sarah would hear the noise as she walked towards the junction with her group of pals 100 yards away.

My group stayed back at the starting grid and watched the carnage unfold. It was exciting I have to say; as I reached the drop-zone at maximum speed, all eyes were on me and there was no turning back. I leant into the turn and grabbed the brake lever. I was sent tumbling down the road alongside the bike, which crashed into the hedge, causing only superficial damage to myself and machine.

The desired results were not achieved, as the only person who did not rush to the scene was Sarah herself. It probably had the opposite effect to what I had hoped actually. What kind of idiot would do that? The same idiot who, two days later, petrol bombed the shelter to burn off the giant love-heart spayed on its back wall, I suppose. Looking back now, I can't believe I did things like that.

I didn't know what to do with my life, so I went and signed up for the army. They wouldn't take me, so I threw my life down on the road. I didn't want to die, but I did get a rush from riding on the edge.

This went on for a few years and I got quite good at, not dying. It made me feel alive. I rode all my machines more instinctively and was generally able to right a loss of control situation without thinking. I'd take stupid risks and loved to ride home at night from the club full throttle, anticipating all the bends and potholes because I knew the route like the back of my hand. If there were no headlights showing, I took that to mean the road was clear and I could take the blind bends as fast as it was possible whilst keeping the tyres on the road. My mum and dad used to say they could hear me coming all the way from Swan Lane and judge which point I was on by the tone of the exhausts.

My CB200 quite quickly started to show signs of hard use. Once I'd broken the Perspex windshield, running the Keeble brothers back down to the brook at the end of a club night out, I stopped bothering too much about its appearance, as its perfect form was compromised.

A month later, just before New Year, the weather got cold again, and I slid the CB over on the ice at the bottom of the pub hill to make my tenth countable bike accident. The next day it happened again in almost the exact same spot.

**Diary extract from 25ᵗʰ March 1986:**

*I hit a car with my left pannier on the bend up Swan Lane by the old children's home; I was overtaking two cars while a transit van was coming the other way doing about 40 mph. I so nearly missed colliding head on at 60 mph, that's a 100 mph impact, by weaving through and cutting it so close to the car I was overtaking that I actually dented his steel bumper with my pannier, which split open at the seams like a wooden matchbox.*

I was obviously riding much too fast in a 30 zone and stupidly began overtaking cars approaching a bend. I didn't see a right indicator and, as the car was going uphill, no brake lights until the very last moment. So, it had never been my intention to overtake this second car at that point, but to cut my speed and tuck in behind it until the bend was clear. I had to overtake, smashing my pannier on the corner of his rear bumper. Otherwise I would have crashed headlong into the back of the car. No time for a decision – it was just an instant reaction and fortunately I didn't lose a leg or hit the transit head on. It was close though, as I almost took the right-side pannier off on the front of the van as well.

A few days after this I saw an advert for a Lambretta in the local paper. It was a Serveta Jet 200, in mustard yellow. I bought it from an old boy in Ashford for £127:50. It was a bit of a lumbering beast and quite old, HKN4E7N. Its engine certainly wouldn't have been described as crisp and its handling wasn't nimble like the Vespa either. But it was the status piece I needed to start going on the scooter rallies, which I planned to do that summer.

These were not Mod runs: the scooter boy style was baggy

army gear, grubby flight jackets with faded/bleached denim cut-offs over the top, and cropped hair or flattops. I liked all this style, as I was right into army gear and craved the camaraderie of the tour patched cut-off which proved that you had actually been somewhere. This ride was going to take me places.

A few days later I had the carb', tank and air filter off for cleaning. My brilliant idea of cleaning parts with petrol, then burning the excess off with a lighter nearly resulted in me setting fire to the machine in the garage, where I was working on it, as well as to the spilt petrol on the floor. I had to throw the burning tank and air filter out of the garage door then put out the floor around the scooter.

This Lambretta was to be my first 'bike' project. I had no prior experience, in stripping down and rebuilding bikes, but would learn on the job. If I'd never touched it and just left it in its original form and colour it would have increased far more in value over time, as it was quite a rare model. I had fun doing it anyway and still sold it for a good profit in the end: about ten years later I got £750.

The week of diary entries I made in May '86 evidences that motorcycles were the most important thing in my life at that time. Despite being actively employed three days a week for Ashford Borough Council, plus another three days back home on the farm, I still found the time every morning and evening to work on them and ride them.

**Monday 12th May**
*I took the foot plates off my Lambretta & adjusted my points and plug gap.*

## Tuesday 13th May

*I got my engine cover off & bolted my down pipe manifold on. It was hanging from one loose bolt. I sheared the main bolt that holds the expansion chamber. I bought some DWF (releasing fluid spray). I have adjusted the plug & points gaps on the Whisper.*

## Wednesday 14th May

*We were hacking a hedge out in Willesborough (at work). I bought a tyre pen (gold) from Cat motorcycles & a front tyre for a 125 that ain't no good (from Victoria road bike breakers), for the back wheel on my CB200. I mended the puncture that I had made putting the dud tyre on.*

## Thursday 15th May

*At work today, John left me in charge & I burned the hedge down & all the dead ferns up the bank, John was mad. I swapped that dud tyre for a decent thicker one & fitted it & took two links out of the chain.*

## Friday 16th May

*I have stripped my Lambretta down now ready for spraying, it took me half the day. I rode my CB up the club with just the down pipes on, it sounds really meaty. I took the bend in Broad Street at the top of Smeed's Farm Hill at 65 & overshot the edge of the bank, the front wheel slipped but I rescued it.*

## Saturday 17th May

*I went to certainly the worst club party I have been to, but still managed to have some fun.*

**Sunday 18th May**

*Me & Dave didn't work today (mucking out) but instead had a good ride on the 250s at home with Derek & Dad. I was riding the Bultaco, it is now my favourite.*

Since the beginning of the year Dad had started acquiring off road motorcycles for use at the weekend activity centre, he had set up on the farm. I was learning a lot about mechanics, as well as trials and motocross riding. I quite fancied taking up motocross, but never got further than the farm track.

We had a Yamaha YZ250 that Dad had bought from George Gimmer and a dangerous looking Bultaco Pursang MK12, also a 250. Apart from the danger of riding these things (and there was nothing safe about them) they were terrible to start. It could take twenty sharp little kicks or more to fire them up; every one of them had to be explosive as the kick-starts were short with limited travel, smacking down on the serrated steel foot pegs and jarring the cartilage in your knee.

We quickly acquired other off-road bikes at the farm. First there was a couple of Honda TL125s, one came with a chromed Sammy Miller frame. Then a collection of 250cc Spanish competition trials bikes: Ossas, Fantics and a Montessa Cota – that one I wasn't keen on.

Trials bikes and the style of riding needed are completely different from motocross, requiring skill and nerve but not speed. We still managed to injure ourselves regularly though. Dad started building banks and digging pits with the old JCB to make trialling more interesting and we used the motocross bikes less and less.

At the height of our enthusiasm, Dad bought a giant Montessa Capra 414. It was a beast and ran on Castrol-R vegetable oil mix, rather than regular two-stroke. The noise was incredible and a blip of the throttle in second gear pulled the biggest wheelie I've ever done. The acceleration flipping me off the back, as it reared up and left me behind on the ground. It was a fantastic bike, but just too big for the ground we had to use it on and not suitable for the kids we were dealing with. Dad had set up the activities weekend centre as Gelt House Education Unit, and within that year it became a full time business: catering for kids, generally from the Canterbury area, who came from very deprived social and educational backgrounds.

I started working Saturdays for Dad as mechanic and trials riding instructor to over a dozen boys aged six to sixteen. It was hectic, but a lot of fun and most of them certainly got a lot out of their time with us.

As time passed and the centre was acknowledged professionally as a useful tool for social services, we got regular calls from Canterbury police, asking us to come and clear out their yard of all the stolen and recovered (but not identified) motorcycles they had built up. These were mostly mopeds and 125s, rarely anything up to 250cc, but sometimes we got some good stuff. We would use these as practice pieces for the mechanics sessions I ran all week, with the prize being to ride them on the Friday afternoon and then for the Saturday boys to wreck.

We mixed and matched and had a lot of fun sticking knobbly tyres on mopeds and customising any other road bikes – by welding exhaust extensions, cutting down mudguards, changing seats etc. We rode them into ponds, into trees and over extraordinary jumps we had constructed. Amazingly no one ever broke a bone, although I for one was rarely without an injury from one week to the next.

**Wednesday 28th May**
*I think I have surrounded the running defects in my Lambretta.*
*For one, my throttle cable was unhooked at the twist grip.*

**Friday 30th May**
*I worked the morning for Dad, added with tomorrows work &*
*some other bits and pieces, he has let me off the £32 for the chrome.*
*I rubbed down & 'redoxided' the front half of my scooter frame.*
*Scootering magazine has given me some ideas.*

At the start of the summer of eighty-six, I was still torn between the distractions of scooters verses bikes. For three months, I was concentrating on customising my Lambretta and having it ready to ride to Doncaster on my first scooter rally. During this time, I had stripped it right down, had loads of bits chromed and re-sprayed it a deep dark purple colour called black tulip. Some parts were black and the toolbox and petrol tank were sprayed the same red as the expansion chamber on the fresco exhaust I had bought for it.

I didn't have time to prepare and spray the side panels, or foot-plates, so they never went back on. I fitted a miniature custom seat, a little chrome back rack and an awkward chrome headlight grill, which was responsible for the poor earthing of the headlamp and periodic blowing of bulbs. I put everything into this creation, but that meant I couldn't really ride it most of the time, although I did do from time to time, in various illegal states of nakedness.

The rest of the Sellindge Magnums; Phil, Dave, Derek and Will were firmly on the heavy rock side of the divide, so had no respect for hair dryers. I think Will didn't really care about style; he rode bikes but was really more into his tractors and a string of crappy cars he kept buying from the local scrap yard. Del's situation was odd, as he had bought a brand new, factory custom bike and wore a studded denim cut-off, while his younger brother Darren was a full-on Mod and took every part of that culture to its extreme. Shane was the only other Mod within our circle (but he didn't have a scooter), Shane left for the army before it got to the choice between two wheels or four. Nowadays, having done his full time for Queen and country, he rides sports bikes, as does Darren. I was the only scooter boy who rode a police motorcycle and we were the best gang of brothers that ever were.

# CHAPTER SIX

## Scooter boys

**Monday 28th July 1986**

*I finished rubbing down my front shield & sprayed it with red oxide prima. I went down Ital foods to view the sorry state of my Vespa (which I had sold to Greeny). I went up the club & talked to Des about doing Dad's KH250 up & Derek said he would help me.*

**Tuesday 29th July**

*I made a fuck up of spraying my scooter shield & went out.*

**Wednesday 30th July**

*I rode my scooter to work in Ashford (without the shield, front mudguard or panels) & broke down, then the police turned up in the car park I had parked it in. I was watching across the park, but I wouldn't go over and tell them it was mine because it was totally illegal, and I wouldn't have been able to explain how I got it there. So, I had to get Dad to come and pick us up in the van at the end of the day. Back home I had to slap all the stuff on my scooter to appear legal but have trouble with the lights, and Neil never brought my chrome parts (some of which are vital to its running) Dad went mad.*

**Thursday 31st July**

*I got my chrome back & spent the evening sorting out my scooter, & I am more or less ready, but have taken the connecter out of the horn button & glued the button. I didn't get finished till 1 am.*

So, I was as fit and ready as I was going to be, that same morning, to head off to the Doncaster Scooter Classic. I had never ridden more than ten miles on a motorway before, the M20 only went from Folkestone to Maidstone at that time and I had only ever been on the Folkestone to Ashford section.

I had very little idea of how tough this ride would turn out to be. My horn didn't work, my hand painted custom number plate was clearly illegal and I had not had time to think about an MOT.

I was up first thing, packed and on the road to pick up Aggi, my old 2-Tone partner in crime, at Ashford station fresh off the train from Lewisham.

We set off at a good pace (60 mph) for a 200cc vintage Lambretta, two up plus camping gear. We were pulled up by the police before we even got to Maidstone, where I was warned about my number plate and given a producer. This ultimately cost me a small fine for an out of date MOT, good job he didn't test the horn.

I wound her up to 70 mph on the downhill before we hit the M25 and it cut out on me. I got her going again and then rode her at fifty to keep it cool, but it happened a couple more times before the Dartford tunnel; so, I took the plug out and found a lump of coke jammed between the arm and the element, showing that my engine was decoking itself. I gave it a good clean and she behaved herself after that, but it still took me half the way to Doncaster before I felt I could trust the lumbering beast.

I had never ridden this far away from Sellindge before and it felt like a great adventure: the two-stroke engine crackling through the tunnel and the headlamp projecting a spider's web pattern on the tunnel walls from my custom chrome grill.

We had some laughs at a service station and were geed up by some girls waving to us from the back window of a coach. The sun was shining, we'd made it north of London and we were feeling good.

We pulled off the motorway after the M11 junction and stopped at a pub to give the engine a chance to cool down. When we came out again, the sunshine had gone. Riding off, I felt the chill pretty soon as I was just wearing army light-weights and a flight jacket. That was the style, so I put up with it, hoping the sun would show itself again before too long. I followed my pre-drawn route instructions and kept it under sixty all the way to the A1, and it ran fine for the rest of the trip.

Pretty soon we started to see other scooters and it felt great to be part of something. The riders we passed, or who passed us, all seemed in good spirits, cheering and show-boating. There was camaraderie and a shared anticipation that whatever happened over the weekend would be worth boasting about when we all got back to our home turf.

We rode along with three other scoots for a while, then kind of got lumbered with helping one kid on a cut down union jack Vespa every time his engine seized. He had no tools and no mechanical knowledge, and it looked like he was never going to make it. Apparently, he did get there though, a couple of hours after we had.

Rain looked inevitable and we just pushed on at our own pace and as more and more scooters joined the road, we all took less notice of each other. There seemed to be lots of round-abouts and coned off lanes, which I was using to undertake the lines of traffic building up. We had one close shave when I had to swerve back into the flowing traffic through a line of fixed bollards, it would have been a safe manoeuvre if I had had any acceleration, but not two-up, which also made the front wheel very light.

When we saw Sherwood Forest on a road sign, we both looked at each other in bemusement. It showed that we were a long way away from anywhere we knew.

The rain had already started as drizzle and we kept going into it as it got harder. It was consistent but it didn't get strong enough for me to consider putting on waterproofs at this point. I was still hoping we would come out of it and the sun would be back to join with the wind and dry me off. Aggi didn't have any waterproofs and I didn't want to be the one dressed in a banana skin, ruining our image.

Of course I took the brunt of the elements and got wetter and colder to the point that we just had to stop at a happy eater or something, where I sat and shivered while waiting for the feeling to come back to all my extremities.

I was regretting my limited choice of clothing and gear for this trip: I only had a Fred Perry T-shirt on under my flight jacket, while the pair of ultrathin perforated black leather driv-ing gloves I had nicked from Halfords would have been suitable for the Mediterranean.

It's hard to feel cool when you're close to hypothermic, but the waterproofs stayed in my pack and on went the army jacket.

This kept the wind out at least, as we hit the road again for what I assumed would be a short last leg of the journey. In fact, it seemed to take forever, and the rain set in steady.

What was really bad, and dangerous, was constantly being overtaken by articulated Lorries, which showered us in dirty spray, stinging my face. Those cool shades I was wearing offered very little protection and I didn't even have a scarf. My mind went back to earlier in the day when we had been singing The Specials version of *Enjoy yourself*, when the wheels were turning on dry tarmac and misery was far from anticipation.

The A1(T) turned into the A1 motorway and it got even worse. I was just hanging onto those narrow grips and being buffeted from the turbulence caused by the lorries, sucked into their slipstream, and pelted in the face by the spray. It was only a short stretch, but it seemed never ending – then, at last, we saw the road signs and rolled into the outskirts of Doncaster… A more dismal, wet, grey, dirty, depressing and featureless place I don't think I'd seen before.

The rally was at the racecourse and it cost six quid to get in. It wasn't quite the exhilarating experience I had been anticipating, although it did feel good parking up amongst hundreds of other scooters, mostly Vespa 150s and 200s in stock form, as well as others in varying degrees of custom modification. Lambrettas make for better custom scoots than the simpler squat formed Vespas. Lammis are built around a frame that looks good exposed, while the side panels on a Vespa are what makes its style and probably half its strength too.

We set up my little canvas boy-scouts tent, which looked very dated (I do believe it was the oldest one on the field), amongst all the modern nylon affairs with vents and flaps and space to move about in. We just lay there until the rain eased off before venturing out, and when we did, the sullen atmosphere seemed as unfriendly as the weather, brooding and intimidating.

There were lots of hardcore skinheads, wearing Screwdriver T-shirts and sheath knives. Back then scooter rallies were places you could get yourself stabbed, apparently devoid of any real security, where a fair proportion of the gangs of thugs were deeply and mindlessly racist. In fact, Desmond Dekker, who was performing over that weekend, had himself been stabbed at a scooter rally the previous season.

Mindsets have moved on a great deal since the mid eighties, when ignorance and confusion reigned supreme, and walking around with cropped hair and Doc Martens in company with a coloured brother of the same faith often provoked a feeling of betrayal from both sides of the divide: that was the ignorance. The confusion came when the organisers of these rallies would schedule ultra-right Oi punk bands alongside Trojan reggae performers at the same venue, with the same confused audience.

There was a 'Scooterist's Disco' going on, but it wasn't any fun and trying to get served rip-off measures of watery larger in squashy plastic glasses just took too long to want to go back for another. We went out to the stalls and I bought a German army sleeping bag with arms and a hood, it un-zipped at the waist and the bottom part folded up so it could be worn like a coat. This served me well on a multitude of trips for years after. They became as popular at bike events as those olive drab moleskin shirts with the West German colours on one sleeve did – you don't see either around now. I never liked the shirts, but, loved that sleeping coat and wore it like a token of nomadic mobility.

Aggi hadn't brought a sleeping bag or any money worth talking about, so I was obliged to let him use my combat jacket for the rest of the trip; it was American style and actually suited him better than it did me – Vietnam War era, I'm sure, I still have the thing in rags hanging up somewhere in a shed at the farm.

The next morning, the camp site looked like a disaster scene. It had blown a gale in the night and most, if not all, of the tents had at least lost pegs, many had parts flapping in the wind and some had been reduced to ripped-open nylon flags streaming from broken fibreglass or aluminium frames. Some had simply blown down flat. My little blue canvas tent, on its simple steel tube A-frame, was totally unaffected and looked pretty good that day.

By mid-morning scooters started riding out to the town centre and so we got ready to go. Aggi had brought some speed for the weekend and my share had been in a paper wrap in my jacket pocket – it had soaked into the paper itself because of the rain on the trip up. I scraped off the excess paste and left it to dry in the tent, and then I chewed the original paper, which remained bitter for some time.

Speed, as we called it, was part of the scene and I didn't do it often because of: A, the price and B, the depressing anticlimactic feeling I got for several days afterwards, guaranteeing me that if I gave in to that come-down, I would be an addict in a matter of a fortnight. I didn't smoke dope, as cigarettes made me nauseous and eating the stuff was seriously unpleasant, without any immediate effect. People only seemed to get hold of resin in those days, which by all accounts was pretty weak stuff, over-priced and over-rated.

I actually became quite anti-drugs, for various reasons. I resented that for some of my mates, it moved on from being an occasional and memorable event, to an absolute necessity, as they didn't feel they were able to have a good time without it. I could have a genuinely good time with a bunch of mates on alcohol alone, safe in the knowledge that I wouldn't want to go near the stuff the next day.

We took the scooter out, following the stream of two-stroke fumes into the town centre area and we found a place to park up beside a bunch of other scoots. It felt pretty good when we noticed an old bloke snatching a photograph of us as we stood by the side of the road, surveying the area before choosing a pub to walk into. We started drinking with a couple of scooter boys from Horsham, Martin and Nick. Aggi was knocking back a small bottle of vodka he had nicked, aiming to get as drunk as he could as quickly as possible. The sun had come out and finally we were having a good time.

Now follows my original first-hand account, as written soon after the event in 1986 (parts of which I am no longer proud of), covering the next three or four hours. I have endeavoured to keep it as accurate word for word (spelling mistakes corrected) as when I first wrote it as a foolish nineteen-year- old.

## Saturday 2nd August 1986

*We found the Doncaster indoor precinct, which was nice, there were Scooterists & Skinheads stomping around like they owned the place. Aggi was pissed by now & that means trouble, he was trying to chat up all the girls, no matter if they were ugly. The place was full of security in dark uniforms with radios, they were actually very friendly but kept moving us along when we stopped*

& hung around.

We played about in the glass lifts & moving staircases, then Aggi was trying to talk to some girls but they disappeared into the ladies. So he followed them in there & we were creasing up outside cause you could hear them shrieking & him shouting & bashing things about, then the security girl we had been talking to before asked 'Where's your friend?' to which Nick replied 'In the toilet, he will be coming out any minute now' & just then the girls ran out & Aggi wandered out, pissed out of his head with a smile on his face. That was classic.

We sat on a step outside in the sun, that was a back door to a bakery, or something. We got some passers-by to take some photos as we sipped cans of beer, this was great. Two local yobs burst out of the door behind us followed by the owner shouting at them and we decided it was time to be getting back to the camp site so we took a slow walk back through the precinct, knocking some dirty mags off a shelf as we walked round the corner. I heard Ag say, 'Hold on' and thinking he had spotted some tart, took no notice. We became aware of two trendies walking behind us & talking to each other insulting us, so we stopped & they walked past & straight to a short wall where there were loads of other trendies & not a Scooter boy to be seen.

I looked around, & Aggi had disappeared too. Then the two trendies came back with a couple more & some girls. The geysers were about our age & the one about my size, handy looking, short dark hair, round face & very bolshy & confident said in his horrible industrial Yorkshire accent, 'Don't fucking stare.' My two mates were arguing back at them while I just stood there saying nothing, my fist clenching my crash helmet strap, ready to smack him round the head with it. I felt surges of adrenaline pulsing through my body as I considered my first strikes.

All the time more trendies were gathering. I wasn't frightened but the odds were stacking up against us, still no Aggi,

'Where the fuck is he?'

They had agreed on a scrap outside, so I said,

'Ok this way.'

They didn't like that and demanded that we go in the opposite direction, through more hordes of trendies, so I said

'Bollocks, this way' & started walking the way we had just come, hoping to pick up Aggi. They couldn't wait, I had my crash hat in my left hand now & my right hand in the inside pocket of my flight jacket holding my short chain with a brass padlock on it.

The split second I saw the lanky ginger haired kid jump my mate from behind, my hand came out of my jacket. The mouthy bastard was on Martin, & Nick was underneath the lanky one, so I whacked him in the back between the shoulders. He arched a bit but didn't roll off, so I whacked him in the head & that did it. I then turned & the mouthy one was grappling with Martin, so I swiped him round the side of the head, he staggered & another one put him down. I smacked the lanky one in the back again as he was crawling & he arched in pain then rolled away.

I saw, at my feet, the mouthy one either trying to crawl to safety or trying to get up & have another go. I thought, or maybe I said it –

'You fuck, you 'ain't' getting up' & gave him the weight of my chain on the back of his big head; he dropped flat out on his face motionless.

All the time their girlfriends were screaming,

'Stop it, leave them alone!'

For that three or four seconds it all happened so quickly before anyone had a chance to jump me, then it came & they got some punches in & knocked my hat off. I was lashing out but couldn't get a decent swing. I thought, 'Shit, if they swamp me, they'll kill me with my own chain.' I ducked out and took several quick steps back so they couldn't surround me. I don't know how many trendies were involved but security was rushing in, breaking the scuffle up. I backed off, or was shoved, to a big thick glass window and side stepped. They were pulling at my crash hat & the side strap had popped open.

I found my feet & distance, as I let go the smack hat & lashed out at the big bastard trying to get at me. I got him on the arm or shoulder &, as I swung again, he backed off into the crowd ring, held back by security. I stepped forwards brandishing my chain & rushed a couple of steps to save my flat cap & the crash hat peak on the floor from the thieving hands grouping after souvenirs. They whipped their hands back & darted away. I picked up my stuff & put my hat on. I could hear the security with their radios shouting,

'Get the Police!'

The confusion was clearing as I put my chain inside my flight jacket and rallied my mates. There was just a wall of trendies behind security. I couldn't say how many or how many had joined in, but we were massively outnumbered, maybe five to one.

I saw that tall lanky one casually walking past, with my blue smack hat in his hand; I snatched it, with some outrage, shouting

'That's my fucking crash hat!'

He flinched & let go immediately. Then I saw a young scooter boy, right out of it, being picked up off the floor by security. He had obviously been kicked to shit by the bastards & I shouted out to the others to get him out with us and find Aggi. We saw that security were looking after the kid, so we hurried off around the corner to be met by Aggi coming the other way, looking bewildered.

No time for talking as we all ran outside to be confronted by three big trendies in their mid-twenties, the biggest one had Aggi's full face crash hat in his hand. Aggi later told me they had attacked him and used his own helmet against him after he had taken one of them on. Aggi was shouting,

'You, fucking wankers!' as he pulled his butterfly knife and flicked it open and I took my chain out again.

They were on the edge of the road shouting & swearing at us and for about thirty seconds we moved forwards & backwards with the railings in between us, no one wanted to risk getting hit whilst climbing over.

Then Police, loads of them, came from all angles. Aggi pushed his knife down his front to hide it then held both hands out, saying,

'Give it to me Jimmy!'

I dropped my chain into his open hands & he slung it over his head onto the precinct roof.

There was nowhere to run to, and we were stopped by some Police after security pointed us out. We told them that the blokes, who were now getting away across the road, had attacked us & nicked the smack hat (which was pretty much true), so they got called back but let go after the helmet was handed over. We were searched but not very well, then again by a different set of cops who lined us all up before we could get out of the scene. They found no chain, I denied ever seeing one, but they did find my lock knife on me and I was arrested.

Two coppers led me to their van which was besieged by trendies, they were going for anyone in a flight jacket, I passed that ginger bastard who started it all; he was looking smug and leaning against the van. I paused & half turned to face him, lifting my top lip a *little & I leant forward aggressively, which took the smile off his face, he could see I wasn't handcuffed. His mate was nearby, having his head bandaged. He was on his feet but looking pretty shaken up.*

*I got in the police minibus, where there was already a Scooterist & a couple of trendies. I still had my camera and was just about to take a photo of the scene outside, through the window, but a cop stopped me. That ride to the Police station felt like being in Quadrophenia, it was so like that scene and a great trip.*

*When we got there we had to line up against the wall & I was having a bit of a laugh with the scooterist, being 'sarky' to the cops & then they saw us one by one & took us to our cells, after having taken our possessions away.*

I didn't enjoy the rest of the experience. It was quite different to how you would find custody in a British police station now. The Police and Criminal Evidence act of 1984 quotes a certain number of rights afforded to persons in custody: forget about your phone call (which actually isn't one of them), by far the most useful is the right to free and independent legal advice. I don't remember being offered a solicitor or any food or drink. I remember the coppers sneering at me and telling me that my mates had dobbed me in. I knew that was a lie. I didn't need PACE and I didn't need some sly legal rep to concoct an account for me. All I had to do was tell the truth, but not too much of it.

*My cell was filthy, the floor was partially wet, with I don't know what. In the toilet partition there were smears of excrement on the walls & over the seat, a dirty pair of underpants was stuffed into the spy hole alcove.*

After about an hour & a half I was brought out to have my prints taken & mug shots. As I was walking to the interrogation room the cocky Scooterist was coming out, he was snivelling a bit & I heard a cop say,

'You won't be silly again now will you.'

As I took a seat opposite the interrogator, I glanced into the waste-paper bin & saw several, blood-stained tissues, from that I assumed they had hit him. I was hoping all the time that they would let me out so that I could see Bad Manners playing, back at the racecourse.

I was about an hour in there, where they took a hand-written version of the interview, while making sneering comments to get me to confess to something. I stuck to my guns, that it was only a camping knife. I said that I never saw a chain & that they jumped us & I never took the knife out, which was mostly true enough. They didn't believe me & I had to take my shirt off for them to check my back for injuries. The fact that one of my tattoos was 'A dagger' fired them up and they started calling me 'Slasher.'

All the time my hands were down in front of me, they were intimidating & I didn't mind a blow to my upper body, but I didn't want one down there. I kept my composure and I was let out eventually.

It was about 6.30 – 7.00 & I didn't know the way back to where I'd left my scooter, or even if it was still in one piece. The only weapon I had was my open face crash hat & I thought that the whole town would be anti Scooterist by now & some yobs might recognise me.

Every time I saw a bunch of trendies, I went down a different street and then, in desperation, I asked a bloke in a newish white saloon car to taxi me around, surprisingly he did. He was dressed for the office like the CID blokes, but none of them would tell me which direction I needed to take.

I was so pleased to see my Lammi, glittering at the roadside, just where I had left her, but just over the road on the corner was a pub with about ten blokes standing outside looking at me. I put my smack hat on in the car for good measure and the bloke said he would wait for me to start the scooter.

I had to unlock the steering, which I was fumbling at. Then I tried kicking it over, but it was in gear & I was getting worked up, half expecting them all to start legging it over to me. I got the engine going & thanked the bloke profusely, then I sped off.

Thinking the pub was on a T-junction I went to turn left but it was just a wide right-hand bend. I wasn't going to slow down though, thinking they might have me off the scooter. I just had to swing wide, right up close to the pavement where the trendies were, and I didn't slow down, or look back.

I was pleased to see the gates of the racecourse again & I came in like a hero, swaggered around for an hour or so until I found Aggi & the other two. They all wanted to smoke dope in their tent & fell asleep; then when it came to the time Bad manners were coming on, I was the only one of us who went out there.

With the benefit of hindsight and a realistic grasp of the potential consequences of violent confrontation, I have questioned myself on this one. As a result of that process, I did edit out some expletives and less sympathetic descriptions about how I was feeling at the time I wrote that journal. I still believe the violence I used was necessary though, under the circumstances. If I had not carried and used a weapon on that day, we all would have been picked up unconscious off the floor by security and gone to the hospital instead of the police station. I didn't start any of the fights I got involved in, I never do, but I will always defend myself and my companions with whatever force is necessary.

Desmond Dekker was on the stage that night too. The first rally he had done since getting stabbed. I remember he came over the mike, stating triumphantly,

'They said Desmond Dekker wouldn't do another scooter rally'

and the gangs of skinheads, all buoyed up after crowd surfing to Buster Bloodvessel had a change of heart. A bunch of them got up there and instead of doing Nazi salutes, they started chanting,

'Desmond is our leader.'

I don't know what drove those people, other than evostik, as evidenced by the glue bags left in the toilets they'd smashed up on the first night.

Next morning was fine and sunny as we packed up the tent and loaded our gear. The ride back south was a lot more fun than it had been getting there. Martin and Nick ,one of them sporting a black eye, said we should head for the M1 and stay on it all the way to the M25, so the four of us, on two scooters, hit the road.

Thirty miles or so later it started raining and it didn't stop. We had plenty of laughs though at the service stations. I was wearing my sleeping bag and, before long, I gave way to reason and put on the set of bright yellow waterproofs that I should have worn on the way up.

We went about a hundred miles in constant rain, battling it out with an artic driver we kept overtaking through clouds of spray. My machine's maximum speed was 70 mph, but it wasn't effortless We'd get past him, then ten minutes later he would be back showering us in filth and we would have to start the long slow manoeuvre all over again. The first scoot through would pull in front to check the lorry's speed until the other one made the pass too.

Eventually the rain got really hard and we took shelter under a concrete road bridge, huddling together, trying to warm our fingers with a cigarette lighter. After four or five minutes of shelter our artic roared past under the bridge with two horn bursts for the spirit of the road. We waved back and then lit a small paper fire using lighter fuel.

That was the last time we stopped and when the rain had eased up a bit, we rode for the M25 and the tunnel. Nick and Martin kept on south when I turned off to meet the A20.

That Lambretta never missed a beat all the way in the rain. I was that pleased with it, but only rode it for another few months before stripping it down again, initially to re-spray the leg shield. With one thing over another, I didn't get it back together and running for another couple of years and by then I'd grown a beard and bought a leather jacket

# CHAPTER SEVEN

## *Riding high*

On 4th August 1986, one of the original five, good old Phil, took the corner at Farthing Common too fast and crashed head on with the school coach. He was killed instantly on a sunny morning, riding his newly acquired blue Suzuki GS400.

We never knew what he was thinking or where he was going that day. He was always so full of life, Nineteen-years-old, riding high, then in the blink of an eye he was gone. The whole village felt it, like a vacuum and nothing seemed so empty as the Monks Horton valley where Phil had lived and worked all his life, under the shoulder of the Farthing itself; a local beauty spot on a bend in the old roman road.

We fixed a Suzuki tank badge from Phil's bike shed to a big ash tree on the corner, under which all the tribute flowers had been laid. It's still there now, each time I pass that spot I pay my silent respects. It's a nice place, with the best views I know of in Kent. You can see St Mary's Bay, Dungeness and Fairlights cliffs on the horizon. Ashford is there and all the villages below the chalk downs; Stowting, Sellindge, Lympne, Brabourne and Monks Horton where we all lived.

I acquired the KH250 from Dad and spent a bit of time getting it running right. It regularly used to neutralise plugs and then only run on two cylinders, which was annoying. I had to keep a stock of them. When the road was wet, it would splash up over the HT caps, leads and coils and cause the engine to cut out. It rattled like hell and poured pale blue smoke from its three exhaust silencers, running black oil from whichever one wasn't firing all through the revs. I loved those exhausts, and the seat, and the tank.

She was a little cousin to the all-powerful Kawasaki Z900 immortalised in the Australian biker film *Stone*. This bike needed constant maintenance, unlike the four-cylinder 'Zs'.

The savage power band and the torque it had from 4000 to 6000 revs was unique and I was hooked. No-one really liked the noise and smoke much and the two-stroke triples did sound rough, unless you were riding one – then you got the whirr instead of the rattle – and the smoke was left all along the lane as witness to a bike which defied the generally accepted standards of safety and mechanical soundness.

I still rode hard, and as fast as I could, most of the time, but took a lot more care with the mechanical safety aspect. I was on a bike that could get me into danger, real easy, so I took greater care over its operation: tyres, brakes, steering etc. and concentrated a lot more on rider skill and staying alert.

Nothing was going to stop me twisting that throttle though; for a while after Phil died, speed on two wheels was the only thing I wanted to live for: that and rock music. I realised I had turned the page on 2-Tone and everything that went with it. Motorcycle culture was alive to some degree in every town and most of the local pubs; it was about finding your own individuality, a lifestyle not a youth sub-cult… and we had lives to live.

September '86 was potato picking season, 'spudding' once again. That was Will on the tractor and me, Rob, Greeny and Sarah on the harvester. We sorted the spuds from the stones and clods of clay all day and then blew our money up at the club afterwards.

I think after the first pay night, when we all went up the club after work, Sarah and I were going out again and life was good once more. Julia Brown was a fanciable lady-friend of mine; although we had never coupled up, she was furious that I was back with Sarah. Julia never knew what she wanted really, until she couldn't have it. Anyway, she and Sarah never got along, I would know Julia for quite some time and we never fell out. I don't know where she is now.

Spudding lasted till early October, by which time the roads held a bit of moisture early in the mornings. I decked my KH twice on the same day, by leaning too far, once around the pub corner (the Black Horse) where the camber falls away and again on the Greenfields ring. Both times it was the front wheel that slid away from me – a technical design fault due to the bike's rear of centre weight distribution; or just me being an idiot and pushing it, beyond its limits on unsuitable surfaces.

The Lambretta came out in fine weather only, due to its chrome and lovely paint work. I only got the finish I was happy with just before the weather turned, and my lasting memory of that first custom build was a good one. Sitting out on that little custom seat we were, parked in the club shelter late one still evening. It was just me and my girl and a first frost catching starlight on the grass outside. It was a chilly night, we could see our breath and for a short while I didn't want to be anywhere else.

Nothing lasts forever and life's beautiful moments, often few and far between, come as gifts to compensate for all the other stuff we have to go through.

This was a year of reflection in more ways than I need to talk about. I got off the dole, developed interests, mended myself emotionally and started living again. I lost one of my oldest and best friends, and out of that I learned to forgive and come to terms with a lot of stuff that was holding me back, as well as spoiling some things too.

I would react against the things I thought were wrong, but, didn't give enough thought about what should be right. One thing is for sure: everything I learned, I learned it the hard way and often I had to learn some things more than once.

The number of motorcycle accidents that I would recognise as such got to a count of fourteen by the end of the year, with no lasting injuries. Not a bad record for the road – if we were talking off road then it was every weekend – still, all these slips and spills came with nothing more serious than a constant collection of cuts and bruises. I really didn't care about the CB anymore, it was my party bike and I dropped it more times than I can remember, mostly on my way to or from parties up at the club.

In December that year, I started to rebuild a Panther M100 engine in my makeshift bedroom that was a space in the loft of our crumbling bungalow. Dad had encouraged me to buy a shed full of parts in several boxes and baskets. He wanted me to move over to good old reliable British bikes – heavy metal with thunder and guts – rather than the frantic, high revving Japanese lightweights that you had to ride at the top of their power range to get any performance out of them.

He hoped I would get excitement out of the grumbling, thumping torque produced by these classics of his youth... So he bought himself a crashed BSA 650 Super Rocket, with frame engine and cycle parts from 1958 to 1960 and '61 models. It was his dream to build a bike like he had when he was my age; more about that later, it didn't come together quickly or easily.

I liked the idea of a Panther, as despite being called Panther 100, it was a 600cc single cylinder engine in a heavy steel frame, with a big fat old fashioned tank. Mine was all in bits after someone had made an attempt at a re-spray, but given up after the red oxide coat. It still sits outside in the shed all in bits to date, as I came to a standstill with the engine build, mostly due to a few missing parts that weren't readily available to me. I never really got that time back again to start a bike from scratch. I keep saying 'one day.' We will see.

My hair and beard were growing like a curly mop and I was never out of denims, leather or wax cotton 'Belstaffs'. My denim cut-off, with the flames painted under the word Sellindge, has been on my back during many great events over the years. It has been drenched in beer and set on fire, I've worn it until the metal buttons have pulled through the holes and the cuts at the shoulders have crept towards the collar. I still own it today and it feels very soft and lived in.

What I must have spent over the years going up the club most evenings I don't know, but that was our place and I couldn't imagine that routine coming to an end. It wasn't always great, but no matter what kind of an evening I'd had, it was always going to be an exciting ride home.

I remember early the next year that I had a close call one night on Swan lane, just before the Moorstock Lane turning, where the bike jack-knifed on black ice at a fair old speed. I managed to hold it on the road without coming a cropper – the trick is not to slow up. The day after that, I went to Wembley stadium with Dave and Tony to see Meat Loaf. We would re-live that experience some eighteen years later at Leeds castle in the rain.

By the end of the first week in 1987, the weather started closing in. More progress was done on my Panther engine, getting the rocker box sorted out, and we got heavy snow. That meant, as always, more thrills and spills on the road. I slid off at the Broad Street onto Swan lane T-junction and then did it a couple of days later at the top of Brook Lane with Sarah on the back. That was actually quite fun, neither of us were hurt and she forgave me. Sarah and I weren't going steady anymore and were meant to be 'just good friends,' but that's difficult in a small village where you all hang out in the same groups at the same places. She could be very sweet at times, but as confusing as I was irrational and that wasn't a good combination.

We were snowed in at the farm for the whole of the next week, it was great. Dad and I rode the YZ across the fields to get to the dairy farm where we swapped a joint of meat for a small churn of milk with Phil's parents, Andy and Pauline. A couple of days later, we took two of the lighter trials bikes to Sellindge to get supplies. The drifts were so high in the lanes that the hedges were almost hidden and it was possible, in some places, to ride right over where the hedges and fences were covered. I liked being cut off and being the only one able to get around. Most of all I loved bikes and the freedom they gave me.

# CHAPTER EIGHT

## *Mad Mile Club*

One Saturday evening in late February '87, Dad and I drove to some place in Essex, just the other side of the Dartford tunnel, to look at a 1962 Triumph Speed Twin. The 5TA was a 500cc machine, also favoured as a police bike in its day. This one did not have a bath-tub fairing or headlight cowling. It was a real Marlon Brando iron horse, in black. The price was £500 and Dad was so keen for me to have it, he signed out ten £50 cheques, which his cheque guarantee card would cover at £50 a time. The bloke wouldn't take a £500 cheque and we hadn't brought cash.

I had arrived on the biking scene and with this cult classic no one could dispute my credentials. It was a fact that most of the bikers I knew of then, rode Jap bikes from the late '70s or early '80s, and I soon discovered why.

The next day my Triumph wouldn't start, which was just typical. Over the next three years to come, I took every part of that bike to pieces, except for the crank shaft itself and Vick Miller at Miller Motorcycles in Hastings did that for me. I used to dread going to that shop, the old boy was such a purist – I just wanted to be able to use the bike; I didn't mind if it had the wrong screws and washers holding it together.

It was a real old fashioned set up though, that shop. He worked there with his son Tony (in his thirties) and on

Saturdays the young grandson would be there. At break times, by the clock, regardless of people queuing, work would stop and all three would sit down at a bench to eat their sandwiches together, whilst customers just had to stand and wait if they didn't want to lose their place in the queue. Anyone under forty got a lecture into the bargain – because obviously they didn't understand British mechanics. You got the feeling he hated greasers too. Vick Miller didn't want your money so much as he just wanted your bike to be right.

I don't think there was a single nut, bolt, screw, bush or pin that didn't have to come out and be refitted or replaced, many of them several times during the period I was riding that bike. I had to change every single bit of wiring too, as the whole lot was brittle and corroded; but did I have some fun on that machine, oh yes.

The following list is an inventory of all the repairs I had to do, that I can remember now, but doesn't include the necessary regular maintenance required to keep any British bike on the road – that all goes without saying. I did however do most of the repairs using a simple tool box kit, a couple of hammers and soft metal and wooden drifts. The Rayburn oven hot-plate came in handy too for expanding crank cases and cast iron barrels, to ease the drifting of crank bearings and tappet blocks.

The inventory of repairs from over a three year period for this Triumph 5TA included:

- Replace broken speedo cable.

- Replace plugs, points, distributor cap, arm and leads.

- Replace broken clutch cable, requiring removal of kick-start/selector side casing.

- Replace kick-start/selector side casing gasket – in doing so, after polishing up the side casing and sealing down my new handmade gasket with red hematite, it transpired that the kick-start return spring had not located its anchor point, so I opted for an old bungee cord to keep it raised until the next time I would need to break the seal and open her up.

- Replace rear stop light of sender and modify mechanism (due to constant problems with rear stop light jamming on).

- Replace several front parking bulbs (the holder was never firmly connected and they kept blowing).

- Reconstruct instrument consul into a less ugly design resembling a pirate captain's cocked hat (with skull and crossed bones design in Airfix paint, for good measure).

- Strip down ignition/light switch combination – very complicated, involving lots of wired up grub screws and lose locking studs. I was never convinced that the multi-coloured wires connecting all these studs were the correct colours or screwed into their correct positions in the first place. I did that twice to clean the corrosion off the connecting studs, as the rubber bung was missing and the whole affair was open to the elements.

- Complete rewiring (every wire except the ones coming from the generator, where the carburettor dripped petrol right onto my connections).

- Overhaul petrol tap and polish it up – I didn't put it straight back in and the cork seal dried out and shrank. It never ever sealed properly after that.

- Repair leaky tank spot around where the tap screws in – I did it with Petro-patch, that worked and is still fine now.

- Seal the copper pipe from tap to carburettor (multiple attempts, never fully successful).

- Bypass ammeter with a spare wire (it was not conducting).

- Replace ammeter – I did pay out eventually, but not for years.

- Construct new front mudguard stays from aluminium tubing (the originals parted due to vibration fatigue).

- Extensive repairs to rear mudguard – I used copper and rubber sheeting as the aluminium guard suffered severely from vibration fatigue.

- Re-spray dent in front of petrol tank, caused by my habit of wrapping a chain and padlock around the centre of the handlebars – one evening leaving the pub, the padlock had fallen between the top of the forks and the front of the tank, jamming the steering and forcing me across the road in front of oncoming traffic.

- Replace multiple stoplight bulbs – foot pegs had lost their position locking serrations, causing gradual pressure on the rear brake lever, keeping the stoplight on and burning out the bulbs.

- Remove the extra capacity float chamber cap from the Amal mono-block carburettor, for polishing.

- Replace two of the three float chamber cap retaining screws because I had not 'locktited' them, after replacing the beautifully polished cap and they had vibrated loose and disappeared. This came to my notice when the engine cut out and I realised that all the fuel was pouring out of the float chamber rather than going through the jets.

- Replace distributor body – various attempts made to repair and secure original body due to it coming loose in its collar block and kicking itself out on two occasions. The replacement one was worse than the original.

- Replace front fork tubes (fitted by Vick Miller who refused to rebuild my instrument consul as he said it was 'Heath Robinson').

- Repair seat and line frame mounting with rubber radiator piping – seat lock was ripped off by me mounting the bike in a hurry to get to the pub and falling straight off over the other side.

- Repair carburettor manifold – originally removed to reseal the flange surface, as air was leaking through and bypassing the carb. This was caused by over tightening the two nuts on the wings and distorting the alloy flange. I struck it on a flat surface to make a flush fit again and made up new gaskets, though I probably should have changed the old cracked and hardened rubber O ring too, its lack of give must have been a contributory factor for why the flange was distorted in the first place. When I tightened the nuts back down, one of the studs just pulled out of the casting like it had the consistency of old chewing gum left on the bed post.

- Repair inlet manifold properly (sent off to SRM engineering in Wales to have threaded brass inserts fitted).

- Remove rocker covers for polishing and to reset tappets – when I put them back on, the studs pulled themselves out of the head.

- Fit steel helicoil springs into aluminium engine head – Vick Miller was horrified at the suggestion of brass inserts, I wasn't too sure but the helicoils have held out fine.

- Replace clutch plates (primary drive casing removed, I can't remember how many times) – initially this was due to clutch slip, but also sticking and heavy clunking on gear changes. I cleaned the plates and filed out the locating tabs and slots. They ended up looser, but looked like they would not jam. The clutch was no better at all, so off it came again and brand new plates went in. Still no good, due to the relaxed springs and terribly worn groves in the inner clutch hub, no amount of filing could ever have sorted that out. Those twenty uncaged roller bearings were hell to get back in place.

- Replace clutch inner hub, including shock absorbing rubber spider and the twenty roller bearings – each time I removed and replaced the primary drive casing I chewed up more of the alloy casing, resulting in more helicoils to fit, more gaskets to make and more tubes of red hematite to buy. I later went onto blue 'Hylomar', as it was stickier, and you could put it on thicker. She still leaked oil from every casing though.

- Replace top and bottom steering headstock bearings, cups and channels – twenty-five years of over tightening had oscillated the whole setup. As the headstock was off, I stripped the yokes using 'Nitromors' and re-sprayed.

- Replace swinging arm bushes (Dad took it somewhere to get that done).
- Replace brake shoes and emery cloth drum surfaces.
- Replace wheel bearings.

I think that was all of the serious stuff, apart from other general maintenance and repairs that I had to do all the time and little modifications like welding a foot onto the side stand (badly). Years later I welded a toe spike onto that, which dug into the tarmac on a tight turn and ripped the whole foot off.

On Friday 6th March 1987 I had the last and most spectacular crash on that KH250. I was speeding along the lanes, doing fifty or more as I came round a bend in a low point on the road. I overshot onto the verge and tried to ride it out rather than lean it on the loose surface. It would have worked but for a dry ditch running between the verge and the hedge. I had no choice but to go down it, or hit the hawthorn on its far side. It took me twenty yards to come to a stop, upside down in the ditch, which was two or three foot deep. I'd hung on in there until the bike rode up the far side, hit the thorn hedge and flung us both back down.

I suffered some scratches to my face where thorns had forced my visor up. My front mudguard and indicators were wrecked and I missed the GP appointment I was trying to get to.

I sold that bike to Dave Keeble the next day for £10, complete with bent handlebars and twisted forks. It would be worth fifty times that now in the same condition.

When the law was changed in the early eighties, bringing the legal cubic capacity of an L plated learner bike down from 250cc to 125cc, all the old 250s became cheap run-a-rounds and the market was full of them. Anyone who had just passed their test could afford one and most riders never intended to keep them longer than it took to save up for a 400 or 500cc machine. 750cc and beyond was serious, and generally beyond the reach of your average teenaged rebel, unsuitable too for the kind of bar-hopping roads we were using before public opinion on drink driving reached out into the green, ultimately killing off most of the countryside drinking holes.

About this time Dad bought a Yamaha RD250, air-cooled of course, from Woody's dad down the road. It was the same eye catching metallic blue as the 125cc version that Phil had had a couple of years before.

I bought this bike from Dad about six months later and rode it for a short time before selling it on. All I remember about it particularly were the Avon Roadrunner tyres, which were quite popular, and its rather straight profiled twin exhaust system.

I have few memories of riding the RD, other than an incident on the same stretch of road where I'd smashed my CB pannier off – it was just past the bend and a car in front stopped to turn up the driveway to the club. Clearly riding too fast and too close, I had to swerve around the car which set off a fish-tail motion, almost causing me to loose control.

I hadn't been used to the handling; the flat profile and narrow, straight bars didn't really appeal to me either. Those bikes are sought after classics now of course.

On Friday 13th March 1987 the unthinkable happened: we were all banned for life from the Sellindge Sports and Social Club. Our whole group were served membership rejection letters, as a consequence of our continued disrespectful and riotous behaviour.

After Melvin and Anna had left, the new barman, Alan, had tried to make the place into a respectable family type establishment. I get his point, but Melv had kept us in tow because he had earned our respect and he liked a laugh. I don't actually remember seeing Alan laugh and so that was that, the end of an era in many respects.

We had lost our meeting place and they knocked down the shelter soon after, as a kind of scorched earth policy. That silly little shelter had been a juvenile hangout for years and we had painted it up, with a huge union jack covering over all the ugly graffiti that was there previously. The mural had covered the whole back wall, and with an old sports bench against it, that was where we parked up our bikes, talked and laughed, smoked and drank, loved and lost. It meant something to most of us.

There was no choice but to start patronising the Dukes Head, out on the main road. Some of us were banned from the Mucky Duck and I was banned from the Black Horse. I kept getting banned by landlords named Alan and Ray and it wasn't long before I got banned from the Dukes as well. We didn't need to be told we were barred from the Plough and the Blue Anchor in Brabourne.

Sellindge and Brabourne were neighbouring villages and there was still a good chance of trouble between the yobs from both sides, which the respective publicans were aware of – and there had been incidents on the last three occasions we'd turned up at their drinking holes. Fortunately pubs changed hands quite regularly, so there were always one or two local places we could get a drink and have a riot at from time to time.

I finished my year on Ashford Borough Council's manpower services scheme, full of misfits and work-shy petty villains that the scheme had dredged from the job centre. It was a three-day week twelve-month starter and the only entry qualification was that you had to have been on the dole for six months.

I was free to start working weekdays as well as weekends for Dad at the farm. I also moved out about that time to a shared house in Sellindge, where I built my own small bike shed out of old church pews and corrugated iron.

Allegiances changed and new oily faces moved into the local biker scene. There was Chip, who I had known when Phil was still with us, he used to go out with one of the girls who hung around up the club. He came from a pretty dysfunctional family environment, living in a house by the A20 where they kept chickens and ferrets.

Chip's mate was Rat-boy Martin who I'd first come across sprawled on the Sellindge stores driveway drinking cider. He was always in filthy ragged leathers and had a foul smelling cut down Z400J. He'd painted it Armageddon black and rode the thing like a maniac.

Greasy Colin was relatively tame, a pleasant enough chap but he didn't stick around for too long.

They all lived in Smeeth but didn't fit with the rest of the village youth there, who were all smoothies in cars. So we became the Mad Mile Club: after a stretch of the A20 between Chip's place and Norrington's garage, which became Bob Fisher's and is now something else. There was a straight mile downhill with a dip at the bottom, where the aim was to get to a hundred before the blind summit at Norrington's.

Despite the fact that I was by this time more Grebo than Scooterist, I came across an advert' in the Motorcycle News for a Vespa Rally 200. I went up to Harpenden, half way between

83

London and Luton, to look at this ugly, dull-green scooter in well used condition and I bought it for £270, which I think was a bit too much, considering it was tatty.

It was great fun to rack around the village though while the Triumph was having a rest and it was always reliable. The thing was great at wheelies, jumps and 'broadies'. I discovered that I could throw it into a bend and when the undercarriage hit the road, I could control the slide like some kind of skidoo.

I don't think I ever actually liked the scooter much in itself – there was nothing appealing about it – but I had wanted a Rally 200 since I first got into scooters, as it was supposed to be a worthy model. Mine looked like it had come out of the Vietnam War itself, which was a popular theme in the eighties, recent enough for a string of cult film classics to burn themselves into our consciousness, but distant enough for us not to have been affected.

We still had the very real apocalyptical prospect of war with the Russians to consider and, as a consequence of that fear, there was a strong element of the survivalist in a lot of us – me particularly. I stocked up on bullets and cans of baked beans; ten years later the corroding rounds were jamming in my rifle and the cans were rotting through their seams in a damp caravan cupboard.

So much for nuclear winter: you can't store stuff in damp holes in the ground and expect to use it in five-years-time, let alone wait out for the end of days. None of us could have predicted that we were only two years away from the collapse of the Soviet Union and the end of the Cold War. Then it was the Gulf War setting the scene, and after that you only had to be involved if you chose to be.

Anyway I rode that Vespa around for a while and then when the tax and MOT ran out, I rode it into the ground.

One funny incident I remember later on in the summer of that year was taking Del back to Kestrels (the house on the main road I was living at with Woz Leggett and Stu 'The Boss' Saunders). We had passed a police car going the other way along the A20 just before the Dukes. I saw it start to turn around, as I knew it would, so I pulled the throttle right back and made for the home driveway. I didn't slow up when I got there, just jammed the rear brake on at the entrance, spinning the back around into the loose grit and shouting 'get off!' to Del. He ran into the house and I rode straight up the drive, across the back lawn and out into the field at the back, where I laid it down in the undergrowth and waited.

The Fuzz did knock on the door and were met by Woz, doing his best to look confused, with Del sitting on the sofa, hair flat back on his head and an abandoned crash hat nearby. They both declared they hadn't seen any bikes coming their way.

There were at least two other incidents of cops trying to pull me over when I was on that scooter. I always doubled back and made it to safety somehow. It didn't help that the back light had stopped working and I'd never bothered fixing it. This was an advert for a pull at night, but I don't think I ever cleaned that number plate and it didn't shine back, so as long as I could get away I kept the points off my licence.

As far as accidents go, I think all I did was slide it over on that corner round the Black Horse pub hill in the morning damp, just as I'd done on the KH the year before.

A year or so later Stuey got himself a Vespa 125 and we both went to the Margate scooter rally. I didn't enjoy myself much, as

I wasn't so much into what scootering had become. The music had moved on and the mindless thuggery carried no class. I did manage to avoid two close calls with the law though.

There was not one thing legal about my Rally 200 by that time, and that was obvious for anyone to see. The best one was on the way there with the boys in blue staked out at the St Nicholas roundabout as we came over the top of the hill down to Birchington. There were ten or so of them pulling every scooter over onto the side, where a concrete track ran parallel to the main A28. They were all searching riders and scooters for weapons (which I did have), or directing us to cruise on to the next officer in the line who was checking documents (which I didn't have).

I was quite worried, but each officer I passed seemed to be dealing with someone else and waved me on to the next. When I got to the last one in the line he was looking the other way, so I just taxied along the concrete path for a bit, then dropped back onto the road and throttled up, heading for the built up area I could see, to wait in a side road for Stu to come past.

I was pleased to be rid of that scooter: when I did sell it the thing had become a complete wreck. To name one example of its many defects: the rear suspension shock absorber was warped at the anchor point, causing part of it to rub on the tire wall under any load. That blew a tire out eventually. When I sold it, the bloke only got a mile or two up the road before the next one went. I still feel guilty about that I have to say.

# CHAPTER NINE

## Run to the hills

In the summer of eighty-seven, I was persuaded to buy a Yamaha SX250 (a four-stroke) from Chris Woods, he was an old mate from school who started getting down the Mucky Duck on band nights. I think I paid £80 for it as a runabout. Chris told me how reliable it always was, but I didn't find it so.

There was a starting problem, so I did what I knew about, I checked the plugs and cleaned out the fuel system. It ran for a bit, then three days later the same problem. I cleaned the carbs again, but no improvement. A few days later, I spent hours fully cleaning out the whole system top to bottom, as petrol just wasn't getting to the plugs. I put it all back together and the bastard still wouldn't work.

With tears of rage, I booted the back light and smashed it, then wished I hadn't. I gave up then and sold the bike to Dave Keeble for £40, he said he left it a day and it ran fine. The problem had been fuel blockages caused by rust in the tank, as I had thought. However, it was after the third clean out, when I actually dismantled the vacuum chambers at the top of the carbs, not really understanding what their purpose was, that the engine refused even to fire.

I had never dealt with vacuum carbs before; I didn't know that if they weren't primed, then an airlock could prevent any fuel getting through. All Keeble had done was leave it to stand overnight, so that they managed to prime themselves and I'd done all the work for him – ran like a dream he told me.

Well, it was midsummer and the Triumph was up and running. I took her out with the gang to the Bull at Bethersden, which was quite a biker hangout at the time. Martin had his girl Michelle with him, her mate Zoe was riding on the back with Dave the Goober, on his black Suzuki GS400, the factory custom version. I think Tone was on the back of Chip, who had just got himself a brand new red Honda FT500 single, on HP. He wrecked that within a year, sold it to Colin and stopped the payments. I don't know how he got away with it, but how do you punish a man with no money or property who doesn't care? I don't think they managed to get the child maintenance payments out of him either for his three kids by different women.

After an evening on the beer, Dave seemed to have won his girl and we all rode back along the dark winding lanes. I became obsessed with riding so close to the back of Dave that I could skim my front tyre against his rear tyre, which was the game. Zoe didn't like it, and when Dave braked I over-shot his wheel, denting my painstakingly polished aluminium mudguard against his rear springs. I knocked it out later, but the scuff mark is still there.

This was a stupid game, I realise that, but not as stupid as Dave and Tony standing in front of the darts board at the Duck and challenging us to throw darts around their heads. To make it a bit safer, they wore open faced piss-pot crash helmets!

Often at the end of an evening some of us would go up to the Farthing to cool off. We did on that night, so Dave could have a smoke and get some peace. I left him and Zoe there and went home to sleep it off.

The next morning I was sick, which was not an uncommon occurrence for the way we were drinking as a habit. Newcastle Brown Ale became the bikers brew and we would drink bottles of the oily muck at parties, it wasn't actually that strong, so we could keep going all night when the occasion called. Dave and I still preferred pints of mild though, when you could get Ind Coope on tap.

The dynamic of our gang of five had changed, but it was still always five active members as a nucleus. Will came and went like some kind of stray dog. He was seasonal, largely due to pretty much running the farm where he worked. He would mostly be out of touch for the best three months of summer, busy with his harvest. The other reason was that he was driven by the wander lust and, like a stray dog; he seemed intent on pissing up every tree he could reach. He was only short, but he seemed to have a good aim.

There were still a few good times left in him over the next year before he did a disappearing act, but he seemed more interested in a string of 'end of the road cars' he kept buying from the local scrap yard. I suppose the girls liked the back seat of a Ford Capri better than a Suzuki GS.

Del had left home and gone to live with a girl called Lynn, who he had met working at the local cake factory. He was out of it, down in St Mary's Bay for what seemed ages, but was probably only a year. He was all loved up and only came out if she did too. Lynn had a brother called Pete who was into bikes - he was quite dark and known as 'Paki Pete' - he had quite a bad motorbike accident at some stage, which left him with recurrent back problems. Pete rode a Honda Superdream and was a good enough bloke, too decent to be much of an animal.

We didn't have a name on our backs but myself, Dave, Chip and Martin (with Tony or Colin as and when they fancied) were the undisputed rough riders of the Mad Mile Club. We wore one set of motorcycle clothing, generally scuffed leather jackets with padded shoulders and cheap market jeans with leather patches sewn onto the knees. I wore a Belstaff Trail jacket, (wax cotton) and ex-army para boots, which were all the rage. The others had all cut down their open faced crash helmets into little pots and sprayed them matt black. I kept mine full face but substituted the visor for flying goggles, just to make sure I had no peripheral vision.

We would race from country pub to country pub for a beer and a laugh any night of the week. Places on the edge of Romney Marsh were good, with names like the Botolphs Bridge Inn, the Shepherd and Crook and the inappropriately named Welcome Stranger – odd little places with few customers, miles from any town, on unlit roads with right-angled bends to take you there: it was great.

A regular ride out might be a meeting at the Mucky Duck in Sellindge, off to the Farriers in Mersham, then a few games of pool in the Ewe and Lamb in Wittesham, and a thrash back to Sellindge, via the White Horse in Bilsington, arriving at the Dukes for last orders. We had to race to get around of an evening, because landlords rang the bell at 10.30.

I do miss British licensing laws; it meant that everyone would be out of their homes by 8pm, 'cause they only had two and a half hours of decent drinking time. Now-a-days people don't go down the local pubs 'till gone 9pm, if at all, even on a band night. Having strictly adhered to opening hours was what helped to make a pub session what it was, you had a limited time slot and all the people you wanted to meet turned up on time. In any case there wouldn't be the variety there was then, within a relatively small catchment area, if people now were to regress to the habits of the good old days.

Most of the small isolated pubs have long since closed down or been pulled down. It would never work now since drink driving has (rightly) become so taboo and no-one is going to shell out for taxis all around the villages.

We lived through an era of youth and mobility that will never be seen again. Now-a-days young people with newish, reliable cars, who are paying £1000 plus on their motor insurance leave them at home. They club in for the taxi fare into town to go to the trendy chain brand pubs to tank up, then queue up for the overpriced nightclubs. They think they have had a cheap night if they spend less than £100 in some place where they can't hear the music or hold a conversation.

No one plays darts anymore or drinks 'Newkie' brown from the bottle, wearing fingerless gloves. I liked it when we could choose our own music on the juke box and a meal in a pub was a pie or a burger at the bar that you could eat while you were having a laugh.

In the first week that August, the Mad Mile Club set off for our long-planned run to Snowdonia, the first real bike trip any of us had been on.

There was Martin on his death-Z, which stank like a sewer every time he hosed it down at service stations to cool the engine. Chip was on his Honda, which he'd just got in order to do the run, the only respectable bike he has ever had. Dave's GS was annoyingly impersonal, as were all factory customs, because there was nothing you could do to them that didn't make them look worse. Dave's contribution to individuality was Maltese cross mirrors, which gave a restricted and distorted view, a Maltese cross rear light, which gave off less red than my Triumph's 6 volt standard Lucas did, and a tank sticker of a naked woman.

My bike didn't have mirrors and my side view was restricted by the clumsy flying goggles wedged into my full face helmet. That didn't matter though: decked out in greasy Belstaffs and farm worker's gloves, I knew I looked good.

The Speed twin with its hand painted skull and cross-bones instrument consul, shaky 6-volt lights and seriously restrictive four gear clunky transmission had the most stories to tell. With its kick-start supported by a ragged bungee cord, it stood at every stop in a heat haze of evaporating engine oil. I had grafted an old Honda luggage rack onto it, which stacked my gear too far to the rear, causing the front to feel a bit light and sloppy. I had a ribbed Avon SM tyre on the front and a brick shaped remoulded side-car tyre on the back, which gave it some flat traction but not a lot of lean.

We left on a Friday evening after work, stopping in Ashford for petrol on the way out and I immediately had to make repairs to the front mudguard. One of the aluminium stays had parted, due to metal fatigue from all the vibration and was threatening to jam in the spokes. So it was dusk by the time we got back out on the road.

We ploughed on up the A20, M20, M26, and then came out onto the M25 west, riding four abreast. That didn't last long. We made the lead off onto the M40, Oxford bound, and stopped for the night on the grass the other side of the crash barrier. We just lay out beside our bikes and didn't waste time putting up tents. Chip didn't even have a sleeping bag.

The increase in traffic caused us to rise early and they all had to wait while I brewed up my morning cup of tea. Martin called 'Let's get on those morgue slabs' and we powered off towards Oxford. We made a garage stop on the outskirts of the city so that Martin could get a rear tyre change. He had been riding on slicks for weeks but the canvas was starting to show through. It did look suitably armageddon, but it wasn't going to make it to the mountains and back.

We were just pulling out of this village square after a stop at a reasonably unfriendly pub when my distributor flew out of the block and there it was, hanging from the HT leads: things looked bad. We examined this vital bit of electrical mechanics and the black hole it had come out from. It seemed the steel pin which held the gear pinion at the bottom of the spindle shaft had worked itself halfway out; this had snagged on one of the gear cogs in the box and thrown the whole thing out.

Right across the street there happened to be a small old fashioned workshop of some kind, with a vice and some basic tools that the old boy there let me use. I pulled the pin right out and hammered it straight, then refitted it, swelling both ends of the pin with a hammer and punch. We slotted the distributor back in, gently meshing the gears in place and had to make several attempts at re-timing the ignition by turning the rear wheel, with the bike on its centre stand and in fourth gear. The points had to be reset, so that they just started opening with the right hand piston at top dead centre on its inlet stroke. Within the hour we were fit to ride.

We left the motorways behind at Telford and took the A5, a

picturesque easy riding route west, heading for Llanwrst on the Conway River valley. This route meandered pleasantly, gaining ground all the time. We cheered when we passed the sign to show we were really in Wales.

It was a hot afternoon and we were all getting saddle sore; we didn't need any more mechanical problems, but we got some all the same. My bike started coughing and spluttering whenever we got to a bend and I had to tease the throttle grip constantly to keep it running. This got worse and worse over the final forty to fifty miles to Llanwrst. Every time we stopped, they all had to push the Triumph further and further along the road to bump start me before she would fire and pick up enough revs to keep the wheels turning.

We looked at the points, plugs, leads and distributor cap, the petrol tap and carburettor float chamber. Nothing we discovered pointed to anything other than an old worn, leaky Triumph engine under load on a hot day.

She was still clawing her way through the afternoon and I was able to cajole the old girl round the last few bends and nurse her into Llanwrst, where we set up tents at a camp site on the edge of the small stone-grey town.

After a bit of a rest we went out on foot to find a pub and some entertainment. The pub we found had its fiercely territorial regulars who weren't pleased to see us. We were at the bar and this old boy in a flat cap came up next to us as if he had lost his ferret and said 'I'll fight the best one of you' – and he meant it too. He was fifty years old if he was a day. The initial hostility melted away after a younger chap decided he wanted to make us welcome by asking a few questions and then we settled in okay.

A couple of local girls, one alright looking and one big old thing who needed a shave, came and joined our table, they were talking about their babies. Of cause Chip said he had one too and when they asked if we liked babies, Chip's answer was 'We like making babies' and everyone laughed. The girls moved on and we stayed till closing time.

We hadn't eaten, so went out and found a Chinese takeaway packed with drunk people eating and shouting. I think that was part of the local culture and a proper end to a regular Saturday night in that town. We made it back to the tents and were just about to crash out, when we were disturbed by those two girls from the pub. They had tracked us down and were trying to work out who was in which tent. I heard the ugly one bellow out 'I want that little one.' Martin was trying to keep his head down and Chip was wishing he had brought his own tent. We managed to get rid of them and sleep off the day's events, finally.

The next morning, I unscrewed the large hollow cap at the bottom of the Amal Carb, the one that encloses the filter and main jet. The three inch crooked brass slide needle came out with the cap. It should have been attached to the top of the slide, but the worn out circlip wasn't holding it and it had clearly just been sitting there, sealing off the needle jet since half way through yesterday afternoon. My engine had been running on air and whatever small amounts of petrol had been able to escape up the shaft of the needle when it rattled and jolted around.

With that mystery cleared up and sorted out, my bike ran fine all round Snowdonia and back home to Ashford without any more concerns.

Over the next few days we visited waterfalls, castles, lakes and a copper mine amongst other stuff, but the main event was climbing Mount Snowdon. I was keener than the others, but Dave couldn't make it due to his bad leg: he never lost that limp after he had snapped his ball joint in a bicycle accident at sixteen.

We undertook the ascent of Snowdon on a hot day in full motorcycle clothing (minus gloves and helmets). Chip and Martin were complaining after the first hour on the trail and I had to lie to them to stop them pulling out. To make it more interesting, I conned them into making our way straight up the inside of the horseshoe, leaving the path way below us.

The theory was that it was a shorter distance and, once we had made the ridge, it would be a gentle walk to the summit, where we could have a beer at the café. I wasn't wrong and if we had been experienced mountaineers with the right boots on, it would have made sense. We weren't and we hadn't, but we soon discovered that once you have committed yourself and then reached a point where it is so steep, you are scared of loosing your footing, and falling to your death. It's even more scary to contemplate turning round, – and probably more risky. I honestly didn't think Chip could have gone backwards in tight jeans and steel toe cap Doctor Martens.

We did get out onto the narrow ridge and made it over the boulder scramble, finally getting to the cairn on top of the highest point in England and Wales. We couldn't see a thing from the top, as the cloud was sitting over it and I don't remember drinking any beer either.

On the way down we used the same tactic: get to the road the other side of our ridge in the shortest time possible. We could see it once we were back on the arm of the mountain and it looked like half of it could be done sliding down a scree slope. So off we went, stumbling and scrabbling down the stony valley, whooping like idiots and expecting that the road would start appearing nearer once we came below the cloud.

Everything is deceptive in the mountains and the scree only took us so far before we found ourselves on uncharted cliffy bluffs, with no clear and obvious safe route. Eventually we got down onto the road, but we were miles below the Llanberis pass where our bikes were parked. Some holiday maker picked us up and dropped us at the start point.

It was good to get back on those bikes. The day was still warm and we caught up with Dave at the small slate-grey village of Beddgelert, after a cold swim in one of the smaller lakes on the way.

I was keen to get back to Sellindge, as I had agreed to be the security at some girl's village hall birthday party the coming Saturday.

Dave decided to ride with me, but the others wanted to stay another couple of days. It was a straight run on a blazing hot day and apart from my mudguards shaking themselves to pieces, everything held out fine. Dave's bike never played up the whole time he had it, as far as I can remember.

The night of the birthday party was one to remember; it was an under eighteen's set up, so what could possibly go wrong? Chip and Martin got back just in time and brought Tony along: Just as well, because there were dozens of drunken rows going on amongst the partygoers. The host was no help, intent on getting off with someone she fancied right in front of her boyfriend.

There were kids throwing up and squaring up to each other everywhere you looked, and we had to stand on all the internal doors as well as the main entrance keeping everything under control. The village copper turned up to close it down in the end, after complaints by local villagers.

A couple of days later I went with Chip and Martin to Paddock Wood Kawasaki centre, as Martin wanted to buy a brand new GPZ-750 turbo. Well, he wanted to part exchange it for his rat bike with its four into one exhaust system cut off short with an angle grinder, rear shocks welded up solid, a little cut down seat and a chromed skull mounted on the front mudguard. Chip managed to mention that it had the remains of a burger shoved into its engine fins and smelt like a toilet, which didn't help the negotiations, so we took ourselves off to raid the complementary customer coffee dispenser, leaving Martin to recover his bargaining position.

A short conversation later and we were riding full throttle back to the village. Martin revised his options and ended up getting hold of an XS650 parallel twin, from which he built himself a weird looking but impressive custom chopper with 666 on the plate. I don't know what happened to that rat bike.

Del turned up down the pub that next weekend without Lynn and feeling sorry for himself. We got drunk and talked half the night about old stuff and new plans. Then he went back to her the next morning. Our gang of five went to the Leas Cliff Hall to see 'Hawkwind' the following Friday night, but left early to go to a party in Brabourne, which was even more disappointing and the year seemed to be running its course... But it all moved up a gear in late November when some of us went to a place called The Lodge, off the A20 in

Charing. A newly formed Motorcycle Club, The Oakmen, based in Ashford, were throwing a party and we got an invite.

# CHAPTER TEN

## *New faces*

The Oakmen owed their foundation to a bloke named Guy, about thirty years old with a short grizzly beard and a thousand yard stare. He struck me as a good president for a bike gang, tough but friendly enough, and genuinely passionate about running the club right. Once fully established the members displayed a side patch with an oak leaf decoration, not a back patch. I didn't understand the politics which came with all this at the time, hey it was only the first real bike club do I had attended.

One or two of the girls looked pretty good I remember, the live band rocked and there were stacks of 'proper' bikes parked up outside.

Martin's brother, Nigel, who was a few years older than us, was there with a bunch of his biker mates. I don't think he ever signed up but he was at all the club do's that I went to over the next few years. Martin began prospecting the following year and Chip a bit later on.

Not everyone I met up with was my cup of tea. I really just wanted a survivalist brotherhood amongst a handful of close friends who would look out for each other and be prepared to hole up in the woods and hills when the inevitable breakdown of civilisation came.

By December that year the road salt had taken its toll on the notoriously poor quality of the chromed parts on my CB200. My front mudguard actually separated at the centre bracket, rusted right through from underneath. I had to weld the front part back on with Dad's mig welder. I hadn't long learned to use it and so the job was ugly and bitty, but it would hold on for another year.

In general 1970s Yamahas and Kawasakis had the thickest steel mudguards and deepest chrome. Things like exhausts, headlight casings and brackets on Hondas and Suzukis only had half the lifespan their rivals did, whether you looked after them or not. It was a fact that Suzuki chrome pealed, off, whereas Honda's chromed parts rotted from the inside out.

Before I took my CB off the road (I kept it on there a couple of years longer than the law would have agreed with), the front mudguard stopped short at the forks bracket, the rear one didn't really exist under the saddle (I think the indicator stems were holding the back of it on) and both exhaust silencers had lost a couple of inches in length, as well as taken on a rather flattened appearance. Throwing it down the road regularly wouldn't have helped much and had scuffed the big fairing to buggery.

The CB was ratty with a character of its own. I had painted it with a mixture of red oxide and black bitumastic, there wasn't a glint of anything shiny left out and the whole thing was baked in a year's worth of road grit and filth.

Around this time I bought a Kawasaki KT250 trials bike, in racing green, from a bloke called Jez, a long haired biker with a big ginger beard. I bought it as a road legal off-roader. It ran on Castrol-R, a vegetable oil that smelt like a grass track meeting, instead of regular two-stroke oil. This competition bike had a wider gear ratio than our Fantic and Ossa trials bikes back on the farm and it had a new motocross tyre on the back wheel which was handy for faster riding in mud and snow.

I kept that bike for quite a while and even took it in the back of a Transit van to Cornwall, where I rode it across the middle of Bodmin moor, right up and over the steep rocky ridge of Rough Tor, and then miles across the moor to Jamaica Inn on the A30. I got ambitious on the way back around and tried to ride straight across Rough Tor marsh, which is a huge peat bog that feeds the De Lank River.

I went for it, rather than skirting all the way round to the north. It was a light bike, with some power coming off that knobbly and I thought that if I kept going at speed I could make it. I didn't get far before the bike started to founder and spun itself up to the rear axle. I stepped off onto one of the large reedy hummocks that mercifully were not too far apart from each other. I kept the bike revving with the front wheel pulled up and managed to turn it and lug it back to firm ground. It took a great deal of effort and I kept the tyre spinning constantly, so as not to lose momentum, throwing black mud all over me until I reached safety. I never tried that again.

At the end of November '87 I bought a KH400 from A1 Bike breakers for £395. It was a 1978 model in metallic lime green with CD ignition instead of the three points and condensers of the earlier models. Not as fiery as the old KH250, but faster and smoother, it had a beautiful sound between 4000 and 6000 revs. It didn't rattle as much as the 250 and those loose parts I did identify, the kick start and gear change mechanisms, I was able to soften somewhat by cutting out thin washers from a fairy liquid bottle, which restrained them to a degree while still allowing them to move easily. For some reason this 'Kwacker' didn't cut out in the wet or destroy plugs, the bulbs didn't repeatedly blow either; it was the most reliable bike I had owned. All I had to worry about was keeping a check on the tightness of the three mikuni carbs, as they had a tendency to work lose and twist round on the inlet manifolds, causing the floats to stick and air to be sucked in through the connecting joint.

I fitted the pair of round mirrors that had come originally from my old CB50 – I had refitted them onto my CB200 as well – I liked them, they were small and neat.

This new arrival didn't have mind blowingly awesome power, but could be persuaded to wheelie easy enough. It was nimble and could reach a ton on the mad mile while laying down a pale blue jet-stream of choking two-stroke smoke for 200 yards behind me.

She always drew some attention at any biker venue, as two-stroke triples had an evil reputation for bad road holding, twisty frames, unpredictable power surges, middle pot seizures and woefully inadequate breaking, not to mention an insatiable thirst. The earlier models certainly did have these faults to varying degrees, but by 1978 I reckon Kawasaki had produced their finest triple. The reputation was set though and it was the end of the line for that breed. Yamaha's RD two-stroke twins had none of those growing pains and eclipsed the 'Kwacker', producing updated models for another decade.

The ancestors of the KH, the 350cc S1 and 500cc H1, were actually the style inspiration for that ultimately desirable classic, the 900cc four-cylinder, double-overhead-cam Z1. If Goose and Toecutter hadn't shown us what the big Zs could do, I'm not sure they would still have held such respect well into the late eighties, given that there were plenty of high performance bikes around by then with lower price tags and alternative badges. A lot of the other super-bikes from the seventies went to the back sheds as chopping material and some came out okay, they didn't have the class of a T140 Bonneville though: that made a proper British chopper.

Another winter went by and in March of '88 I bought a CB400N from Derek's dad, Brian, as it wasn't running properly. I thought I could make a rat bike out of it, but I just couldn't get it running right either. I did discover that the woodruff key was sheared off so the rota wasn't locked in place, but it still didn't run any better once I'd put that right. When Chip offered to buy it from me I cut my losses and sold it for £50, I think I had paid Brian £90. Chip rode it away popping like a gun, with just the downpipes on. He rode it around a bit, then sold it on to Colin.

In early April, Martin held a 21st birthday party weekend at his place in Smeeth. It was down a small lane off Stone Hill and his back garden was a steep slope, with the bonfire at the top and some straw bales to sit on scattered about. Martin's party rules were for everyone to be as wild and barbaric as we felt able and we made sure we didn't disappoint.

Will had resurfaced; presumably his woman must have finally woken up to reality and kicked him out, as he was on the prowl for fresh meat. Dave Bish, who didn't show up until the Sunday, had been fazing himself out of our activities ever since he started getting serious with his new girlfriend Sharon. He was getting ready to settle down and become a family man and soon we would lose him. That weekend at Martin's was the last time I remember that all of us were in one place at the same time, drinking, laughing and playing the fool. They were good times, when all we had to concern ourselves with was beer and petrol.

The party kicked off after a regular Friday night session down the local pubs. Del brought Lynn and Pete, then forgot about them, as we got out of our heads on cider and psychedelic mushroom dust. Chip was doing the music and Fat Rob was charging around like a bull on speed. As a party trick, I let him pour a litre of cider into an old Triumph mudguard that was hanging up in the shed. It worked like a sluice channel, cascading out of the lower end while I drank as much as I could of the alcoholic road filth.

Beer was thrown in people's faces, initially as a sobering up method, where Tone got most of it, as he needed the most sobering up. We'd brought hoppers of it from the pub and mostly it was just for fun, as there was plenty of drink to go around. Will disgraced himself by getting caught snogging Martin's new bird, who's name was Sarah. Martin let it go at the time, as just an act of drunkenness, but that wasn't the end of the story. I think Will did him a favour really and then ended up paying for it for the next twenty years of his life.

All the local bikers turned up and there were some other molls and misfits too (Nigel's crowd), some I knew, some I didn't. I don't remember how it wound up or how everybody got home; maybe we slept by the fire, which would make sense.

It took me most of the next day to recover and I realised I had smashed the glass of my Swiss watch again. The plan was that after a day's rest, the party would kick off again on the Sunday afternoon.

I had yet another accident on my CB that Sunday, speeding

over to get there once I finished work. I ran her down the short steep slope where Southenay Lane drops onto Stone Hill at a blind summit, and my brakes weren't good enough to stop me short of the junction. I saw the car gunning it up the hill just too late, so laid off the brakes and went for it. If I'd held back, my brakes would probably have stopped me smack in the middle of the road.

I almost made it, the car (that happened to be driven by the landlord of the Plough public house in Brabourne) couldn't stop either and despite his wheels locked solid, he had enough momentum to skid forward, smashing into the rear of my bike just behind the foot-peg, then carry on a few yards down the other side of the hill. I was left standing, as I'd merely stepped my leg up and let go, while the bike was pushed further down the road to the sound of growling metal and squealing rubber. I paid the bloke £8 for his broken number plate, picked up my bike and rode it to the party, getting there as it was just starting to warm up.

There were the usual crowd (plus some Oakmen) as well as half the Dukes Head regulars. Some straw bales were broken and strewn down the bank like a carpet. We amused ourselves by dragging each other down this straw slide by the ankles, Stuey took offence and kicked me in the mouth, which I probably deserved.

As the sun set, we moved on to the Dukes. Needless to say, beer was thrown around and then, when we had outstayed our welcome, it was off down the Duck for more of the same.

On Friday 22nd April, a group of us set off on an Easter camping break, for the West Country this time. I was on my KH400 with Will on his cut-down GS550 and Pete still with the Superdream. Del didn't have a bike at the time, so he was on the back of Pete. We stopped for a beer at the Duck on the way out of Sellindge and, after a silly moment with little Craig, resulting in a broken glass and beer over both of us, we were chucked out and I was banned from the place for the second time.

We took the road to Rye, then Hastings. Just beyond Eastbourne, when we hit the downs, I chose an old chalk quarry for us to get our bikes off the road and sleep the night. We didn't set tents up; I don't even know if Del and Pete had brought one. We built a fire for some cheer and Del got a cinder in his eye. It was a windy night and the bikes didn't give much shelter from it. In the morning Del appeared to be blind in one eye, said he needed a doctor, so Pete took him home to Lynn. Will and I rode on to the New Forest. I remember the road sign, turning off the dual carriageway, and then all of a sudden we were in it. The area was quite pleasant and we stopped at an inn called The Green Man, which was fitting.

We rode about till we found a camp site. It was a sunny afternoon and there were New Forest ponies and cattle ambling around on the roads and verges with no fences to restrict them. I remember quaint little villages, thatched roofs and squirrels. We both had to sleep in my little tent as Will didn't have one and the nights were colder than we had bargained for. That first morning in the forest when we got out of the tent, the canvas had frost on it.

We had trouble finding a pub that wasn't displaying a 'No Bikers' sign and when we finally did get to sit down with a beer at lunch time, we found that the local brews were a fair bit stronger than what we were used to. We rode back to the site in a state of drunken euphoria. We raced through the roads and villages taking turns to lead and I got the front wheel up a few times Then back at the site we had a go at catching a pony, failed ridiculously and crashed out in the tent. When we woke up, it was just about dark and getting cold.

The next morning there was a harder frost than the previous, we had to light a fire to warm up before riding north to Stonehenge, making up the plan as we went along. We camped at a site in the village of Orcheston in a little hidden valley with a stream running through it. That night we were treated to a sound and light show courtesy of the British Army; we hadn't known we were on the edge of a military training ground.

The following morning the weather was much the same: cold bright start, warming up by mid-day. We packed up and hit the road. The bikes were going well and we rode west to have a look at the Avebury stone circles. We parked up and hiked about two miles past the giant man-made prehistoric hill of Silbury and up the other side of the valley to West Kennet long barrow.

I was still dressed in my wax cottons, over top of denims and carrying my rucksack with all the camping gear that I didn't want to leave on the bike, as well as my crash helmet. We left the sleeping bags on the bikes and Will didn't have any other gear to carry except crash hat and leather jacket, so he was alright, while I sweated and chaffed like a bastard. That was as far as the trip took us and we rode back to Sellindge that same afternoon.

Only a few weeks after getting back from the bike trip, I had my twentieth motorcycle accident and the only one I've had on the Speed twin. It happened one misty night, riding across the marsh back from Del's place in St Mary's Bay. I was pretty much disorientated in the mist, which sat in drifts here and there, interspersed with clear road and I was getting frustrated at the lack of road direction.

The roads down there make no sense and were obviously laid out hundreds of years ago to follow the winding water courses before the place was properly drained. Suddenly, the lane I was following bent round at 90 degrees and I hadn't seen it coming. I leaned for it, but slid on the grit straight into a hedge part way down one of the dry ditches. It didn't cause much damage to the bike - just a few scuffs and scratches really.

Twenty minutes later, I had found a wider, straighter road and the air was clear, so I got some speed up just before hitting another blanket of mist. I skidded and snaked my way round the wide bend it was shrouding and managed to pull out the other side, just about alright without going over the edge into a dredging. I knew where I was by now, the aptly named Donkey Street, I was out of the maze and not far from the base of the hills.

Chip held another party at Martin's bank one Sunday afternoon in May. The band named Roadhouse was playing and the same sort of crowd showed up for it. After the band finished, Fat Barry led the convoy into the Dukes Head car park by taking the turn too sharp in his drunkenness and tipping his 'plastic pig' over on its side, shattering the windscreen. The 'plastic pig' was a popular machine favoured by bikers who had not passed their car tests, but wanted to cart people and stuff around. The 850cc three wheeled Reliant Robin in a fibreglass shell could be driven on a full bike licence and a lot of people converted them into cheap instant trikes. They looked like a fairground bumper car with the shell on and never appealed to me as a trike: you could see what they really were.

Reliants were very light and usable. Del used to work at the Swan Lane garage in Sellindge, pumping petrol and polishing 'pigs', till he got the sack. I remember a bunch of us one night trekking up from the Duck to the Dukes and stopping at the forecourt where the Reliants were parked. It was right opposite the police house and Dave thought it would be funny to turn one over on its roof, I think it only took three pairs of hands.

About fifteen years later I met the old village copper, also called Dave, in the refs lounge at Ashford cop shop. Whilst reminiscing about his time as the village bobby, he told me that the funniest thing he remembered was one morning coming out of his driveway and seeing a Reliant Robin on its roof. In truth, I don't think there was much sympathy for the garage owners, Del said they used to rip off customers for servicing etc. I don't know.

Colin had a 'pig' for a while; it didn't have enough clutch friction to make it back up the hill away from Martin's place when he was round one day. Martin used his Z400 to push it from behind and help it on its way. I can see the scene now: Martin on the bike grinning amidst the smoke and the smell of hot exhausts and slipping clutch discs.

I was as busy as ever with motorcycles at work that summer and still riding trials bikes with great enthusiasm. Often, Dad and I would ride them after the day school kids had gone home. We hurt ourselves regularly, but the rule was to get straight back on so you didn't lose confidence. The worst disasters were when a bike got tipped over in one of the ponds, stalled and sucked in water. It would run with the exhaust submerged, until water clogged the air filter and was drawn in through the carb and then the exhaust would fill.

Those trials bikes didn't have a lot of electrics to deal with, but if a bike went under it meant a three hour strip down, which had to be done right away to minimise any long term damage. The quicker you could get them sparking and flushed through after a splash the better.

I remember one time I took the Sammy Miller Honda into the pond and lay in the muddy water underneath it, with the exhaust burning my leg, trying to keep the vital parts clear long enough for Dad to get down in and pull it off me. It's funny: we always ran to recover the bikes after a spill before aiding the fallen rider. Fortunately, no one ever needed hospital treatment because of bike accidents on the farm – and there were some good ones too.

It was the bikes, above all, that helped us keep the 'juvies' in order, but we were all enthusiastic and I often helped the boys modifying small road bikes and mopeds so they were fit for scrambling, with some interesting looking machines as a result. There was a green Honda C70, over-sprayed with silver and fitted with worn out knobbly tyres, that was great fun to hack about on. You could do jumps and 'broadies' and it even went down into some of the pits we had dug out with the JCB. If you went fast enough, you could ride it out of them too.

I did hurt myself on that little tin bike though, racing around the wood with the boys, following tracks we had cut. The way it got ridden tended to make you stick your knees out and I whacked into an old hazel stump, cracking my knee and bending the foot peg, as well as pulling the stump half out of the ground. I felt sick after that, but the pain wasn't as bad as the time I kick-started a big Yamaha XT500, following a top end rebuild. Because it was a big single, it needed a full-on jump to kick it over. It fired and kicked back right at the full extension of my leg, with all my body weight on it. It was as much as I could do just to slump over the tank and keep the bike upright, while some of the boys came to my aid and took hold of the bars for me. I had to sit out for a good five minutes before daring to join in again.

I never did regain my confidence to kick that bike over again with the same positivity it needed to guarantee a start. I liked it though, it was a serious lump of metal, heavy and quite rough on the take up, not very suitable for the kind of riding we were doing and what the kids could get out of it, so it didn't get used that often.

In 1991 the barns (and our old bungalow) caught fire after an oxy-acetylene spark up and 95% of the school bikes were destroyed. It was a sad day and we all had to live in trailers for a couple of years afterwards, until the new farm house was ready. Of all the twenty or so bikes that burned that day, only the XT had enough metal in it to pour out a twin stream of molten aluminium five feet long. It set on the barn floor like a piece of art and hangs up to this day in the kitchen of the new house, nearby the bullet hole in the wall that Dad made when he was showing Mum that the rifle wasn't loaded.

Back to the June of 1988, Derek turned up at Kestrels one day all morose as he and Lynn had finished with each other. So we went out drinking at the local pubs, until he physically couldn't drink anymore. That was Del, he would start slow, rush to the point of becoming paralytic and then if you put a pint in each of his hands, he would drink them both, order two more and pass out. I always thought that was stupid, as he would work through the regular part whilst still miserable, then have half an hour of great times and miss the funniest part of the evening, the part that cost as much as the first two put together.

Del liked Kestrels so much that he eventually moved in, and it became the best party house in the village. It was ideal for a crowd to get back to after a night at the Dukes. Stuey's sound machine would be blasting out Springsteen. Sometimes things got a bit silly and we would have to rush around on a Sunday morning to clear the mess up before Roger, our Irish landlord, came over to cut the lawns and check on things.

Wozzy, our other housemate, worked for a construction company and would sometimes bring a new door back to replace the one he had put his fist through the night before. Roger came back one time while he was screwing the hinges in – that was quite an amusing situation. Roger knew how things were, but he liked the money that never went through his books, so rarely made a fuss. He rarely did any proper maintenance either. There was no heating and the upstairs bedrooms leaked every time it rained heavily.

It was good that he didn't mind the bikes; he was a sensible enthusiast himself, who rode a Honda 400-four and used to go to the Isle of Man TT races every year.

We ran amok at that place while Roger was away; I often used the upstairs landing as an airgun range between the bedrooms either side of the hallway. Drinking and vomiting were common place, but we had a 'no drugs' house rule which was strictly adhered to, while Woz and I were living there anyway. Nothing but good old fashioned 'milk and alcohol' – we nicked each other's milk and we never had enough chip pan oil between us, but there was always beer in the fridge.

Stuey seemed to eat best, as he worked at the local butchers; I filled up on meals at work while Del lived on packets of crisps and litres of cheap ice cream. Wozzy just ate down the pub most nights.

Our old group was starting to spread out by now and we didn't all live locally anymore. Will was in Ealham, Chip and Martin had moved out to a caravan in Bethersden, but Del had come back to the home turf, also Dave and Tony still lived in the village. We weren't as close as we had once been, but we weren't ready to shatter and split yet and we still didn't think we ever would.

We all had full time jobs and there just wasn't the time anymore to hang around each other's places aimlessly, talking crap and listening to records. We were all moving through life on different wiring plans it seemed. I was becoming more insular and to be honest, I think I was looking for some spiritual guidance.

I hadn't been to church since primary school and we had never been a religious family, but I still knew that there was a force for good and a bent for evil at work amongst mankind. The signs, as indicated in the Nostradamus quatrains were slotting into place. Wars, pestilence and natural disasters: the earth would cleanse itself and make way for the new dawn. I wasn't quite ready to repent, but was quite busy working out my strategies for surviving Armageddon.

Although finding a remote Scottish island to retreat to as a hermit, eating seaweed and shellfish, was a practical possibility, it wouldn't be as purposeful as roaring around the wastelands on a turbo-charged suicide machine, or anywhere near as much fun.

# CHAPTER ELEVEN

## *Heavy metal thunder*

The annual bike show weekend was fast approaching and Del still didn't have a bike, so I lent him my CB200 for a week or so and we went down there at its new location, Snargate in the middle of the marsh.

The Triumph made it down there, smoking and dribbling oil, it was never the best bike at any gathering, but it brought no shame either. There seemed to be so many more people and bikes there than when it had been held at Stowting. The fact that the site was close to the long lazy drag that ran between Hythe and Hastings was good; that route was dotted with small distractions along the way and made for a good ride out the next day.

It was warm and the seaside towns were heavy with leather and hot metal. Everyone was out to show off and Saturday was good. Del went back to Lynn on the Sunday, so I went home too and worked on the Triumph. Dave came round to Kestrels and I helped him clean his carbs through. Then the bastard shook his tank out over Roger's lawn – it didn't occur to him that petrol might kill the grass.

Below are a few diary entries that rekindled some memories:

**Tuesday 19th July 88**
*I bought a Honda 550 four K today from the Victoria Rd breakers.*

*I am very happy with it; it's big, fast, powerful & clean.*

**Thursday 21ˢᵗ July**
*I took about four hours this afternoon to clean and service the four carbs on my 550. I went with Tony & Martin to the Bull.*

**Friday 22ⁿᵈ July**
*I went with Martin, Tony & Chip to the Bull & the Six Bells in Woodchurch. I ran out of petrol & we used a siphon pipe & drank our beer with it in the pub. We rode into Ashford & I filled up my tank & rode off.*

Actually that Friday was a monumental evening, one of the best. It also happened to be the last time the Mad Mile Club, as we were, rode out together. When I ran out of petrol between the Six Bells and the Bull that night, Martin towed me back to the Bull, where the landlady lent us a washing machine pipe to use as a siphon, so we could transfer fuel from Martin's tank to mine. Back in the pub, we were larking around siphoning slops out of the drip trays. By chucking out time it was teaming with rain and Chip and Martin were staggering around trying to get onto Martins bike. Tony was on the back of me and we rode into Ashford.

We filled up at Beaver Road and I stayed on my bike while the others went in to buy snack foods and beer. Tony was still dawdling inside the shop when we fired up and started to pull away. It was hilarious to see him running from the shop like a fugitive and made it look like it was him who was nicking the petrol. He jumped on the back of mine as desperately as a man wearing two pairs of tight jeans can, then we rode hell for leather in the pissing rain back to Sevington, where Martin had another caravan set up.

We were soaked and the first thing that went on the fire, once it was lit, was that washing machine hose. I didn't realise Martin still had it. The kettle went on the boil, the mushroom dust came out and we drank beer, told jokes and laughed hysterically all night like the good times would never end.

I took a day out on Sunday to recover and on Monday I put a side stand on my 550 and a reserve tube in the petrol tap. I did my washing over at the farm too; we had no facilities at Kestrels and using the old leaky twin tub at the farm took half the day from start to finish.

Washing day was a big chore and as it was always at least a fortnight's worth, I dreaded it: that Hotpoint twin-tub with its separate washer and spin-dryer compartments churning, shaking and thundering. Two of its wheels were missing and it had to be dragged out over the worn floor boards to the kitchen sink, so it could be filled up with cold water. We had no hot water at the farm, but the tub had its own element. When anyone in the house wanted a bath, the twin-tub had to be used to heat some water, and then the whole thing dragged into the bathroom and pumped out into the bath.

I had never used a modern washing machine, something that didn't need to be pumped out and refilled by hose in between washes, something that didn't splash, leak and shudder. The spin drum was unstable if not carefully loaded to balance out the centrifugal force and the machine would judder itself around the kitchen. In any case, you couldn't wash many clothes at a time.

When spring came around and I had moved back to the

farm to live in a tiny wooden gypsy wagon, I came up with the brilliant idea of using the big diesel-engined concrete mixer to wash my clothes in. This process took a matter of ten minutes or so from start to finish. Denims came out 3D clean, but it broke buttons on my shirts and snagged any synthetic materials. It was great for working clothes and I still use this method for tarry old boiler suits.

The 550-four was another of those mid-seventies classics, with four real exhausts and that unmistakable early Jap four-cylinder roar, like a leopard in an oil drum, in contrast to the throaty growl of a Brit.

My new Honda was a 1978 model and an earthy metallic brown colour. It would do a ton on the flat without a game plan, and was the closest I came to riding a similar type of bike to most of the others in my peer group at the time. Having said that, I didn't actually know anyone who owned that same model at the time when I had mine. The Z650 was the affordable bike of choice for those on a budget to be able to feel like they were riding a Z9 or GS1000.

I always liked something a bit different to what everyone else was using and all through my riding career I don't think I've ever known any one of my pals to own the same make and model of bike as me, unless they happened to have bought it from me in the first place, like Stuey did with one of my KH400s – on reflexion we were more alike than we wanted to admit, both being Sagittarians may have had something to do with it.

Twenty years later, by sheer chance, I happened to meet Stu back in Ashford. He had been living in Australia and New Zealand for a decade and we'd had no contact. It turned out that we had both bought the, quite rare, KTM 640 adventure, in orange. An Australian desert epic was planned with great enthusiasm, but that's as far as it got. Stu went back to Tasmania and we both ended up selling those bikes, which I regretted.

# BOOK TWO

## Exodus

But God, led the people about,
through the way of the Wilderness
of the Red Sea: and the children
of Israel went up harnessed out of
the land of Egypt.

Chapter XIII verse 18

# CHAPTER TWELVE

## Free bird

When I make a plan to go somewhere or do something, I'm quite serious and if it doesn't work out first time, I have been known to go to great lengths to see that commitment through.

Our gang didn't make it to Cornwall, which had been our big plan, so I was going to get there on my own. This was the first time I was to set off alone on an adventure. As it turned out, I quite liked the freedom and solitude and the feeling of accomplishment when I had made it there and back, relying on nobody but myself and my machine.

I left about midday on Wednesday 27th July 1988 and took the same route along the coastal strip to the new forest, with only a short rain break in Rye to contend with, that I sat out in a café.

Before too long, about 5pm, I reached the 'Rufus Stone', a rock set in a grassy clearing centuries ago to mark the place where William Rufus, the second Norman King of England, was killed by an arrow in a hunting accident.

I scouted out a hidden glade in the forest where I could secure the bike and set up camp. After cooking up some food on a small camp fire, I walked out to the nearby Sir Walter Tyrrell pub, named after the man who loosed the arrow which killed William II. It was a real nice country pub to have a few drinks in and the locals were friendly enough.

I had great difficulty finding my way back to my camp in the pitch black dark, but eventually found the hidden clearing in a dense bit of forest and laid out under the stars on a bed of ferns, feeling like a knight on a quest. I could hear the neighing and stamping of wild ponies in the night, but none came close.

About six in the morning, a gentle rain began, which lasted about an hour. I made a star fire and cooked my breakfast, then made it out to the road. It was quite slippery going, uphill through wet vegetation. I'd chosen the spot so that my camp wouldn't be stumbled upon, not for its ease of access.

I followed the coast through Dorset and the rain started again at Abbotsbury, only stopping just short of Plymouth, where I got my first sight of the pink and grey granite rock the peninsula is made of.

I crossed the Tamar River in the late afternoon and was in a different country, both geographically (Cornwall is almost an island, as the Tamar starts only a few miles from the north coast and empties into the English Channel in the south) and in a sense of perception, as Cornwall was a land of mystery and legend to me; It was King Arthur and all the Celtic magic thing that was popular with us transient wasters at the time.

It was raining again the next morning when I packed up and left the Mount Pleasant camp site, a few miles past the river. I rode to the top of near-by Kit Hill, to view the lie of the land and plan my day. There were storm clouds spreading up from the south west, as if they had come to flood the whole peninsula.

I got going and skirted the south east of Bodmin Moor, riding up through two wide flooded valleys, then up onto the moor itself. I stopped at Dozmary Pool, a roughly circular moorland lake, claimed in various tales to be enchanted. One legend has it that this was the pool of still water that Sir Bedivere threw Arthur's sword Excalibur into, after the battle of Camlanh. I was fascinated by the whole Camelot thing (as was Hitler for one) and quite superstitious generally, so I got a lot out of this trip, visiting several sites of similar interest.

I loved the wild barren moor with its wind carved rocky tors, isolated settlements and ancient stone monuments. It was a place where men had been drawn to in ages past, leaving sad lonely reminders of their presence.

A great meeting place for bikes is Jamaica Inn, at the crossroads right in the centre of the moor. This historic coaching inn, made famous by Daphne du Maurier's novel of the same name, is a remarkable building with five foot thick granite walls, slate hung outside to keep off the driving rain. It is set down off the road behind an uneven cobbled court yard. Apart from the shop and restaurant sections, I found a proper local bar full of character with a huge fire place and a resident scarlet macaw. The place was still a genuine inn, offering accommodation which included one reputedly haunted room.

The next day started with the same weather pattern, rainclouds being driven up the backbone of the land until midday, when they seemed to blow themselves thin and then offer some sunshine to break through at times over the afternoon. I rode around like a hornet, trying to get to as many places as I could from the list I had drawn up.

The bike behaved great, with no problems at all and not even any maintenance required. I quite understood why other bikers rode these mid-range fours; it was a great bike and I wish I still had it now. Sure the thing used a fair amount of petrol because, as Martin had said, it had four C90 engines running all together, re-bored and tuned up. It was a comforting thought, as I knew the C90 had the most unbreakable engine ever created.

The highlight of the day was late afternoon at Tintagel Head, the legendary birth place of Arthur Pendragon, where the ruins of a C12th castle sit on evidence of an older settlement on that impregnable rocky promontory. It rises sheer out of the crashing Atlantic waves, reached only by a low narrow bridge of land with a precarious stairway carved into the black rock.

The next day was a Sunday and I explored the south coast from Looe to the Fowey Estuary. One small fishing village called Polperro, where cars were banned, had a lane leading out of it so steep that my rear wheel started to lose traction as I came up on the gritty side of a bend. I had to put my foot down but made it out OK.

I was up and gone the following morning by 7am. I rode to Slaughter Bridge, which may have been named after the site of Arthur's last battle near Camlahn. It would have been a likely sort of place for two opposing armies to meet, across a gentle grassy valley with a stream dividing it: a natural division in the land, defensible from either side of the water course.

I walked upstream half a mile to find the flat stone slab, seven feet long and carved with some ancient characters. All weathered now and softened with moss and lichen. This grave marker stone has been shielded from the world in its peaceful hidden gorge at a twist in the stream for well over a thousand years. It felt quite spiritual, shaded by mature trees and I stayed there for some time. It's not known who the stone was really laid there for, or why in such a secret place.

In the dark ages, great chieftains and regional kings were buried on high places with mounds raised over them, open to the sky, not normally in a quiet secluded place like that. In the Doomsday Book, Cornwall was known as Kernow and it was a sovereign Celtic kingdom with strong links to Brittany and a language similar to present day Welsh.

I made it back home in the evening that same day, taking a route along the north Cornish coast and up through Devon into Somerset. I made a stop at Glastonbury Tor, then on over Salisbury plain, before hitting the motorways back to Kent. I had put over 1000 miles on my clock in that few days and then sold the bike shortly afterwards, for a small profit actually.

So why did I want to sell it, as I couldn't fault it in looks or performance? Why didn't I upgrade to a 750-four, instead of setting my sights on the notoriously unpredictable and disaster prone big two stroke triples: the 500cc H1 and 750cc H2. Because they breathed fire and I still needed a little danger in my life – the Honda was just too sensible.

I continued to ride around on my CB200, without much consideration for personal safety or mechanical upkeep. I would say that both aspects were connected and one form of neglect feeds the other. I rode that bike at full throttle wherever I was going: generally it was just around the local lanes. The bike had no MOT and was not fit for one – no tax either, so I couldn't park it in town. The fact that I had no insurance on it bothered me less.

One day I met a huge 4WD tractor with a seed drill on the back, coming down at me on a steep little lane near home. We both skidded and the tractor locked up, still carrying a lot of momentum. It stopped at a twisted angle in front of me, touching the banks both sides, but I was already off the bike and about to run for it. I really did think that tractor was going to roll and I reckon the driver had that thought too.

Thinking back, the fact that I was always in a rush to get to work on time, or get to the bank before it closed, would be one reason for riding full throttle. Another reason was that it felt raw and wild and gave me a sense of purpose. Riding a bike to its limits requires a high degree of concentration and that made me feel alive. I don't remember any further bike accidents on the roads for a while after that incident, although I had plenty of stupid ones about this time with a transit van I was racking around in.

I took myself out of the circuit for a couple of months that autumn and stopped going to pubs. I wanted to be something and trained up to dive with the British Sub Aqua Club at Folkestone, I was also going to the swimming club at Hythe on Monday nights and boxing on Tuesdays and Thursdays in Ashford. I was looking for new horizons and preparing myself physically for some great challenge that would come in the future, I didn't know when, where or what. I just knew I was going somewhere and it was going to be tough.

Over the Christmas period, I helped Dad to fit the tyres onto his rebuilt BSA Super Rocket wheels. They had stainless steel spokes and the rear wheel had been reduced in circumference so that it could take a modern (post 1960s) 410x18 Dunlop. The hubs were stove enamelled in electric blue, as were the engine barrels.

The engine had already been down to SRM engineering when it was at Carmarthen, to be completely rebuilt with all sorts of modifications:

Needle roller bearings throughout instead of bronze bushes, SRM special sump plate with magnetic swarf catcher, 12 volt alternator ignition conversion in place of the mag-dynamo system, quick change external oil filter fitted onto the old dynamo body, oil pressure gage plumbed into a machined bronze connector at the magneto end of the timing case, crank case top opening machined out so it could take 750 barrels if we ever wanted to fit them and I'm sure Dad had said that all the threaded holes in the casings had been fitted with brass inserts so they wouldn't strip.

The frame and forks were another matter and were not ready and assembled for a year more at least, with stainless nuts, bolts, screws, shafts and washers.

Dad had to wait quite a while for that bike to hit the road, about another three years actually until it got MOT'd and fully fit. We built it and then stripped it again to modify bits on the frame, had it shot blasted for the second time and the tank reconditioned. With the paint and chrome parts all done and ready, I built it up again.

The wiring and primary drive parts were fitted by Roadstar, an outfit half way up the Dover Castle hill, run by a couple of shaggy, bearded mechanics who worked in and amongst a jumble of old British bike parts. John and Steve have been there for decades without sunlight or heating, they don't seem to mind, always ready to help out or offer advice.

Roadstar fitted a Triumph Bonneville clutch, in place of our worn out corroded BSA one. Apparently the Triumph clutch is stronger than the original BSA.

Because of the alternator fitted to the crank shaft splines

that powered the electronic ignition, the original primary drive casing couldn't go back on and we were lucky to acquire purpose made original inner and outer covers. These items were only produced in very limited numbers and are pretty rare. I read that the Dorset Constabulary had required a fleet of A10s with the upgraded 12v set-up, because it was the best bike for the job, doing away with the extra maintenance involved on the mag-dynamo system. It was years before the Japs caught on.

1989 had started with me leaving Kestrels and moving back to the farm, where I was working every day anyway. I moved into the little wooden caravan that was housed under the shelter of the huge new pole barn I had been building for about eighteen months.

I had a bit of a barn warming party one windy night in February, inside the empty section of the barn. I had driven a handful of the Sellindge crowd from the Dukes Head to my new place in the Transit. No Will or Dave, but Chip, Martin and Colin turned up half way through the evening. By the end of the night it was just Chip, Martin and myself, plus a crate full of Guinness bottles that we had found under a hedge amongst the old scrap vehicles. The labels had gone and the tops were just crusts of rust, but when everyone's drunk and wild and all the good stuff is gone, it is amazing what people will resort to. We were knocking the necks off the bottles on bits of angle iron, drinking it and chucking it over each other.

Something changed in me in 1989; I became aware that there was a global village out there. There were whole new experiences to be had and none of them were connected to Sellindge and the people I already knew.

I had wanted to travel for some time, but needed a shove

to get me started. I got that when Wayne Gifford came to work with us that year. It was Easter time and Neil Smith, the bike mechanic, was with us then too. Wayne was from a local farming family and fresh back from the 'Grande Tour' of Israel, Egypt and Greece. I was encouraged by his tales of back-packing and especially about life on a Kibbutz.

The Kibbutz system was set up after the state of Israel was declared in 1948, as an organised network aiming to build a country, defend it and turn the desert green. They are part farm, part factory. My impression was that it would be a kind of survivalist commune based on fruit farming with a gun in every chalet. I knew very little about politics and any opinions I had then were very blinkered.

Wayne recounted stories of sweating in the fields under incredible heat as well as visiting archaeological sites. I wanted to see the places from the Bible and experience the camaraderie of life as a volunteer. The menace of the Intifada (the Arab uprising) didn't put me off, it seemed like this was a point that my life had been leading up to. I was going to Jerusalem, the pyramids, the Dead sea and the Nile, to Bethlehem and the ancient town of Meggido in the valley of Jezreel; Armageddon itself. I did all that and more. It changed me more than I could have imagined.

I'd been working long hours and seven day weeks from spring till autumn that year and spent most of the time on the farm. I was still frequenting the Dukes Head, but not getting around much otherwise. One Wednesday night in May, I got bored with the inertia amongst the local crowd and decided to check out the band at one of the pubs in the next village. A lot of places had band nights mid-week as well as weekends and they were usually packed. As I left the Dukes Head, and as a bit of a statement, I held the front brake on whilst revving up and dumped the clutch. The burn-out started off OK, but then the KH front wheel slid forward and I shot off, ploughing straight through the wooden bill board that stood outside the pub door. I promised the landlord I would be back the next day to fix it and sped off to find some action.

I came across Martin and Colin and we had a good old time at one of the country pub band nights. Then back out in that car park it happened again. I was drunker this time and dumped the clutch at maximum revs. The bike hurled me forward across the tarmac and into the side of a parked car with such force that my rear wheel left the ground on impact and I was nearly thrown over the top. I didn't hang around and was lucky not to crash it again in my desperation to get clear of the place. I still do feel bad about that.

It was nearly three months before I got the bike sorted out and back on the road. The mudguard was ruined, the forks bent, as were the handlebars. Even the lower steering yoke was twisted. I had the old 250 in the shed that I could swap bits with, but I got the bars and forks straightened all the same.

# CHAPTER THIRTEEN

## *Burning out*

Just before the 1989 custom bike show, I bought a blue Honda C90 from Dave Keeble for £20. The plastic leg shields came off straight away. I took the tank off, turned it around and bolted it to the stem at the front to look like a real motorbike. I used a sledge hammer to re-shape the seat by thumping it down into the void where the petrol tank had been, then welded it onto wherever it touched to form a deep saddle. Then I painted the whole thing, including the tyre walls, with the tar paint we used for the corrugated iron barn roofs. Finally, I chucked coal dust over my creation for some sort of wasteland effect. It actually looked quite good when it was done.

Due to the KH front end being in bits and the Triumph having been temporarily transferred to Dad's ownership, I decided to take the C90 to the show, it would certainly draw some looks and that's what it was all about.

Four of us met up at Sellindge stores on the Friday evening: me on my coal-black flat-tracker, Tony on his shitty 125 Superdream, so gutless that it couldn't make it up Lympne Hill in first gear without Tony jumping off and running alongside it at the steepest part. Tritton and his new bird were on my CB200, as I had resorted to renting it out for £20 a week. Last but not least, Keeble was on some crappy Yamaha RSX100.

We decided to add insult to injury by all buying a Kinder egg each, from the Sellindge stores and sticking whatever plastic toy came from inside it to the front of our bikes. I think mine was a blue Pluto dog or something similar. A gold tyre pen turned the 90 on my side panels to 900, and we were ready to go.

It was a hot weekend and we stopped at the Ship Inn in Dymchurch for a beer along the way, where the landlord actually assumed my bike was some rare vintage model. Coming through the centre of the little town, I noticed a panda car on the sea wall road. I think he saw us as easy pickings, because he started moving just as we approached the main junction before the lights. For several moments a row of buildings blocked our line of sight and I made a break for it. I swerved straight across to the right, off the main road and raced off towards the marsh on a minor road with the others in tow. I kept us going until I was sure that plod was not on our tail.

We made our way across the marsh to the show site and joined the mass of smoking, popping machines on the track that filtered through the gates. It was really funny and some of the hard core riders around us didn't look that impressed that we were bringing down the gravity of the event. To cap it off, I had mounted a squirrel skin complete with head, legs and tail to the top of my crash helmet. It looked like it was clinging on for dear life, as it had set rigid in a sort of flying position (barmaids hated me for that and had banned me from having the helmet on the bar beside me at the Dukes). However, a lot of people did think it was a funny sight.

We chose an open spot in the camping field and arranged our bikes like a wagon coral, so that we could stretch a sheet of polythene building membrane across the lot of them, using blue bale twine to secure it to all the handlebars. That became our communal sleeping shelter and it looked a right mess. The funny thing was that, as the field filled up, no-one wanted to site their tents and bikes anywhere near us and have their credibility undermined. The result being that our camp got left in an oasis of grass in the middle of a ten acre thicket of tents, bikes and guy ropes.

Here are some more extracts from my diary, written at the time:

### Saturday 8th July 1989

*We had without doubt the worst bikes & the worst tent there. We went down New Romney & a group of bikers thought my CB200 was great & took photos of it with me. We were all sitting in the road drinking & I kept buying cake. Then Triton took his bird home & Tony went too, on a doubtful excuse. Back at the tent (which was now only a plastic sheet sagging between two bikes & looking quite inadequate), people had lightened up & were laughing and taking pictures of the C900, the stupidest bike there. We met Martin, Chip, 'Sick George', Colin & Nigel. I spent the rest of the day eating fruit & burgers.*

### Sunday 9th July

*We packed up camp & I decided to go out showing some style by revving the bike up & doing a few donuts before burning off back home. If it displeased some, there were just as many laughing, as I was.*

The gear I was wearing and carrying was all (what I would have called nomad biker stuff) as if I had just ridden in from the wasteland, all rags, and a coal sack roped to my back instead of a proper bag. It was all a bit of a send up at the expense of those in the motorcycling fraternity who took themselves a bit too seriously.

I spent the next nine hours in bed when I got back home, then worked a couple in the evening. I sold that little Honda three years later as a non-runner for £7.50 to a bloke called Shaun who had moved into the village and set up in a new party house where the village no-hopers would be round there playing cards and watching Cheech and Chong all weekend. When I got back from six months travelling around Central America, I found Del living there in a haze of dope smoke. Shaun was an alright bloke and into bikes, he bought loads of crap from me to do up and sell on. He eventually joined the Oakmen, as it happened.

A few days after getting back from the show, I bought my Triumph back from Dad. I don't remember quite when I had relinquished it, but it was Dad's idea to keep it in the family. I had been planning to sell it and he didn't want me to lose it, so he said he would buy it and sell it back to me if I wanted it in the future, which I did.

The next month saw me down in Hastings visiting Vic Millers again, more than a couple of times, for parts for the Triumph and BSA. I dreaded an audience with him, as he always scolded me for not knowing the part numbers for the bits I wanted, or for asking about quick fix solutions to practical problems. He just saw that as sacrilege. I wanted to buy a tube of plastic metal for some kind of crank case repair. Although the product was displayed for sale in his shop, the disgust in his voice was as if I had asked him to bodge a repair with 'polyfilla'.

I didn't buy the resin. Like him or loath him he was quite well respected; Mr Miller was like a godfather of British motorcycle engineering perfection. Well that's the impression I got, and he didn't even look as if he rode bikes: neat hair, clean hands, buff factory floor style overalls and brown leather shoes. 'Yes young man; what can I do for you?'

On Saturday 15th of July (I'm sure Will didn't record the date), I was in Ashford and happened to ride past St. Mary the Virgin church in Willesborough. A wedding procession was walking out of the building up the path to the gate. As I had to pause at the road junction, I just looked down the path at the scene and rode off. I found out later that Will had been married at that church on that Saturday.

Not one of us had been invited and I hadn't even been aware he was engaged. It was eighteen years later that Will would come back to look for his old mates. Divorced and bitter, estranged from pretty much everything outside of farming. We would meet during a difficult time in all our lives. And then we would ride again.

I filled up those pocket diaries with the smallest writing I could manage. Here is the entry for Saturday 5th August 1989:

*I went to Hastings on my KH, nice hot weather. I had to wait an hour and fifteen minutes for Millers to open so I went to The Carlisle pub on the sea front – a right rough biker's pub. I met a couple of blokes talking about my KH. Everyone was drinking outside and sitting on the wall by the parked bikes. Someone who claimed to have a garage full of KH bits was wheel spinning on a metal drain cover, to the cheers and calls of the rabble. I made some contacts, then when I left I pulled the best power wheelie yet* and kept it up down the road to show some class.

I rode to Ashford and got a kebab then rode on to Martin's caravan, tailing a Z750 at the outskirts of Ashford that was going the same way. He tried to lose me but I kept up with him all round the bends and he stopped at Martin's. Allen his name was and he was going on about brewing wine from tea. Klumsy Chris was there too and Chip was living in the old caravan next door. He didn't seem to mind that some old bloke had died in it only a month before and it hadn't had a make-over. When I left I was pulling wheelies for Martin's camera out on the road, then I shot off into the bend taking it too wide and smacked the end of my exhaust silencers on the side of a car coming the other way as my rear whipped round, I straightened her up with more throttle and was gone.

### Sunday 6th August
I drove my transit van down to Hastings to the Carlisle to meet some blokes about some bike bits. I had to go back to Toad's place with Spider to take the gear box off his A10 chop. I bought some side panels and a tank, plus a spare 5TA tank with a rack from Toad. They were all right to me after Toad's initial reserve. He had half a foot missing from a bike accident and had seen a lot more of the outlaw bike club scene than I had – and had owned and ridden a lot of the 1970s superbikes that I wished I had.

Spider (he had a spiders web tattoo on one side of his face and a road rat style haircut), was clearly dangerous. He had been to prison for stabbing another biker in a confrontation up north. He said the bloke pulled a knife on him first.

I decided not to get on the wrong side of Spider as he was probably a psycho, but I liked Toad and met up with him a few times over the next couple of months. By October, Spider was back in prison – Toad said he'd cut someone with a knife.

About this time Tony (Heapo) had a bike accident with a car on a sharp bend near Bonnington. He wasn't badly hurt, but his bike was written off and it must have shaken him up as he never rode again. Tone got himself a haircut, some stonewash jeans and a girlfriend; he still came to the bonfire parties I threw every now and again but he'd turned a corner and I didn't see him in a leather jacket again.

### Saturday 12<sup>th</sup> August 89
*Tony came with me to Capel St Mary near Ipswich to pick up a really tatty KH400 & another almost complete one in bits for £100. It ran badly. When I got back I tightened & checked the carbs, cleaned the plugs & it goes fine, spent some time sorting through the bits.*

### Thursday 17<sup>th</sup> August
*I started to sort out documentation that I will need for the Middle-East. I cemented one side of my Rayburn hearth (in the barn I built). I rode my KH400 to Hastings & changed my 5TA clutch hub but he left a hub panel out so I must go back again. I went round Toad's house till 10pm & met a little bloke called Titch. Good ride back.*

### Friday 18<sup>th</sup> August
*I drove my van to Crowhurst & Toad took me round some bloke's house to buy a load of KH250 bits. I went back to Ashford to draw out £1,300 for triples tomorrow & I got in a parking difficulty & reversed into a Capri, had to give my insurance and registration details.*

**Saturday 19th August**
*David Keeble came with me to buy two Kwak triples, an H2B 750 and a KH500 from Southend and Luton, costing £775 & £450. They are well worth it. I went to an Oakmen bonfire party in Brook. There were lots of people I knew there. Shaun Hammant, the old council rockabilly turned up on a CX500. He had broken away from Harry & them & turned biker. Some of the Hastings lot were there.*

**Sunday 20th August**
*I sent off my passport application & managed some 40mph wheelies on my KH500.*

Shaun and I had worked on the council together years before. He used to drive around with a nutter called Harry in a bright yellow Bedford HA van, with a Dukes of Hazard air horn set under a bonnet that had a confederate flag painted across it. Shaun became known as 'Knuckles', due to having fingers missing on both hands.

I remember that bonfire party well, it was great. Guy had brought so many good people together and the atmosphere was perfect. It was loud music, motorcycles and the open sky. The party never fizzled out as people dropped out, it just became more intimate. We sat around the huge camp fire drinking, laughing and puking 'til the sun came up, and by that time there were just three or four of us awake out of hundreds. One by one they had succumbed to the damp comfort of the scrubby grass, littered with beer cans and other debris. Trog was still opening cans as the early drop-outs were waking up to the morning.

This was the first time I had taken the H2 out, first day I got it and every time I did it caused a stir. It was a big bike and had been customised cosmetically but not structurally altered. It was sprayed a dark swamp green, frame as well. On the tank, side panels and tail box were some quite good scenes from the Greek myths. The seat had been re-covered in pale green leather, it had KNN air filters and the original silencers had been changed for Microns.

I was ready to join a motorcycle club at that point: I had the bikes and the contacts.

The best known local clubs at the time were: the Ashford Oakmen, the Romney Marsh Body Snatchers, then the Highwaymen and Rejects Brotherhood (both of the latter from the North Kent region). I had rubbed shoulders with members from all these clubs for a while at local events, but only the Oakmen had not gone full back-patch. I thought to do so would be selling out the independence of the club and most people agreed with me.

A back-patch club falls, to an extent, under the protection and exploitation of whichever one-percenter club has a representation in their region. The big clubs were bullies and rode rough-shod over any affiliate club which they perceived to be getting too big or was not subservient enough. I wasn't interested in all this pseudo politics, I was just keen to show that I was as big a rebel as anyone else out there.

I didn't see the point of prospecting with any club just then, as I was all set to leave for the Holy Land in October and didn't rightly know what was going to happen or where it would take me. I expected the trip to be a life changing experience, but when I came back in the new year, my horizons had widened beyond all expectations. I had new goals and ambitions which were not all dark and heavy.

I still loved bikes, but I loved travel and culture too and saw more opportunities for adventure with a backpack and a passport than I did with a motorcycle club patch. After that first trip abroad, I didn't feel a particular desire to belong and conform to a set of rules and commitments imposed on me by anyone.

Before the end of the autumn, I would be off to 'the land of milk and honey' and living on Kibbutz Ramot Menashe. But as a last thrust I rode out to meet the Oakmen, who were at a Body Snatchers do in a field near Lydd aerodrome.

I turned up fashionably late on my KH500. It was a really good looking beast, like the 400 in style, but heavier all round and there was more than the extra 100cc of power in there. The colour scheme was crimson and sand – I think that's all the plus points. The gear selector operation was very much hit and miss and the engine itself rattled and clattered like a tin bucket full of spring washers. I wish I still had that bike though.

The fact that it wouldn't run in rain would not be an issue to me anymore: who wants to ride in the rain? I look at my motorcycles now as having usable tolerances and keep them within those parameters.

I only remember using that bike a handful of times. Burning down the 'mad mile', I was overtaking a car with a pretty girl in the back and some fool pulled out of a yard entrance near the bottom of the hill, head onto me. Once again, I had to shout at the devil and chicken run between the two vehicles, narrowly missing both. By rights, I didn't deserve to keep my legs and to this day I still wonder how I've lived this long.

When I got to that party, I pulled up amongst the Oakmen camp and gave it a couple of blips, my throttle cable stuck on full opening, creating clouds of smoke and an engine scream to wake the dead. I'd made an entrance.

Everything was great, there was entertainment in the way of a wet T-shirt contest, a bonfire, a free spit roast, a burger stall and beer tent as well as trade stalls. Chip and I entered the yard of ale drinking contest, more for the free beer than any hope of winning. Our crowd cheered the loudest as we poured ale through our beards and soaked up the tail end of the eighties.

Bikers I knew from Hythe, Hastings and Ashford were there, as well as from further afield. But a small delegation from an internationally renowned back-patch club appeared to be making their presence known, once the party was in full swing. Most of the Kent back-patch clubs put in an appearance but it was the first time I'd seen the Hells Angels turn up to a party I was at.

It seemed the host club had traded their independence for a dance with the devil; they didn't attempt to exert any influence over the way things would play out.

The atmosphere definitely changed, there was a band playing but only one gang hanging out in the beer tent. Toad and I started walking into the lion's den to buy beers and changed our minds as two other blokes (one with a leg missing) were punched and kicked to the ground right in front of us. 'Not a good time to be in the beer tent.' Toad said, and I had to agree with him.

Later in the night there were more reports of unprovoked violence and I don't know if the Body Snatchers made any waves that night, but it wasn't their show anymore. That stunned me at the time and I spoke to a club member a week after the event about it all. He fully subscribed to accepting and supporting any actions carried out by the one percenter club they owed their patches to.

In fact, it turned out that a man who had been at the party was stabbed on that night, in the back, in a phone box just down the road from the camp field. I even heard someone say he deserved it for trying to make that call. What does that tell you? We all knew what the message meant. I was glad the Oakmen were content to display their patches where you could see them, which meant they got left to do their own thing and respected for it.

Toad and I chatted for a long time before I went back to our camp. He told me about Spider being in Lewis jail and that Titch was with the hippies in their converted ex-army truck that was parked up behind our camp. It was really just an old Bedford they had bought at an MOD auction and fitted with a pot-bellied stove and some benches in the back. There was a tarpaulin stretched across a frame they had made from fresh cut branches.

It was inspirational to me though and I really liked the idea. I got invited in and it felt like being in a cave. I didn't like new-age travellers in general but there was a part of me that envied something they had. The girl had something positive about her, but I couldn't really see where her partner was coming from. It was warm in there though and Titch sat so close to the fire that his lighter exploded in his jacket pocket.

Back at the tents, Guy had made sure no one was unaccounted for, everyone was on edge and either drunk or stoned: it wasn't a nice feeling and it wasn't our party, but for sure if trouble came our way we were ready to stand up for ourselves. We heard the big Harleys start up and they were gone. Soon after that it was the ambulance sirens.

Once the atmosphere settled down and people mellowed out it was good once again. We talked till four am round the little camp fire we'd built and roasted a rabbit someone had hit on the way in.

This should have been a party to bring the eighties home in style and a coming together of our carefree, largely peaceable society. A fraternity where we rode motorbikes, lived in caravans, got drunk on brown ale and expanded our minds on the fruits of the earth. We relished our rejection of conformity to the fanatic aspirations of the yuppie class, wore scuffed leathers, patched jeans and buck knives.

Mostly we were not big earners and none of us even cared, a warm place to sleep and a damp shed to work in at weekends was alright. When I look back at that October night, what I see is echoes of Altamont and the death of the sixties. I never went to another big do like that; I like to know who I'm getting out of my head next to. In any case, the nineties, for me, was a decade of travel and exotic foreign adventures. I worked and saved for those trips and nothing else.

I gave up regular drinking and shunned all forms of mind altering substances. It irritated me that a lot of the people around me weren't looking further afield. Come the millennium, we would all be very different people. Most of us with heavy responsibilities, having lost the incentive to party like a maniac until the sun came up.

# CHAPTER FOURTEEN

## *The promised lands*

Going to Israel changed me in some ways. It opened up my eyes to the fact that there are good and bad people on either side of any conflict. Also that hanging out with a bunch of hippies, soldiers and university graduates from far flung places in the world was fun. It was inspirational and I discovered that to love thy neighbour was good. I had to fight my room-mate first, 'to clear the air' he said, after feathers got ruffled during a late night drinking session around the camp fire. There were only three of us left out there, all English of course. Alan (the engineer) set out the ring in the dirt yard using bed frames.

Phillip (an ex-squaddie) went in for the kill. He was fast and I was a bit taken aback by it, but I managed to get him into a decent headlock and made him tap out, whilst I kept his head pushed into the dirt. We turned in after that and the next morning we were fine.

The foreign girls were so sweet, I couldn't even swear around them. It was so nice to realise I could be valued by people as a human being and I discarded some of the armour I had worn for so long. I found many of the Israelis to be arrogant supremacist bastards and some of the Arabs I met most certainly were dirty lying bastards. But both groups had their share of the decent and righteous, existing in an unfair but impossible situation.

As far as Armageddon was concerned; I went to the biblical city in the plain of Jezreel, where the Book of Revelations warns that the Four Horsemen of the Apocalypse will ride out from, to begin the final conflict. I nearly met my own fate there at Har Megiddo.

While climbing through the rough thorny scrub covering the ramparts to the ruined site, I'd got two thirds of the way up and almost stepped on a coil of venom the colour of the hillside itself. The Palestine viper reared up instantly, and whipped out at me in one movement as I stepped back fast. I turned and leaped away and, as I landed with my front foot, I saw the scaly brown body in that extended S shape, with its head inches from my trailing ankle. I don't care what anybody says about snakes not chasing people, 'cause I was there and that fucker flew as fast as I could on that steep slope, and it wasn't stopping.

My body moved so fast my legs couldn't keep up and I went head-over-heels, again and again, all the way to the bottom, where I scrambled out of the thorny scrub and my legs took over again to get me clear. It must have been a sight to see, I was dressed like Indiana Jones and all cut and grazed and stuck with needles and thorns.

I think I came to terms with how I saw myself fitting into the world and what my reasons for being in it were, on a trip the Kibbutz ran to the Dead Sea. It can be depressing wondering what it's all about and I felt quite melancholy sitting on a block of salt that evening, staring out in the dark over the lowest point on the earth's surface. No epiphany came to me and I eventually wandered back up to Ein Gedi settlement where our lot had been put up for the night.

Being met by the friendly welcoming faces and voices of the volunteer group, it just all clicked into place. I knew it wasn't about surviving the future, but experiencing the present. Live for today and love the ones you are with. My spiritual awakening was realising that I could like people I had nothing in common with, and what was more surprising was that they could like me.

When I got back home at the end of January, I was happier than I had been for years. I enjoyed the frosty mornings, which lasted into March that year and was often up and walking the fields to catch a clean sunrise. It was a year of hard work and saving up for my next planned trip, with Stuey to South America. I still got out and around but no longer just because it was a Friday or Saturday night: I was busy with a whole lot of plans and the world was opened up before me.

The nineties saw the beginning of the epic ten year Triumph 5TA rebuild. The catalyst for this had been an obsession I had about riding to the western extremities of the lands of Britain. It was Wales this time and I had set off on the tried and tested mount. I did know she wasn't fully fit for the job, but I had faith that, taking it gently, we'd make it together.

There was a fair bit of smoke coming from the right hand exhaust once I hit the M25, but I carried on all the same and sadly didn't get much further before the head gasket blew. I later discovered I had burned a hole in the top of a piston.

A good spirited motorcyclist pulled up within minutes and offered me a tow to the nearest civilisation off the next junction. I gratefully accepted and he secured a bungee cord to the hand grip at the back of his bike. I had to grip my end of the cord with one hand (arm reaching right forward) and steer with the other. It was torture controlling the bike and keeping it in a straight line. The hook kept snatching in my hand when he accelerated, yanking the steering, but I couldn't let go in case the cord whipped back and smashed his light or got wrapped in his spokes. Once the tension took up, I had the full weight of my bike and pack being taken by one arm stretched out over the steering axis.

Somehow I kept a hold and several miles later we were off that motorway and in a couple of hours more the bike and I were in the back of the Transit van and going home.

I wouldn't be deterred and wheeled the H2 out of the barn, untried and untested with no tax, MOT or insurance. I would see what it was worth. I changed a cracked top yoke, gave her a quick service and swapped my baggage over after a reselection of my tool-kit make up. Then I went to bed, ready to head out again the next morning on this unfamiliar machine that was totally unsuitable for touring.

It started out feeling OK, but I think I was under-using it by keeping the revs down to run it in gently and that engine was not designed to run sluggishly below the power band. What I didn't like was the nasty finned plastic grips which felt too big, cut into my hands and transmitted the vibrations up my arms.

I got onto the downhill section of the M25, between junctions five and six and I started to run her fast, then bang! The rear wheel locked solid. I think the weight of bike and luggage kept me in a straight black line and I got the clutch in before she could whip, freewheeling over to the hard shoulder for the second time in as many days. There was no turning that engine over: it was seized solid.

I later discovered, on inspection, that the middle piston

had melted and welded itself to the barrel lining. This was to cause me a great deal of time and expense: stripping down, rebuilding and running in again. All for the bike to seize on me three or four times over the next couple of years – I finally got rid of it for a pittance because I needed some money for travelling, all the plugs blew that same day and good riddance to the 'Widow Maker'.

That evening, I decided that I would not be beaten and it was my right to ride to St Davids and look out over the Irish Sea. The H2 went back in the barn to worry about later and out came the trusty lime green KH400. I took a bit more time with the servicing and felt a lot more confident when I set off on the following day – third bike, third time lucky.

That fine sunny day I had ridden west for hours, stopping only for petrol and to admire the Cherhill White Horse carved into the chalk hillside in Wiltshire. I rode on through Bath as a curiosity, but, far from being quaint, it was crowded with traffic and I was hot in my Belstaff suit. So I just rode out for Wales, to try and get as far west as I could before stopping for the night. I just kept blasting past those motorway junctions, into the evening.

Just before dusk I took an exit slipway and rode into the countryside a short way, looking for some cover. I chose a field track leading round the back of a small wood and concealed myself and machine in the thicket. I brewed up a cup of tea and made myself comfortable for the night.

Back in those days, sleeping under the stars was no discomfort and the risk of rain in the night was one I was prepared to accept. I would generally be up at first light and gone before I could be discovered.

It did rain that morning and I stopped on and off for shelter on the way to Pembrokeshire. I camped at Manorbier village, where there is a pretty good Norman castle.

The sun was shining all the next day and I walked a couple of miles along the spectacular coast to the next village called Lynton or something. The cliffs had vertical strata a hundred feet high and great rifts and narrow chasms, just with the sea reaching right inland, splitting the rock like wedges.

When I got back, I had a little ride to the walled town of Tenby, where they used to do speed trials on the long flat sandy beach. I made it to St. David's Head the following day, the most westerly point. Then I continued on up the coast, north east to Cardigan Bay. For some reason, my desire to go on sort of petered out and I made the decision to head back home. I suppose I had fulfilled my ambition and been to the most westerly point and so the mission was complete. I did enjoy doing a bit of sightseeing, but as a by-product of the journey, not for the sake of it.

I rode through the Forest of Dean, thinking I would camp there, but was disappointed, as it seemed to be an entirely managed unnatural plantation of non-indigenous pine trees, with a main road running through it. Even though the land-scape was rugged, it seemed sterile: nothing grows under dense pines other than the odd toadstool.

I do remember dreading coming back through that area of the M25 where I'd broken the two previous bikes. I was very superstitious, but also defiant. The bike made it through okay, but I lost my cherished cream coloured scarf. The wind had managed to loosen it from my neck, as if by the frantic scratchy fingers of a whore in the night. I felt the scarf whip as it was stripped from my neck by the road harpy, just as I was coming out of the same stretch of hill where the H2 had bought it going down.

I was very much a believer in fate and that I would survive risky situations because my purpose had not yet been revealed and my time, until that point came, was unlimited. This explains to a degree my contempt for road safety, although it's certainly no excuse. If I'd been born a hundred years earlier and riding horses instead of bikes, I would have done so with equal irresponsibility I'm sure.

Once I stripped that 5TA down, I discovered that, not only had I holed a piston, but one of the big ends needed replacing. What followed has been described by some mates as the longest rebuild in history. A complete engine rebuild by my own hands, which lasted ten years.

I had to take the block in to Vick Miller, as I didn't have the tools to split the crank case myself. He removed the old bushes, reground the crank-shaft and unblocked the sludge-trap I didn't know it had. He said the only way any oil had been getting from one side to the other was because the bushes were so worn, the oil had been able to bypass its correct route within the crank-shaft and spill through them.

I had ridden to Miller Motorcycles (about an hour to Hastings from the farm) on my KH, with the engine/gearbox unit, minus the primary drive, head and barrels in an army surplus rucksack on my back, which nearly broke me. When I went to collect it, it was all in bits. He told me I couldn't afford to pay him to put it back together and I suppose he was right. So with all the new parts I needed, a proper gasket set, a good torque wrench and the Haynes manual, I rebuilt it from scratch – every single nut, bolt, screw, spring and washer.

Some of the job I enjoyed, I have to say, but not that bloody primary drive, or the tappets, 'cause you have to do it with the rocker covers on and there is no room for a regular feeler gauge. I bought one new con-rod, as the old one was cracking near the bottom end. I fitted a new bronze bush for the gearbox to primary drive, as it was split and not supporting the shaft. I had the barrels reconditioned and fitted a new tappet block and push-rods. The head and barrels went to SRM to be re-bored and the valve seats were re-ground and seated with new valves and springs. I had the oil pump and pressure valve reconditioned too: new pistons, rings and pins of course.

Since the rebuild it produced so much oil pressure that it was blowing it out of the breather at the back of the primary drive, so I stuck a tube on it and fed it back into the oil reservoir tank initially, but that mucked up the oil tank breather pressure, so the pipe is now clipped high up the frame. I'm still working on this and the electrics, but the old girl doesn't come out of the shed too often these days.

I was back working with the boys anyway, repairing the trials bikes when they broke them and teaching riding skills. That didn't stop me pushing myself and the machines to the limit, with big jumps and all sorts of manoeuvres that I'd developed. The huge mound we had in the main field was the centre piece and I would ride any bike straight up the steepest edge. If it started to flip I'd just step a foot off and let it wind round the back wheel, then twist and throw myself back on, aiming the front wheel at the bottom. I never wanted to let go of the bars.

We did have some fantastic accidents, amazingly without any serious injuries, as the only protection we generally wore was an ill-fitting crash helmet, welly boots and gardening gloves. We used to pull discarded wellies out of Folkestone harbour quite regularly, hose them out and match them up as pairs. Often we would actually come across the other genuine matching boot, but mostly the kids looked like they had been outfitted by Stig of the Dump.

On one of my triples buying sprees, I had got hold of a couple of 400s that were partly dismantled. One of them was a crimson coloured KH that didn't take much putting together. It was a really good looking bike. I used it a few times, including taking it up the Castle pub in Ashford town centre on a Saturday afternoon. Stuart saw it and liked it so much he bought it from me that evening for £700. The next weekend I sold the KH500 up there for £625. As long as I got to ride a bike for a while, then sell it on for a bit of profit, I was happy.

The Castle was definitely the place to go, everyone seemed to get up there and lounge around outside on a sunny afternoon, showing off their metal. I didn't see it myself, but I was told that someone we all knew had come out of the pub in front of a crowd, revved up his 1000cc four and pulled a wheelie without unlocking his steering. It was confirmed for me, years later, that the bike and rider had ended up through the glass window of a shop opposite. Trevor Laker was always a mental case: I thought so since I first met him at the Stowting youth club, so I can actually believe that story. I have seen him quite a few times since, most recently with a Highwaymen patch on his back when he was close to fifty – good on him.

At the end of April, Stuart and I took our 400s to the New Forest. We camped near the Rufus Stone and then rode to Poole the next morning.

Stu had to be back at work on the Monday, but I went on into the West Country, getting to Dartmouth that evening. I found it an interesting little place, a steep sided little bay where the River Dart meets the sea. I chose a bench in a little park area up by the castle and watched the fishing boats coming and going down below, as the evening darkened. It was warm, so I didn't put a tent up and just lay out in my army sleeping bag.

I was woken about midnight by the growls of a large Alsatian dog. This frightened the hell out of me, as my face was exposed and the beast was right there in front of me, snarling like a hell hound. I felt sure that if I moved it would attack and I wasn't in any kind of defensible position. I decided the safest thing to do was nothing and not even look at its demonic eyes. It seemed to circle me a bit, as I heard its growls from various directions, then after a minute or two it was just me alone on a wooden bench in the dark.

These diary entries record the rest of that ride:

### Monday 30th April 1990
*I rode to Start point, the most southerly point of Devon and walked down to Hallsands, the remains of a fishing village destroyed by the encroaching sea earlier in the century. I rode along Plymouth sea front, quite nice really and on to Bodmin moor where I took accommodation at Jamaica Inn. I took a two and a half hour hike to the summit of Brown Willy and back, the highest of the granite tors, then cooked sausages and beans in my room on my camping gas stove.*

### Tuesday 1st May
*Excellent breakfast, rode to Padstow for their May day 'Obby Oss' celebration, which was a bit like a Morris dance through the*

streets, great atmosphere. I ate Cornish ice cream and drank the local brews then I had my palm read by a Gypsy woman. It was remarkable, she read me like a book for £5 a hand; the left one for where I've got in life and the right one, where I'm going.

### Wednesday 2nd
I hung around half the day in Padstow then decided I had to go back and live up to my future, as newly revealed. I rode back across Dartmoor and through the hilly land of S.W. Dorset with the sun setting behind me. I stopped at the Walter Tyrell Inn for sustenance just before dark and found my bed for the night near the Rufus stone.

### Thursday 3rd
I woke up in the forest again, very comfortable among dry leaves and moss, feeling both refreshed and enchanted. I lost no time in getting home, eager to seek my rightful fortune.

Looking back, the gypsy woman had given me good practical and financial advice, but I ballsed up the romantic part by backing the wrong horse from the limited selection of prospective soul mates who got up the Dukes that I was sweet on. I snubbed the advances of the sexy one, to play hard to get with the cute one. In the end I forfeited both to keener players, leaving myself high and dry. I think I gave up on landing myself an English Rose about that time and concentrated on preparing myself for going to South America at the end of the year.

### Friday 8th June 1990
I went to thoroughbred stainless in West Ham (near Eastbourne), for some of the missing stainless steel fixings I needed for Dad's BSA.

*I then went to Millers in Hastings and he didn't have anything ready that I had asked for a month ago. I went up the Dukes.*

**Saturday 9<sup>th</sup> June**
*I started work on my Triumph, did a few things right & fucked a few things up. Went up the Dukes.*

I decided to throw a midsummer party in my caravan field. So the word went out to Chip and Martin, who turned up at the Dukes with ten or fifteen of the Oakmen. We caused a bit of a stir in the pub, as the landlord and his fancy lady didn't like the rowdiness, or Martin's sick jokes, and my fox skin headdress was banned. Actually, it wasn't long after that that I got myself banned from the Dukes Head altogether. This complimented my long list of achievements in the art of social ostracism: the Black Horse, the Plough, the Mucky Duck on various occasions and the Sellindge Sports and Social Club. That's not an exhaustive list, but just covers the pubs within a two mile radius that I was no longer welcome at.

I left the pub early with Stuart, Del, Sue and Tony on a mad race back to my place to get the bonfire started and light the way for the club bikes with flaming torches. The Anti Nowhere League was playing as the bikes rumbled up my driveway, recently built by hand with huge concrete sleepers, slabs and blocks, then superficially covered with rubble. There was about seventy five yards of it around the edge of the field and most of the bikes were choppers. They all complained that they had bashed their sumps or exhausts on lumps of concrete sticking up like shark's fins. Martin's brother Nigel actually did split the fibreglass belly pan on his brand new XJ900 in half.

My parties were legendary and once this one got going it went like a pocket full of Chinese bangers. There was the obligatory fire dancing and then Stuart found a stack of antique refectory chairs I had picked up for sale or repair and foolishly left too close to the fire site. When I saw him hurling them onto the fire I protested initially, but the scene was so anarchic it just seemed the right thing to do, so the lot went on, about twenty five in all.

When the fire settled down and we could get back near it, I brought out a bottle of Arak that had come back with me from the Kibbutz; so that went round – I always hated the stuff and was pleased to find a use for it.

Derek got himself blind drunk and wanted to go home, but Sue (his new bird) didn't, so he threw their sealed bottle of vodka in the fire to emphasise the point, to no effect. Sometime later when he was stomping around in the embers, the fire exploded and burned his legs. We never knew if it was his own bottle that went up or an aerosol can Martin Greenhill had stuffed in there. Del had another go at dragging Sue away, but she wasn't done, not by a long way. A shouting match ensued and then they took it in turns to slap each other round the face. Sue was a great girl, one of the gang. So, honour satisfied, she just sat right back down and took another drink, while poor old Del took a walk.

Things calmed down and some party goers drifted off in the early hours. One of the funniest things was seeing Knuckles crashed out by the fire and big Andy trying to wake him up by heaving an empty forty-five-gallon oil drum over beside his head and belting it repeatedly with a lump of wood. No effect whatsoever!

By about four am there was just me, Tone, Sue and Andy still awake and we were cooking sausages. Then out of the dawn mist, Del came striding back in. Sue knew it was time to go home, and she'd made her point. Del had made a tonk of himself and Tony, the lovable fool, took it as an invite to go along for the walk back to Sellindge. I don't know what they all talked about.

The parties we had were wild, irresponsible statements of anarchy – and they were perfect times; for each occasion there was a theme or a particular motivation which justified the event and every one of them was memorable. In recent years I've made efforts to re-invigorate that culture, with some success. I've been able to bring back together various people who went their own way decades ago. And we're still mad.

# CHAPTER FIFTEEN

## *Home roads calling*

I never bought a new tyre for any of my second hand bikes, tyres and chains were things I was tight on. When I was stopped on my green KH on the way back from Cornwall, they noted that my rear tyre was below the legal limit, which is only about a millimetre. I was given a ticket to fit a new tyre and present the bike at a testing station within a certain time period. Well, I fitted a second hand one I got from the bike breakers, a Swallow, I'd never heard of the make. Andy said 'Oh yeah, Swallow tyres, they're a substitute for a proper tyre.' He was right there, as it altered the handling, with a tail whip whenever I crossed a centre line on the main road. I got the bike tested at Nackington traffic police centre, outside Canterbury, where they passed it as legal. Then I went straight home and changed it back for the old worn out Metzeler that I knew. Old tyres are like old friends.

A1 bike breakers had once sold me a tyre which looked all right, until I had forced and pried it on to the rear wheel of my CB200. It was all wrong and when I checked the markings on the side wall it clearly indicated that it was a front tyre. When I took it back, they suggested I might have got the tyre pressure wrong but begrudgingly changed it for a rear tyre, which was what I had asked for in the first place.

**Wednesday 29th August 1990**
*I took my Vespa to Warehorne and got a rear wheel blow out on the Aldington-Lympne road. I rode it home, (3-4 miles) like a wounded chopper; the tyre was cut to ribbons.*

**Thursday 30th August 1990**
*I helped Derek fix the CB brake & centre stand spindle (that bike was falling apart and any form of maintenance was just to keep the wheels turning). We rode to hollow lane, near Nackington, to hunt down Will who had disappeared from the scene; his woman told us he wanted nothing to do with his old mates.*

We didn't see Will again for another seventeen years. I don't know what the truth of the matter was and it doesn't matter anymore. But it was kind of strange at the time.

In December 1990, Stuart and I took off to Latin America for six months. We bought return tickets to Mexico City and the plan was to be in Rio for Mardi Gras. We had many adventures out there and made it as far south as the Amazon, using local transport: boats, trains, trucks and busses.

We never got to Rio, but what the hell. We did trek through the Darien jungle, carrying everything we had for ten days from the last road in Panama to the first road in Colombia. We braved snakes, ants, panthers, ticks and clouds of mosquitoes.

There were Indian villages where the indigenous people helped us and some stole from us. I was also bitten by a dog. There was a tense situation where we thought we might actually get shot by a furious negro boatman with a .22 handgun. It was strange; a couple of villages we stumbled into were entirely populated by Africans, the legacy of the old slave days, isolated deep in the jungle. Those people weren't shy like the Indians: the blacks were smugglers who wore pistols and machetes and loved to drink and fuck (there was no mistaking that), their villages were untidy, but colourful and we felt that if we were going to get into any kind of trouble, it wouldn't be with the native Indians.

It struck me that, according to available records at the time, no one had actually made it through the Darien on a motor-bike and I kind of fancied my chances. I spent years afterwards assessing the qualities and disabilities of every half-suitable bike on the market, hoping that one day I might go back there with something that could get me through and still be fit for the road afterwards. I understand that a good deal of the jungle we sweated through at the start has now been cleared on the Panamanian side, so the challenge will have lessened somewhat. I'd still do it though, if Stu was on board.

Whilst winding things up in Kent before we left for the Americas, there were a whole host of things I felt I had to put right and store away for the future. I didn't know for sure that I would be back the following summer – it would depend on what I found when I was out there. So that autumn I worked like a fiend, there was so much stuff that was important to me.

I had spent some time and money overhauling my H2: new pistons, rings, gudgeon pins, needle roller bearings and circlips. I'd had the barrels re-bored and had just put it all back together in time for Nigel's Guy Fawkes do in his girlfriend's back yard in Ashford. I didn't get there till about 11pm, but the bike looked fantastic at night. The street light glinting off the polished chrome and that deep alligator green paint-job set with magnificent murals depicting Jason and the Golden Fleece.

The evening was in full swing when I arrived, Martin was chucking up, Chip's woman had her top off and Bearded Andy was turning the paraffin-tainted sausages on the barbecue. We started chucking paraffin and petrol on the bonfire and running through the blaze for laughs. My denim cut off actually caught fire at one point.

I felt pretty bad the next morning and had to throw up. It was bright sunshine though and we were all set for a ride out. I opened my drive casing to adjust the widow maker's clutch and found that my front sprocket nut was completely loose. Then, whilst sorting that out, someone pointed out that my petrol pipes were leaking. A few corrections were made and the bike was safe to go.

We rode out en masse to the Stonebridge Inn at Woodchurch, mostly windy roads, but once we found a bit of straight, I throttled past Knuckles on the inside to take the lead. I looked back to see that I'd choked him out in the cloud of blue smoke I left down the road every time I opened her up. That was the best day out I had on that bike.

Although everyone who saw it commented on how beautiful it was, no one actually wanted to buy it. The reputation the H2-750 had turned out to be pretty accurate. It ate spark plugs, the carbs and air filters were always vibrating loose and I could never stop the middle piston from seizing in the barrel whenever it felt like it.

People used to say that fuel consumption was so bad on those bikes that you should be able to hear the whistle of air being drawn through the vent in the petrol cap. I never got enough use out of it to fill the tank more than a few times and those after-market exhausts must have drowned out the sound.

I virtually gave the bike away a couple of years later, after failing to get anything near what it had cost me. I needed the money to fund my travels and that bike was in the way and picking up rust. I do, from time to time, wonder what happened to that rare classic that must be worth ten to twelve thousand on today's market. Did the lucky bloke who thought he had bought a donkey from me have it restored to original spec, or is someone admiring that custom paint job right now?

On Friday 7th December, just before I left for Mexico, I held a bonfire party out in the caravan field. We hit the Dukes first to get revved up. Then about 10pm a convoy of vans and bikes made it over the bumpy muddy back track to my site. The fire was lit with a blazing oiled rag torch and a whoof of waste petrol and oil mix I'd been saving up. It was cold out, so we had to get some heat on the go quickly.

People got settled in around the fire, so I went to the caravan to get the firework display started. Wearing a motorbike glove, I launched the first rockets, from my hand at about 30 degrees, to screech over the fire site, laughing as people dived for cover. If you came to one of these parties, you were accepting that you might go home injured, as often was the case. Whether it be broken glass cuts, a red hot nail through the boot during a fire walk, or second degree burns with hair and beard loss, as I suffered myself during a surprise welcome home party six months later, when an acrobatics trick went wrong.

For this midwinter see off, I had prepared food for the guests in the form of two whole chickens, bought from the local butchers specially. I left the bagged up giblets inside each. There was no barbecue set-up, I just slung the carcases, still in their carrier bags, into the fire and stamped them down a bit, to some mixed reactions. The plastic soon burned off them as, probably, did the first quarter inch of skin and fat – they were big chickens.

I provided some fire irons and people got into the spirit, ripping and gouging lumps of half charred flesh out. Stuart turned up late with a car load from Ashford and drove straight through the fire. Most of the meat was gone by then and he picked out a blackened hook shaped object from the selection, Martin polished off the giblets while Stu gnawed away at his chicken neck. That was how 1990 ended for me. Sue got the hot nail through her tucker boot and someone burned their fingers pulling it out for her.

When I did get back in the summer of ninety-one, I was keen to get straight back into my old lifestyle. The bikes came out of the barn one by one and they all worked. I found out that the Duck had changed hands, so I could get back in there. Word from the Dukes though was that I was definitely still barred.

Thursday nights at the Duck were band nights and I went down there with my wild bushy hair and beard that made me look like an escaped lunatic. The Oakmen were there and all the Sellindge boys. Beer was thrown everywhere and we laughed and bundled each other, drank and rioted.

We were always obnoxious, but never actually started any real trouble ourselves. I think people knew it was safe to be in the same bar with us and we'd only get rough amongst our own crowd. I remember putting Matt Godden in hospital once with a ruptured kidney, when he jumped me and I threw him off my back onto the pool table. He carried on drinking and pissing blood, he said he'd thought it was neat Pernod and black coming out. The next day his girlfriend made him go up the hospital. When I went to see him there, he was laid up and plugged into tubes, his missus was not happy.

About a week later, I caught up with the Oakmen at the Pilot on the edge of Dungeness for a lunchtime session. We left in time to get up to Ashford for the evening, where Guy was running the Castle. It was their pub, no doubt about it.

As I'd thinned down my collection a bit, it was time to get some use out of that black KH400 I'd picked up a couple of years previously. First trip out, the chain parted up on Stone Street and I had to push it home. A couple of days later I ran out of petrol on the way back from Ashford on my green KH, so pushed it to Del's new digs in a communal doss house in Sellindge. Claire and Shaun ran it by getting lodgers in to cover the upkeep. They all worked through the week, but at weekends it was a dope fiend's crash pad.

The next morning I chucked some fuel in the tank and kicked it over and something went loose and tingly. I thought I had done the piston rings, but it turned out my lower generator had disintegrated.

That's how it went one day to the next, as each bike broke down in its own fashion; I'd just wheel out the next one in the queue and ride that for a while until I got the time to fix the first one. You don't get that kind of relationship with vehicles nowadays. Everyone has modern machines that can only reasonably be fixed at the recognised service centre for as much money as I used to spend on getting another run-around that I knew I could fix myself. You can't even change a tyre yourself on these modern bikes, let alone diagnose an electrical fault.

Well I got that black KH fixed up, including changing a rear wheel bearing, which was shot, and started using it. I didn't like it at first, with its narrow bars and rear-set foot pegs, but as the CB was really just scrap by then and I needed a bike I didn't have to clean, it did fine for the ten mile thrash to my old, once a week, gardening job at Warehorne, where I'd worked for a few years.

I loved thrashing my old rat bikes there and back along those windy country lanes, pikey country. I never taxed, MOT'd or insured that Black KH. Just put petrol and two stroke oil in it and tightened up the carburettor flanges every month as and when they wore loose.

I just loved racing through country lanes and back ways with just the noise of the engine and the connection I felt with the road. The smell of the land was great. On cold fresh winter mornings, close summer evenings, just after a shower or through that glorious golden fortnight, almost guaranteed in late September, with still air and the potato fields freshly turned. Just me on an iron horse, the noise and vibration fused into one, blazing a path through the English countryside. There's no more perfect a feeling of freedom.

# CHAPTER SIXTEEN

## *Starting the fire*

Del had been without a bike since before I'd left for Mexico. After I got back, I lent him my CB200 to use, until he'd worked up the money to buy it from me. Unsurprisingly that never happened and the bike was a virtual wreck when I got it back from him. Nothing worked on it and one spark plug hole had the thread stripped from it, so that from time to time a plug would fire itself out of the head. Amazingly it still ran, but that was the end of its life as I knew it.

About three years later I sold that bike as a non-runner (at the Sellindge Steam Rally), to a father and son who wanted a project. I think I got £25 for it, which wasn't bad considering. I hope they had some fun with it.

Before Will disappeared, he had left an old Suzuki GT250 round at my place and it had stood against a shed until the top end had seized. Del thought he would take it on, so I helped him get it over to his place and we stripped it down and unseized it. That was as far as that plan went. The next I heard, he had sold it on to keep him in dope for another week.

I wanted to break this negative cycle and re-map his brain by taking him travelling, thinking it might broaden his mind and offer some new horizons. I had my thoughts around South East Asia. Del had been working as a grounds-man at the Philippine Village, a less than popular tourist attraction in Brookland on the marsh, and he persuaded me that the Philippines would be a good place to start. So we saved up and bought tickets on Pakistan International Airways. We left that November.

London – Bahrain – Karachi – Bangkok – Manila. That was a long haul flight, and when we got there we discovered it was typhoon season. We couldn't do most of what we had planned; we got ripped off almost every step of the way and hadn't brought enough money anyway, but we still had a laugh and managed to get back home in one piece, without even being conned into marrying anyone.

One stormy couple of days hanging out in nipa-palm huts, surrounded by rotting coconut husks, we composed some alternative lyrics to the 1989 Billy Joel hit – *We didn't start the fire*. With some poetic licence, I think our version pretty much summed up the experience. It went something like this:

*Pakistani Airlines Mabini street and bar fines,*
*dog shit Del Pilar street hypodermics in my feet.*
*Abra NPA her mother says you've got to pay,*
*gonorrhoea diarrhoea why the fuck am I here.*
*White beach nipa hut, Suzy is a lying slut*
*Jeepneys Bulacan typhoons and Pagsanjan.*
*Garlic Zosima sugar cane the floating bar,*
*Coca cola dried squid, there goes my 500 quid.*

- chorus-

*We didn't start the virus*
*It's the planets answer to the worlds disaster*
*We didn't start the virus*
*But I think I caught it and I even bought it*
*We didn't start the virus*
*Think I should just go home, and live alone*
*Alone.*

Three months later, after doing a bit of research and a load more work, I flew back out there, on Gulf Air, to this exotic archipelago of 7000 islands. I completed a proper island hopping circuit, left the beer and bars alone and took an advanced open water diving course. I explored caves, mountains and jungles, as well as getting up close to dozens of tiny desert islands. I even got to ride a 1965 Honda CB450 around the voodoo island of Siquijor; that was a strange place. I only wanted to go to strange places and never considered any of my travels to actually be holidays.

There was only one more bikers' bash I remember going to about that time, before I stepped away from the scene. I still met up with the club members at the pubs from time to time, but wouldn't get to another full-on party night for about another six years after, that was when I made it to Klumsy Chris' wedding reception up near Chartham.

The Oakmen used to rent out Bethersden village hall for party nights and they were good events. I took the H2 on this occasion; it seized on me twice on the way up there but made it back all in one go. I thought maybe that's because I actually opened it up on the way back rather than playing safe: I was still technically running it in from the last rebuild.

There was a lot of speed going around at that do and I ended up accepting a couple of hefty dabs, first time in about four years. I had a great time, as did everyone there. I think we were all on it and that was the deciding factor for me to opt out of the scene.

I just wanted to ride out, have a raucous drunken evening and make it back in time for work in the morning. I didn't want to be getting back half way through the night, unable to sleep until the following afternoon, then loose interest in food and everything else for about the next three days until the come down had run its course.

There's nothing good comes out of habitual drug use: once or twice under odd circumstances can be described as 'an experience,' but then it takes more and more to get the same feeling and before you know where you are, it's become a dependence. Solvents were a suicidal adolescent craze and magic mushrooms a free earth self-realisation journey, the main danger being what you might do in your psychotic confusion.

Generally, most free spirits were smokers anyway, so naturally gravitated to dope smoking. That scene bored me; a bunch of twenty year olds sitting around a communal house with the curtains closed wasting their weekends and all their spare money on Leb, Rocky Black, Pringles and Patchouli oil.

I was anti dope because it dissolved people's ambition. Amphet was a different case; once people started down that route they didn't seem to be able to have a good time without being on a chemical high, it wasn't like you could take it or leave it.

Actually, as I concentrated more on work, in order to fund my growing addiction for overseas travel, I would eventually come to shun alcohol as a habit, only drinking if an event warranted it. This stance saved me a lot of money, but I began to lose connections with most of my old mates and for a number of years it was only Del who I kept in regular contact with.

I never sold all my bikes or burned my denim originals, I didn't turn my back on the past; I just looked to the future. To me, the nineties were all about packing my rucksack and marching out to explore the exotic and desolate. My idea about travelling was that if it was easy, I wasn't interested. I wanted to challenge myself, to go out into the world and come back a better person.

In the intervals when I was home, every now and then, I would get one of my old neglected motorcycles out and complete some repair that had been waiting years for me to get round to it. From cleaning out the carb on a trials bike and giving it a turn around the field, to spending six hours in the barn re-fitting pistons and barrels on a two stroke triple by the light of a paraffin lamp.

There were the long term projects too, like the Triumph engine still in bits since 1989. It would be three years from when the engine blew before I'd even get around to reassembling the crank shaft and con-rods in place, along with securing the cases as a bottom end unit. It was another few years before I slid the re-bored barrels over the new pistons. Actually starting and running the rebuilt and refitted engine for the first time had to wait until the last few months of the millennium.

Travelling was breaking up any possibility of consistent motorcycling activities, social or mechanical. For example:

**Tuesday 26th May 1992**
*Got up late. Put the gears & clutch back in my Lambretta engine.*

**Wednesday 27th May**
*I put the engine and wheels back in the Lambretta frame.*

Then nothing till June relating to the same project:
*I smoothed down my Lambretta leg shield again & re-sprayed red oxide & then did the front half black then ran out of paint.*

Two months later the July 31st entry reads triumphantly:
*I finished my Lambretta today, as far as I shall work on it this year anyway. So for the first time since 1986 I rode it up to the phone box & back. The lights don't work, the front brake cable snapped, the back brake stopped working, I lost the first gear selection and I couldn't find the speedo. But I think after seven years in different baskets it's a miracle that it actually works, oh I have two different shades of purple on it.*

After all that time I had really lost interest in scooters and I never rode it again. It was stored away in the barn until I needed some money in 1997, when I sold it for £750 I think. It would have been worth a few hundred more if I had left it in its original boring dirty yellow colour.

During 1993-94, Dad and I had painstakingly acquired, modified and made from scratch the remaining parts to complete his 1959 BSA 650 Super Rocket, to almost Rocket Gold Star spec. With new satin blue metallic paint and chrome in equal measures, she looked a beauty, all topped off with stainless steel nuts bolts and screws.

It was Dad's dream bike, created from a crashed Super Rocket he had bought about the same time I picked up my Speed Twin. A lot of pain and effort went into re-building every part of that bike and there were times I hated it.

Dad had wanted a replacement for his old 1957 Road Rocket that he had had at college in the sixties. I remember the stories of how he had stripped that first bike down and then rebuilt it, piece by piece in his upstairs lodging room, before riding it down the stairs and out of the building.

He always said the colour was Monaco red and I found the old registration book recently showing it as TLW932. He never got the thrill of a Beezer engine out of his system.

Roadstar had sorted out the clutch and rigged the primary drive arrangement, a rare special for an A10 requiring an almost unobtainable primary drive casing to cover it. Roadstar did the wiring at their odd little workshop place beneath the shadow of Dover castle, crowded with new and second hand bits as well as part broken, mainly British bikes, which fill any space they don't need to walk on. There are mudguards, lights and cables hanging from the walls and ceiling and greasy tools as old as the bikes themselves, still the best things for the job.

It is the only place I go for British stuff now. They will find things, repair them or get them made and even let you advertise bikes for sale on their board, if you can find room on it.

Dad and I had become members of the BSA Owners Club in 1987, same as the Panther Owners Club, but my Panther is still in boxes out in the shed. The Beezer made it out into the light of day in October '95, but it wasn't on the road till May '96, with an MOT and a final bill from Roadstar.

We had gone through the process over the years of making

lists, then stripping it down and doing a first build, then making more lists and then repairs and modifications to the frame, sand blasting (for a second time) and delivering all the parts to a workshop at Old Surrenden Manor for paint and chrome.

Finally the modified and reconditioned engine went back in the frame. Dad had had that engine made ready when SRM were still at Penarth docks; the barrel was stove enamelled, as were the wheel hubs: I don't remember who did that, but SRM went to town on that engine and nothing was left to chance. It was certainly no easier putting the bike together the second time. Absolutely everything had its own awkwardness, from re-building the forks to re-fitting the chain guard.

The bike received an Amal TT9 carb, a halogen head-light bulb, Hagon shocks and stainless fork springs. We fitted Avon tires onto the rebuilt QD sports hub wheels by Radaelli Italy: 19" front and a reduced 18" rear with stainless spokes. Everything you could see with a thread on it had to be stainless, all from Thoroughbred Stainless at Potts Marsh near Eastbourne.

She looked a serious motorcycle, with an oil pressure gauge nestling below the pair of Smiths clocks on an extra bracket we made. The old dynamo casing at the front was converted to take a replaceable oil filter. There was a lot of other stuff including a Spitfire cam conversion, but I'll stop there – she was ready to hit the road.

# CHAPTER SEVENTEEN

## *Golden Triangle*

19⁹³ was the start of an entirely new section of my life. Always looking for adventure, I had started the decade in the deserts of the Middle East, followed by the mountains and jungles of Latin America. Now it was time to follow the dawn to the land of smiles. I had great plans for an entire circuit of South-East Asia, which I did do, in a roundabout way, over the next few years. I got to most of the places I had aspirations about, and each trip I undertook would change my outlook on life for better or worse.

That spring, I found myself living in a hill tribe village in Thailand's Golden Triangle region, playing Tarzan and wondering how I was ever going to be the same again.

Things were moving way faster than I could have imagined, after meeting a young Akha girl called Abu, which simply means girl in the language of her tribe. It was not all paradise and making love in the forest though; we had a hell of a lot of pointless arguments – mostly over cultural things and I know I could never have truly been one of them.

I loved the times we would go out together to collect food, as there was a natural timelessness to the whole aspect of being – and everything was a delight.

Fate eventually intervened, as the pig I had bought as a part of the engagement process strayed into a villager's rice field and got shot before the ceremony could take place. This was taken as a bad luck portent and I didn't argue too much, or buy another pig. We cooked and shared the pig meat out amongst the village and they all seemed happy. I kept the two lead bullets which were dug out of the carcass as my own souvenirs and everyone ate well that evening.

I never forgot Abu and nothing can take away what we had, we were both too young at the time though to make it last the way it had been and I left that hilltop village soon after, with a heart so heavy that I needed some form of excitement and danger to lift me up again. That was most easily found in the form of various smallish, two wheeled machines; mostly sporting the Honda badge and Thailand was great motorcycling territory.

The MTX 125 I hired from Boon Bun-dan guest house in Chiang Rai town took me deep into the hills, using jungle trails and elephant tracks for the first day. Then following unmade roads as much as I could, I headed into the border areas – where things are always more interesting.

Red and grey dust roads running through colourful villages, then narrow, stony trails to less accessible places with great mountain views. I came to a place on top of a hill called Santikhiri. Totally Chinese, it's where a remnant of the Chinese National Army had ended up when Mao's revolutionaries turned China Red. There was no going back for them and the 'Jin Haw' were stranded in the land of the free, which is actually what Thailand means.

On the way back to town at the end of the ride, I had to pass through an impenetrable cloud of dust on the main road. A big machine was sweeping the opposite lane as part of a resurfacing process and the wind blew the dust all across my lane like a dark blanket. I watched trucks with their headlights on emerging from the cloud and then I was engulfed by it. I could actually feel the dust and grit covering me for at least 100 yards and could see nothing at one point. When I came out into the light again, I was on the wrong side of the road facing the oncoming.

A few more miles down the road I realised I had a puncture and a mechanical problem to boot. The rad water was really low and I couldn't find any oil in the sump base. Fortunately, it being the main route back to the town, there were some small mechanics shops alongside the road, just shelters really, with some tyres and bearings and things hanging up. A Thai gave me a tow to one of these places, where I got the puncture fixed for a start.

Topped up with fluids, I made it to the next repair shack when my faltering engine had had about enough. The mechanic put a squirt of oil in the bore and changed the plug for me. He sent me on my way (no charge), telling me not to stop till Chiang Rai.

Two Thais stopped to help me the next time the engine lost it and towed me the thirteen km back to the edge of town. I restarted it to get me back to the guest house lane, then switched off to coast it the last fifty yards, so I wasn't seen pushing it and no one would hear the knackered engine.

That bike's problems were down to a lack of maintenance and skimping on repairs. This turned out to be par for the course on rental bikes all through South-East Asia. Add to that poor roads, low grade fuel and intense heat and it's a wonder any of these bikes lasted more than two or three years, probably lots of them didn't.

There were no Haynes manuals and people didn't fix or maintain their own machines, as street side garages were so numerous and cheap. I remember watching, in amazement, a one handed mechanic refitting a moped tyre and wheel at night, without any assistance. Instead of a hand, he had a metal cup with a drill chuck fitted to his arm, into which he clamped screwdriver blades etc. to help him complete the job.

To start out from a base closer to where I wanted to ride next, I took a bus to the small border town of Mae Sai. From my new guest house on the river bank I watched the people going about their business in the Burmese town of Tachilek, the other side of the water. Simple lives, not always peaceful though.

The long civil war that had been running on and off pretty much since the British pulled out often spilled to the border areas and disrupted the regular people's lives. In these sorts of places, remote from central control and days from a major city, it makes little real difference as to who is actually in charge. Life stays the same, Thais swam and washed clothing in the shallow water their side and the people from the Myanmar shore did exactly the same.

I swam the fifty yards across the Sai river, as it was the dry season and the water was not much of an obstacle. The people on the other side were really quite dark, a bit like Indians, but with a hint of the East. The women were slender and quite beautiful in a mysterious way. They wore colourful sarongs and a kind of gold dust compound applied to their cheeks and the bridge of their noses. Oh the Thai women were beautiful too, but the decades of close association with western influence took away that element of mystery that bewitched me during many of my travels away from the beaten path.

My taste in women had developed not unlike my taste in motorcycles: functional and uncomplicated with a twist of the exotic. I respected sophistication but never really felt comfortable beside it. I wanted my rides to be reliable and good looking in their own way, but not too common or over beautified. There had to be something a little bit obscure for me to find appealing. I've been the keeper of thirty six different motorcycles to date and can pretty much guarantee that wherever I went on them no one else had one quite to match mine in style or uniqueness.

The next day I hired a Yamaha 225 Serow, a small framed four-stroke trail bike built for the Asian market. Not a lot of fire in its belly, but simple and reliable. I rode it on a circular route to Saam Liam Thong Kham where the Ruak River coming from Burma meets the Mekong from China, with Laos away across the other side of the wide expanse. This river would intoxicate me and draw me back to the region time and again for years after. To the jungles of Laos and the baking plains of Cambodia, to the steamy sprawling Mekong Delta hundreds of miles south in Vietnam, where the sea can't be far away but there's no road to reach it and no reason to try.

The Serow took me south along the river to Chiang Saen, once the ancient capital of the region. Then back inland for some trail blazing up Doi Tung, before taking a mountain road back to Mae Sai.

I didn't drink much, or often, when I first went to South East Asia. I was looking for something enlightening and it wasn't marijuana or opium. I was searching for a pureness, a way I could feel clean, something alien to popular western culture. I don't think I ever really found it, although I felt I got close once or twice.

What I did discover was I could eat some pretty strange foods; snake, dog, various types of insect both cooked and raw. Also small birds, deep fried and whole. I would try almost any street food, until I had some large freshwater snails on the pavement in Saigon one day. I offered one back to the vender who declined, indicating something by scratching her forearms and screwing up her face. A passing street kid shook her head at me and put her hands up, showing me blisters on her palms and I remembered reading about snails infected with blood flukes.

I went straight back to my room and put my fingers down my throat repeatedly. Then I drunk a litre of water and did the same again, until there was nothing left inside me. This pissed me off, as I'd just had a decent meal prior to trying the snails. After emptying my stomach, I felt hungry again and had to go out and buy myself another dinner.

# CHAPTER EIGHTEEN

## *Practiced forced landings*

17<sup>th</sup> April 1993 was the date I arrived in Phnom Penh, the capital of Cambodia; ironically it was also the anniversary of the fall of the city in 1975 to the Khmer Rouge Maoist revolutionaries. Nothing I saw that day, or ever, indicated to me that the recent historical tragedy was recognised or acknowledged by the vast majority of the people.

Their liberation by the Vietnamese, beginning on Christmas Day 1978, had resulted in a decade of occupation, right or wrong. Then, with the war still dragging over out in the countryside and the Paris Peace Accords freshly signed, the country was swamped with 11000 UN troops, plus administrators, aid organisations, international criminals etc. The door opened for independent travellers a couple of months prior to the UN sponsored elections and I was on one of those first few flights to the strangest land I'd ever experienced.

In this country, more than any other in the region, the Honda C90 was king. It was the life blood, versatile, indestructible and pretty good looking for a moped. The original 70cc and 90cc Super cub versions were the best. Later the 100cc Dream took over – the electric start option was loved by the middle class kids and anyone who wanted to show they didn't do manual work.

When I got there in ninety three, the classic kick-start version from the 1970s was the only way to get around if you didn't want to be sitting on a sack of rice on the roof of a clapped out Peugeot, or in a trailer crammed full of assorted people and animals. I took to it like a duck to water: anything bigger on those roads would have been asking for trouble anyway.

At some shitty back-packers guest house in a noisy part of town, I think it was the only such place open at the time, I got talking with a Swedish bloke called Jurgan, who came in from Bangkok on the same Russian plane I got. We decided to hire a couple of these bikes for $5 a day.

The traffic was madness, not many cars, but Hondas everywhere you looked. It wasn't jam packed like Saigon was, in fact there were no traffic jams at all, just a constant flow of mopeds weaving around the pot holes at a sedate speed on any side of the road, going in any direction. There was no highway code whatsoever and no one used brakes, you just timed your manoeuvres and swerved to avoid objects, people and potholes.

We took a ride out onto highway no.1, twenty or thirty kilometres into the countryside following the Mekong to the east, where I nearly had a head on with a Peugeot 404 while overtaking a bike pulling a handmade trailer full of people in colourful scarves and wide brimmed hats.

This major highway, direct to Ho Chi Minh city, very quickly deteriorated into a broken tarmac causeway with steep red clay banks either side, straight down into flooded fields full of water lilies. The road got so narrow that two Peugeots loaded up (roofs, bonnets and open boots) with people and sacks of rice could only just pass without going over. Nothing was safe and that was part of the thrill of the place.

The next day, we flew up to Siem Reap in a small Russian

plane which must have been a hand-me-down to the Vietnamese during the cold war and passed on to Kampuchea Airways when it became less serviceable. It was a worn out Antonov turboprop An-24. With no proper air-con, it was hot inside to start off with. The land was so flat, with many swampy lakes and the Tonley Sap lake itself was like an inland sea.

As we started to lose altitude during this short trip, the upper quarter of the whole cabin filled with thick clouds of vapour. It was coming down from the luggage racks, as well as leaking in from the doors that didn't seal properly. There was no safety equipment and I noticed at least one broken seatbelt.

Arriving in Siem Reap, it was immediately clear that we were in a war zone. UNTAC (United Nations Transitional Authority in Cambodia) trucks, Toyota Land Cruisers and helicopters were very much in evidence in the daytime, KPAF (Khmer Peoples Armed Forces) everywhere at night.

The Khmer Rouge, otherwise known as DK (Democratic Kampuchea), had recently pulled out of the election process and were stepping up attacks on the ethnic Vietnamese settlements, as well as targeting electoral staff, in the hopes of de-railing the whole process. The owner of our guest house told us, with a smile, that we could rent bikes and go out to the lake to see where the Khmer Rouge had slaughtered thirty seven Vietnamese boat people.

My journal at the time records some of my feelings and experiences:

*These people are unreal, death and cruelty has been bred into them for so many years that most of them don't understand human- ity. We hired the bikes to go to the Rulos group of temples out on highway 6. We passed many people waving and saying 'Hello UNTAC.' There were trucks full of people and bicycles on the road and government soldiers hanging around with AK-47s and RPGs; they weren't alert, just lounging around with those chequered peasants scarves on like the KR wear. They looked lethargic and unperceptive of reality, it was a little scary.*

*We got to the first temple, Preak ko, (9th century). It was deserted, quite small and fitting naturally into the vegetation around it. There was a dead snake on the road, long and thin and dark greenish brown with yellow stripes down both sides. We rode on to the next temple, along a dirt track, it was called Bakong, incredible, like a scene out of Herge's adventures of Tin Tin. The heat was 37-40 in the shade, with a breeze (that's about 100f).*

*There were many Buddhist monks in their saffron robes who came out to stare and accept cigarettes. Then there were the handful of locals living outside the weed choked swamp moat, drawing water from a well, all wearing kramas (those chequered scarves) on their heads, round their necks or waists.*

*There were no souvenirs or soft drinks, no entrance gate, sign posts, guides, nothing. Just this wonderful complex of statues, carvings, walls, towers and platforms, all this was surrounding the main pyramidal structure. We rode off south east on a dirt track with homes dotted along on either side, but back from the road. All the children shouted 'Hello, Hello, Hello' waving and jumping up and down as we passed, it was so funny.*

*We reached Roulos town, really a small lineated village of wooden stilt houses either side of a dry river bed. We stopped the other side of a bridge and the children flocked to us. It was so beautiful, and so sad that their country is entrenched in violence, insanity and hopelessness. Statistically, unless the war ends, many of these children will become involved in one way or another.*

*On the way back to town some people shouted at us, some smiled or waved and some just gave cold stares. They could be supporting either side, we don't know, but we didn't want to break down along that road.*

*Back in town we chatted to some British Paras who told us that highway 6 is mined every night. We have learned that all sorts of robberies and killings go on all over the country every day. Only last week, on one night, four Vietnamese restaurants in Phnom Penh were hand grenaded. There are regular pogroms against the Vietnamese refugees to drive them back down the Mekong and the Khmers don't give a shit. Several UN people have been murdered, two only last week. Also there are disgusting looking frogs in the bathroom.*

That evening we went to a place the paras had recommended to us called the Minefield bar, run by a self-styled mercenary from New Zealand. I wrote in my diary at the time:

*The man is addicted to war and death and has a psychological need to surround himself with it.*

Graham told us a lot of psycho war stories about his life in the Special Forces. Don't know if it was bullshit or not, but we know he had been a Buddhist monk in Thailand before coming here. Anyhow, he had to have been crazy to ride a Honda 750 sports bike from the Thai border straight up to Siem Reap, through a war zone, on a mined road only fit for trucks.

Instead of agricultural tools and fire implements on the walls of his bar, he had hung hand grenades, mortar bombs and bits of shrapnel, plus photos of carnage, war slogans, flags etc. The place was full of UN soldiers, administrators and journalists, and staffed by a bunch of quite demure taxi girls, with limited communicative vocabulary. Dire Straits was playing and Victoria bitter was a dollar a can.

While we were in there, we learned there had been a mortar attack at the Angkor temples about four km down the road and we watched the KPAF APCs rumbling down that road past us as we held our beers and lived for the moment.

I stayed in that town for about a week and decided to apply for a job as a UN volunteer, driving about to polling stations and overseeing the voting process. The electoral authority said they would hire me, as they were two UN staff short: they had been shot on the road by soldiers the previous week. I was so excited about the proposition of sticking my neck out to try and do some good in the world: I would gladly take the risk.

Walking back late from the Minefield bar with my head full of plans, I took the wrong street in the dark – Cambodia didn't have street lights. A group of Khmer soldiers roused themselves from hammocks in the garden of a French colonial building. They came scrambling out shouting challenges and I heard the AKs being cocked. If I hadn't been drunk I would probably have been pretty nervous, but as it was, I just calmly waved an ID card, said 'UNTAC' and walked back the way I had come. I couldn't sleep for quite a while when I got back to my room.

The next day I got into a Hercules transport plane. I was being sent to Phnom Penh to register for the UNV role. I got to the head office with my letter of recommendation from the Siem Reap electoral department and a feeling of destiny.

I was knocked for six when told I needed to fill in an

application form, which would need to go by post to Geneva. I would apparently not expect a reply until July, which would be two months after the elections!

I was going to go straight back to Siem Reap, but the KR had launched an offensive right into the town. All commercial flights were off, due to a plane coming under fire whilst in the air, as well as the damage sustained to the airport itself during the attack. I would have risked travel overland or up river if there was a job for me when I got there, but I wasn't going to do it just for the thrill.

I hooked back up with Jurgan and we travelled on the roof of a train for fifteen hours, all the way through southern Cambodia to the port town of Kompong Som. The ticket cost pence, but would have been free if we had chosen to ride on the flat car the trains pushed in front of them to detonate any mines laid.

About eight hours into the trip, going through a lightly forested area at the foot of some hills, there were three gun shots and the train came to a stop. It was a worrying few minutes when no one knew what was happening, but it turned out just to be the regular army stopping the train so they could have logs loaded on. If it had been the other team things wouldn't have been good.

Some days later, a train in the north was ambushed and people died. I spoke with a couple of backpackers who had been on it. They told me they had ditched their gear, jumped and run across the rice fields with the locals. It could easily have been a similar story with my train: anything could happen at any time. During the following year, the southern train was ambushed and three backpackers were captured and taken to

Phnom Voar in Kampot province. They didn't come back.

For people visiting Cambodia now-a-days, or even fifteen years ago, there is no comparison and only travellers who were there in the '90s can have any understanding of the day to day experiences I had in that place.

We got to Kompong Som at dusk and jumped on the back of moto-dops (dirt poor taxi riders on C90s). They set off immediately, ducking under a swing down barrier designed to stop trucks. My rucksack snagged on the beam which took me clean off the back of the bike, to the amusement of the crowd. No harm done, I was back on the seat and my moto-dop sped off after Jurgan's into the weird gloom of a sea-side town with no lights.

The majority of homes were lit only with home-made paraffin lamps (which were just a wick in a can). The only other illumination anywhere was the tube lighting above fruit stalls on the pavements and the soft florescent red outside the brothels. Most people just stayed home after dark.

Things got more laid back at the beach for a few days; I liked it though, because it was a tropical haven with white sand, clean blue water and palm trees for shade. There were only a handful of fishing huts and a couple of low impact restaurants serving quite nice food. There were UN Land Cruisers around as always and a few vendors, three or four back packers that I'd already met in Phnom Penh or Siem Reap and that was about it. I went back there ten or twelve years later and it was horrible: completely built up, filthy, crowded and it wasn't even cheap anymore.

I got the train roof half way back to Phnom Penh, stopping off at Kampot town. A 'motodop' ride took me fifteen miles east towards the Vietnamese border to a place called Kep. This was the old French resort town, reduced to rubble and ruins by the KR in 1975. It was interesting: a ghost town with squatter families living in some of the bombed out villas that were being reclaimed by nature. The beach wasn't special – shallow brown muddy water with views out to several islands belonging to either Cambodia or Vietnam.

Looming over Kampot town and the primitive landscape for many miles to the West is the ominous Bokor Mountain. Shaped like the back and shoulders of a buffalo, its wide south facing slope is immensely steep, with tree cover right the way up to the brooding cloud blanket that sits over the broad bare plateau. When I was there that April, the cloud curling over the top was a grey blue colour and it looked like it would be raining up there. It seemed to spill down over the edge, melting away into the thick jungle and the heat below.

Bokor was a no go area. There was only one vehicle trail up to the top which, due to its condition, took an hour and a half and the KR had been occupying the place for years. I went up there on a dirt bike years later after the war was finished, very strange place. It had been developed by the French as a hill station in colonial times.

On top was a ghostly collection of ruined buildings including King Sihanouk's private retreat, the shell of a Catholic church and a Casino building clearly modelled on Monte Carlo.

I actually crashed that bike on the way down the trail, going too fast on loose stones and injuring my foot. I limped for weeks after and was lucky to get away with that: all part of the fun. When the war finally ended – effectively in 1998 – Cambodia revealed some of the best adventure motorcycling routes in the world. There's no question, Cambodia got into me on that first trip. It changed me yet again, there was no place like it and it took a long time to shake out.

I didn't ride much when I got back home that summer, but concentrated on earning money for my grand plan. I decided I was going to become a pilot and then try to get a job as a missionary in New Guinea or some other jungle refuge the other side of the world. It seemed a natural progression to substitute the thrills of the motorcycle ride, as I knew it, for the adrenaline rush of flying a light aircraft through a mountain valley and putting it down in places no one would believe.

I'd had a one hour flying lesson back in January in a Cessna 152 training plane out of Headcorn aerodrome. It had been good. The air was clear and still and it was a perfect first flight experience. The two seater cockpit was the size of a bumper car and I had a quite attractive posh young female instructor (we actually ended up hating each other by the end of July), she taught me climbing turns, descending turns and night flying. I learned practiced forced landings, stall and recovery, as well as all the boring stuff. Landing the plane in the middle of a heavy rain shower was quite exciting.

By August, after sixteen hours tuition, I was flying solo and I started teaching myself some of the stuff I wanted to be able to do; low and slow in different wing configurations, lots of forced landing practice, with the wheels almost skimming the seed heads in the fields, before I'd throttle up and climb out of it.

I pushed it close on more than a couple of occasions; once coming into Rochester airport, way too high, instead of going around in the recognised circuit pattern, I just aimed for the ground and put it down halfway along the runway. Brakes were never going to stop me before I got to the fence where the industrial estate began, so I veered off into the long grass to the side and made a snake trail to lose some velocity. The blokes at Rochester control tower joked with me about smoking tyres when I went up there to sign out, but they still grassed me up to the Headcorn team, who were not impressed.

I had learned sixty-degree turns pulling 2G, with a new instructor who also taught me how to climb at an angle that meant the wings couldn't hold onto the air. Then close the throttle, twist the control yoke to full lock and the plane starts falling out of the sky in a flat tail spin. The only way to recover from this is to level the yoke and force the column right forwards, aiming the nose at the ground. Opposite rudder arrests the spin and full throttle in the dive will bring up the air speed you need to pull out of it, otherwise it won't respond. All this must be done before you lose too much height, as there is a minimum altitude that you can safely pull up from, but the air speed indicator must show that you have enough to do it. It's pretty nerve wracking watching that altimeter spinning backwards and the ground getting bigger.

A year later when I checked out with the more powerful Cessna 172, I took it over the downs above Stowting where there are three deep natural coombes, like bites out of the hillside all in a line. Two or three hundred yards from the base line of the hillside, the electricity pylons carry high power cables up from Dungeness power station and I wanted to find out if it would be possible to use the flattish clearing at the bottom of Coombe Wood to land a small plane in there, just in case I ever got a flying machine of my own.

The only approaches to this hidden field would be underneath the high power cables and straight in, which I didn't like the thought of, or flying parallel to them on the inside and turning sharp right into the proposed landing strip.

I planned out a clockwise rectangular approach course, flying along the top of the ridge then closing the throttle and sinking down into the deep field coombe, spilling air from the wings in the turn. This worked out fine and I was still losing altitude as I came out over the cornfield below. I throttled up again to make the corner turn, allowing the plane to slip a little lower so that I was below the height of the cables and midway between them and the base of the hillside. A bit more throttle to make the final quarter turn and I cleared the fence at the base end of the landing site at a speed I knew I could put it down at.

That far it had been text book and it all fitted into my calculated theory. The big gamble was to see if the plane could climb out of the steep wooded coombe that I was still flying into: it was like a finger of green, hemmed in by very steep wooded banks. The ground rose in front of me as fast as I could get the lift, the clearing wasn't very long and the huge bank of mature oak and ash trees towered above me to the crest of the hill. I had full throttle and full elevation on and I was gripping that control pretty tight.

I made it out with about twenty feet to spare beneath me and the exhilaration was immense. Wood pigeons were breaking out of the tops of the trees in panic and I have to look back and say that was one of the most ridiculously dangerous things I've ever done. Man did I feel alive though.

My black KH400 kicked the bucket during the 1994 Whitsun bank holiday. The Sellindge steam rally was on and I foolishly let old village boy Craig Gammon take the bike out for a test ride. An hour later he was pushing it back seized up, swearing he would help me strip it down the next day and put it right. He still hasn't turned up.

I sold the bike on with some other spares to the mate of a bloke called Jeff from Ramsgate. We called Jeff 'Universal Soldier' and I'd met him that summer when I got carried away with the voluntary humanitarian aid scene at the height of the Bosnian war.

I was spending all my spare time that summer preparing for trips out to the former Yugoslavia in various aid convoys. These were hastily grouped together collections of miscellaneous donated vans (I actually supplied my own), driven by a collection of do-gooders, religious nuts and would be mercenaries.

It was fun and we got a sense of doing good in the world – even Universal Soldier discovered some compassionate empathy when we got to the refugee camps. Regardless of how little difference we were really able to make, it was clear that a lot of communities we delivered stuff to did appreciate our efforts and, even if it was only for that day, we made it a happy one for them.

# CHAPTER NINETEEN

## *Fighting for new frontiers*

19<sup>95</sup> started with me on the Trans-Siberian Express, trying to make my way around the world by land and sea. The idea was to stop off for work when the opportunity arose for something interesting and rewarding to get involved in. I'd got myself to Hong Kong by train, bus and river boat by the second week in February.

I couldn't bear going back into mainland China after welcoming the relative civility of British Hong Kong as it still was. I didn't want to be re-infected with anyone's cold virus, as they all seemed to have one in the People's Republic, as well as having no perception of personal space.

Overland travel in China was just so punishing and I couldn't see a direct uncomplicated crossing into South-East Asia, so I opted out and bought a plane ticket to Bangkok. By the time I got off the bus in Chiang Mai (twelve hours north of Bangkok), the cold I'd had for over a month had dried up. The climate in the north of Thailand during winter months is the finest anywhere, pleasant in jeans and T-shirt. It's so far north of the equator; it's almost subtropical and guaranteed to be dry from November to April.

I settled in, for what turned out to be about three months living in one of a row of wooden stables that fronted a Muay Thai training yard. I had nurtured this dream since my first trip out there: to train solidly, full time in a Thai boxing camp and get to the point that I would be fit to stand up in the ring against a Thai fighter. I couldn't move on until I had fulfilled that ambition, win or lose. I would commit myself and stick to it, no matter how much I wanted it all to be over.

I met a whole lot of interesting characters out there, each with their own take on the philosophy of life. Once again the motorcycle was central and gave us the freedom, and mobility we needed to keep us sane. The Honda cub or the updated Dream 100 with electric start was not merely the bike of choice but generally the only affordable option. I came to love that unbreakable purring kitten. I acquired my, well worn, version from an old Air America pilot who had stayed over after the 'Secret War' in Laos.

David lived a reclusive life in a villa on the outskirts of the city, under the shadow of the Doi Suthep mountain. This was the same plot of land that Lanna Muay Thai boxing camp was based at. People said it belonged to some Princess of the Chiang Mai royal family, which David had bailed out to save her embarrassment at a gambling venue after a bad loss. This discreet loan apparently allowed her to save face on the night and, in return, she let him live rent free at the rundown property.

David was a cantankerous, stubborn old bastard, who would take no one's point of view but his own, he didn't care how unpopular he made himself and he seemed to do his best at that.

Because I was the only non-Thai living in his back yard, we ended up talking quite a bit of an evening, sitting out on his porch. He was old and ill and wanted some company after twenty years of bitterness and solitary living, since his Thai wife took off, with everything she could get out of him.

He was a notorious whisky drinker and an occasional visitor to the Moon Garden bar in town, where he was tolerated by staff and customers alike. This all changed as did he, he cut out the drink and let me have his bike on permanent loan so I could go out and get him milk, bread and painkillers.

One morning I came back from the routine early morning jog up the mountain and David's porch light had been on all night – it still was an hour later after breakfast and I hadn't heard anything from the villa – so I went over to check it out.

David was stretched out in the doorway, stone cold dead. We gave the old boy a traditional Buddhist funeral and I carried his wreath behind the coffin float in the front basket of his old Honda. His villa had been sealed off with long ribbons (part of a religious ceremony by the monks) that same day I found him, and the boxing camp was put on hold for a few days.

I had been training for a month by this time and didn't mind a bit of a break from the relentless schedule: six days a week, morning and afternoon.

There were four or five other 'Falang' (foreigners) training there under our Dutch-Indonesian mentor, Arjan. He was a very likable and humorous character, claiming to have come from the Amsterdam underworld. He had lived in Thailand for years and had a lot of cultural knowledge, fluent in the language and a professed Buddhist, as well as being an accomplished gigolo.

Arjan rode a red VF750, drank anything and smoked marijuana with Andy and his Thai wife Pom (founders and owners of the camp) every evening after training. They all later fell out over money soon enough, and Arjan disappeared eventually.

He was a great organiser though and had brought in a Thai associate called Kom to train us, a bona fide Lumpini champion, a veteran of the main Muay Thai stadium in Bangkok and a good friend to all the boxers. After that, the camp really started picking up, more decent trainers turned up and the place is still going strong today.

Anyway, Arjan said we had to do things properly for David and send his spirit on its way: it was some wake. The Thais stayed away and Arjan bought a bottle of some horrible Chinese rice whisky called Shaoxing (it's really for cooking), some incense sticks and cigarettes. We said some words and saluted David's spirit by the little wooden house shrine set up on a post like a bird table. Well, that bottle didn't last long, so Carl went out down the lane to get more.

Carl and Derry were a couple of rough looking maulers from Nottingham in vests and tattoos – they had recently arrived in Chiang Mai to train. Derry went on to fight, settled down with a local girl and stayed out there for years. Carl went home, got mixed up wrong and went to prison. They were great blokes to party with.

Before long, it was dark, Arjan had already sent me down the road on his 750 to bring back more Shaoxing and that was gone too. We were steaming drunk. For some reason, Derry thought it would be funny to throw an elbow technique at my face, but failed to pull it and it smashed me right in the mouth, splitting my bottom lip wide open.

Blood ran down my chin and splattered onto the cement floor while I tried to comprehend what had happened. Derry was as surprised as I was, and insisted I hit him back, he grabbed my arm and smacked himself in the mouth with it several times. Then we proceeded to punch planks out of the bike shed wall and break furniture with our bare hands and feet. Carl was just finishing off a teak bar stool, when a group of bemused looking Thais turned up in a big car. Arjan said 'Shit it's the Princess,' I don't know if it was her and her assistants, or not, but they weren't working class, that's for sure.

Arjan handled the dialogue and excused our drunkenness, telling them that it was customary for Europeans to drink to excess at wakes, but that we were all done and would be leaving straight away. I don't know what they thought looking at us, but we wound up, jumped on our bikes, fell off them, got up again and headed into the city.

I don't remember much about that ride except an impact to my shoulder when I hit someone crossing the road by a vegetable market. A bag full of produce took to the air but I didn't look back in case I hit someone else: stopping didn't seem to be an option and probably wouldn't have been wise either.

When I got to Moon Garden, I didn't see the others, I just ordered a drink and collapsed into a deck chair.

Apparently Arjan had found me out the back in a haze of mosquitoes, and somehow put me on his bike and delivered me to some tart's flat. I think I was too drunk even to throw up that night and when the woman got in after the bar closed, she found me on the tiled floor, where I stayed until mid-morning, when I staggered out to reclaim my bike. It turned out that we all did make it to the Moon Garden that night, but each of us thought we were the only ones who had.

I didn't drink for another month after that, just trained, ate and slept until the big fight night.

Del decided to dump his life in Sellindge and came out to

Chiang Mai to be in my corner for the fight, which was scheduled for the beginning of Thai New Year and the Songkran festival. The idea was that we would then continue around the world, travelling and working, as was my original plan. I did appreciate that he came out for me, but to be honest, he wasn't sacrificing much by leaving the village.

Other people around at the time who were associated with the boxing camp were Scott from Australia and his Thai aromatherapist partner Aree. I liked them both, so it was a shame when she kicked him out later that year and took his 750, so I was told.

There was Paul Korones from New Zealand; he made part of his living exporting silver jewellery and teaching Wing Chun. He'd done well for himself and seemed to have it all worked out. Then there was Russell, another Kiwi, great character to have at a party, but a bit rough around the edges and not everyone's cup of tea. I don't know what he really did for a living, but he had been kicking around for a while and he could tell a fair tale or two.

Max, the long haired, British owner of the Moon Garden, was a strange one. A dope head and very laid back, until something spiked him.

Nuit was a pleasant dumpy young kitchen girl living at Moon Garden, she was like a little sister to the streetwise bar staff there. Nuit was sweet on me, but played a confusing game of it. I liked her but didn't have time for all that. It was nice that she was part of it all and I was sorry when Moon Garden closed.

Marcel was another Dutchman, who owned a small wooden partition guest house called the Flamingo, where we always met before and after the fights in town.

Marcel's wife persuaded him to take on her young country cousin Kem as general help around the place. Kem was an ethnic Karen hill farm boy from the northwest. He was pretty much deaf and, as a consequence, part dumb too, only sixteen and tubby, with feet as tough as a crocodile's. He had no grace then, but that boy could kick like a mule.

Marcel farmed him out to Arjan and so Kem came to live at the camp too. He was ideal as a sparring-partner for me, but after his first decisive fight he quickly became a lethal weapon, famed and feared throughout northern Thailand. Within two years there wasn't a promoter in the north who could match him up with a suitable opponent and he had to take his fights in the main stadiums in Bangkok, as well as across the border in Burma, where they still did it the old way with just cotton wraps on their fists.

Eventually Kem went to Japan as a celebrity fighter and earned his fortune. In 2012 he came back to Thailand after some years and bought a modern 1100cc sports-bike – and broke his back in a high speed crash. I visited him in the hospital, where he had been for three weeks after the accident. He was black and blue, but joking that although he couldn't feel his legs, when a nurse gave him a bed bath there was still some life left in him. Kem rides a custom manufactured trike now: functional, not flashy. He married and moved back to the little mountain town of Pai, where natural hot spring water runs piped through his home.

There were other people around the camp too, and more who we would meet regularly at our favourite Friday night spots, but these were the everyday companions we had.

The worst thing about going into any fight is the feeling of hollowness you get a few hours before the time. It didn't matter that I had trained for months and was fit and ready for the job, on that day it was the last thing I wanted to do. My stomach was empty, and my limbs had no fibre in them.

Arjan and Aree mixed up their special concoction of raw egg, vitamin C tablets and Kratingdaeng (the original Red Bull concentrate). They told me there was also a secret ingredient that would make me fearless. I'm sure it was a placebo, but I felt better all the same. After everyone else finished up eating (I had been told not to eat after midday), we walked from the Flamingo to the venue.

It was a pretty seedy place and the poster at the gate just said: *Songkran special. A European man will fight with a Thai boxer plus Sadist show.* I felt good though, walking between the collections of small bars with my team behind me. There was music and drinking going on and Thai men looked at me with narrowed eyes, I hardly noticed the girls.

I was the last on the bill, after the Thai fights and the Sadist show. It was gone midnight before I got on and I hadn't eaten since 11 am.

Arjan led me out, in a brand new, red robe, with Lanna Muay Thai embroidered on the back. I had the traditional mongkon (braided head band blessed by monks) and we paused at the steps before I climbed to the edge of the ring. When I got there, I just vaulted over the ropes and I was in. I didn't much notice my opponent, but walked the boundary of the ring to the wailing sound of the horn and drum music, stopping at each corner to bow and privately pray for the strength to give a good show, the winning or losing was irrelevant. My opponent was younger and heavier than me, but certainly not as fit. I'd never been in the ring before and was nervous, thinking 'What the hell am I doing here.'

The bell rang and I tried my first technique, straight kick to the abdomen, which worked. The left jab also connected and then he was on me. His style was to move forward like a tank, throw a kick then grab me, using his knees to strike for the ribs and diaphragm. My knees were ineffective against him, but I could grapple.

I soon realised however that I wasn't scoring that way, just sapping my energy. Breaking free, I tried to keep him at bay with straight kicks and punches. I couldn't stop him coming for me, each time I threw a punch he just dipped his head and took it on the skull, he didn't care. We clinched again and I took some knees, but broke out to the side and got a knee and a right hander in. The crowd screamed out at every blow we took and the bell rang for the first break.

My team had me on a stool, pulling my hair and rubbing ice water all over me. Then, I was standing and my arms and legs were being stretched out. Arjan and Kom were shouting at me in Thai and English and I knew I was doing alright. But looking across the ring at the other bloke, I saw he was just standing, casually waiting for the next bell and staring into my corner.

Round two started similarly, but I picked my shots, trying to conserve energy. I knew my style was better than his, but he was relentless. Kicking uses a lot more energy than punching, so my kicks were losing power by the middle of the round and I couldn't seem to hurt him. I landed my best straight right hand, full in his face as he came in: it checked him, but he just shook his head and smiled back at me, to say 'No you'll have to do better than that.'

It's funny, but once you're in the middle of a fight, you don't register each blow as pain, just the degree of force absorbed. The shin on shin impact when a kick is blocked is just a crack of bones at that moment, but once the adrenaline has left you, the pain that was really there all the time can make you hardly able to walk. The bell rang, once again, and I hardly remember the interval. I was exhausted; Arjan said the Thai was tired too and I hoped I could believe it.

The third and final round started fast. I unloaded my best combination, which put him on the ropes, his head rocked back, and the crowd were screaming. I thought I had him, but his arms came back around my neck and the clinch started again. I could see the crowd over his shoulder, but the sound didn't register, I know my corner were yelling at me to use my knees and I tried one, but it slipped off him and the chance was gone.

When we broke off after another clinch, I tried a full-on low kick, but it didn't topple him: he had legs like teak logs and he just kept coming. I got caught on the ropes myself by two or three punches, and I swung at him and missed, causing a clash of heads that I did feel. The rest of the round was pretty ragged and we both slogged it out to the end with no let up.

When that bell rang, we just hugged each other out of the relief that it was over. I almost forgot about the result, but the ref took both our arms and held them up as a draw. Neither of us cared right then and I'd never been so happy.

I heard the music and the cheering and before I could get the gloves off, Arjan had passed me a bottle of Singa beer. I looked around me and there were all my friends. *No woman no cry* was blaring out from the nearest bar and I wasn't tired anymore. It was total euphoria.

I went to the washroom area and tipped a tub of water over my head, then joined the party. Kom gave me my pay from the promoter, 600 baht, which equated to about £18. I gave him half of it straight back. The rest would be gone before the night was out.

Del and I ended up drinking at a nearby bar with the bloke I'd just fought, whose name was Arth. He told me he'd had fifty fights, then I felt pretty good about it all. We drank and danced till three am, then Del and I made it back to the Flamingo for a beer with Arjan and Marcel. Del had been drinking all evening and swung his leg over the back of my bike, falling straight off into the road.

We eventually made it back to the training camp before first light. The following day, when I did get up, I just walked around slowly and sat in the shade. I could eat and drink what I wanted and didn't have to run up that mountain anymore.

It was time to move on, but I kind of liked it out there. The place had become home and the crowd were like family. I loved the freedom of doing what I wanted when I wanted – riding back from a hot night out with the breeze cool all around me, no crash helmets, no boots – it was hot and steamy, and the monsoon was ready to break… This happened in two ways; it actually did start raining, but also that sly old serpent sat on my shoulder and whispered to me her lies.

Her name was Yui: a beautiful hostess at a pool bar, with model looks and a body like a serpent. She had long wavy brown hair and eyes like melting muscovado sugar. The gold jewellery she wore, as if she were royalty, marked her out as a powerful independent woman, in her own setting.

My ticket was that she had seen me fight the Thai that other night, was clearly impressed and that was good enough for me. I felt like a gladiator and she felt perfect, close behind me on the back of my bike, as we cruised through the night.

We sat cross-legged, face to face, while she fed me segments of mangosteen, an exquisite and exotic tropical fruit: firm and dark on the outside, soft and heavenly sweet within and we ate slept and made love until well into the afternoon of the next day. I knew I had to leave and thought I saw a vulnerability in her face as I rode away, that I hadn't expected. I deliberately didn't make contact for several days; I knew that an involvement would scupper plans for the next leg of the journey.

Del and I were to do a tour of Indochina, before heading down the Malay peninsula, and into Australasia, but I had to see Yui again before we left. I thought that would be it, but she turned up like a vision, alighting from the back of a blue tuk tuk like a queen bee, as we waited at an open air restaurant to catch our bus to Bangkok and I knew I was hooked. I knew Del and I would be returning to Chiang Mai before leaving Asia behind.

Our, month long jaunt took us around Cambodia, where I got ill, into Vietnam, where Derek got ill, then back into northeast Thailand by way of a punishing truck journey through Laos, crossing the Mekong back into civilisation at Mukdahan. This trip wasn't without incident, but the highlight was taking an old Russian two-stroke bike, a Minsk I think, on a dirt-road track so bad it was only fit for horses. We went from the coastal town of Hoi an, deep into central Vietnam, to find the ancient Cham city of My Son; a fantastic place, despite having been bombed to ruins during the Vietnam War.

These old battlefields were worth visiting at that time, it was only twenty years since the communist victory and, with those regimes opening up to the world, you could actually speak to the people who had been there. Indo-China had a very poor travel infrastructure and the sites were virtually deserted. Any maps available were all old military ones or pre-war colonial, and the only information signs were the classic red 'DANGER MINES.' At Khe sanh, the kids who followed us around as self-appointed guides couldn't actually tell us anything, but saw their role as making sure we didn't step off the paths that they knew had been cleared of UXOs (Unexploded ordnance). The mortar shells, bullets and bombs were just lying there on the ground at the edges of fields and by the sides of the trails. The DMZ (De-militarized Zone) still had a real frontier feel to it.

When we got back to Chiang Mai, I decided to sign up for a second boxing match and went to find Yui. I discovered she had left her job and moved out of her guest house. I found her dancing in a go-go bar called Spotlight and she told me she was going to Europe to work for a Polish nightclub boss. She indicated towards an unpleasant looking bear of a man, about fifty, thick set with Michael Caine glasses. The man was sitting in a corner, in conversation with another hefty bloke: the pimp who was setting up the deal.

The music changed and so did the dancers, Yui took her break and I thought I might as well order another beer and get on with my own life. I stared over at the two men in the corner and it looked like the bill was being settled. Then Yui walked straight past me and out of the door with the Pole. I did nothing, for best part of a minute, then threw the money down for the beer and walked outside. As I came out of the door, there she was, just about to get into a tuk tuk, and without any kind of plan, there I was too.

The conversation was short and when he took his glasses off, I hit him. I held him down in the gutter, pounding his head with my right fist, as the 'mama san' of the club shrieked like a banshee and clawed at me. Other girls had come out of the bar and I knew I didn't want to hang around. As I left the scene with my shirt torn and my mind all over the place, I realised that my hand was also broken.

Kom's attempt the next morning at massaging counter-pain balm into my broken hand, so that I could still fight the following week, was painful and unsuccessful, so I eventually went to a hospital just a bit too late and had to have it re-broken and set in a cast.

I found that having a cast on my hand was a great way to start a conversation, so, as I couldn't do much else, I was out every night till the bars closed. Then I would hitch a ride back to the camp, or not get back till morning as the case may be. I'd sleep till the afternoon, eat, sort my washing out and then start all over again.

I found myself a less complicated girlfriend, who wanted to take care of me whilst my hand was in plaster. Nithaya, she was really nice, a bit older than Yui, but cute with an open honest face. I could have settled down with Nit, but Del and I decided we needed to get back to Kent, ride out the summer, earning money on the farm and come back to fight again in October. That way we could gather enough dough to carry us through to New Zealand before having to work again.

# CHAPTER TWENTY

## *Total eclipse of the sun*

I had been aware of an impending total solar eclipse, passing right across South-East Asia on October 24th and, as the trajectory passed directly over the Angkor temple complex in Cambodia, I felt I just couldn't allow this prophetic occasion to pass without bearing witness.

Considering the warped sense of reality and logic trained into the minds of a large percentage of the Cambodian population, coupled with their reliance on fortune tellers and witch doctors, I was sure that this would be a momentous occasion: a portent. I had some pretty open spiritual beliefs myself and was deeply interested in astrology, but I also had to fit another Thai boxing match into a ten day window I had left myself, between returning from an aid convoy to Chernigov in the Ukraine and getting off the fast boat in Siem Reap the day before the eclipse. It was going to be tight.

We soon discovered that booking the cheapest flight to Asia had its drawbacks. It was fine into Moscow. Sheremetyevo airport was just as dingy and lacklustre as the last time I had passed that way. It was early days, for the new Russia and it looked like they didn't have enough electricity to run more than 20 percent of the light bulbs in the place. They were installed in bunched up black tubular silos suspended from the high ceilings, as if designed of a more sinister purpose.

Our Aeroflot plane was delayed without any explanation, or any updates for twenty hours. It was hell; the place was full of African migrants. Some of them said they had been in transit for up to a week and were living on meal tickets the authorities supplied. This caused huge scrums when they were handed out from a service window at limited set times through the day. They were all sleeping on the floors on bits of cardboard and kept in check by drunken Russian police officers.

Eventually, by way of a popular uprising, our passenger lot crowded the departure lounge, blocking the ticket desk so that no other flights could load. This seemed to work and brought the manager downstairs. He promised us another plane to get us out.

When we did get into the air we were only up there for twenty minutes before I realised we were changing course. My suspicions were confirmed when I saw all the fuel being jettisoned from my wing; the plane was preparing for an emergency landing.

Back on the ground at Sheremetyevo, the word going around was that the landing gear was jammed open and that had been the original cause for our delay. The assumption was that they had not actually fixed the problem, but just stuck us on there to get us out and hoped for the best.

We spent some more hours waiting around before they managed to get us onto a Lufthansa plane and we finally arrived in Bangkok. What with the airport delays and then a day in Krungthep and a night bus to Chiang Mai, we were cutting it fine.

By the time I got to start training, I only had a week to get myself re-familiarised and ready for the fight.

This Muay Thai fight, at the Bar Beer Centre again, turned out easier for me than the first. My opponent was more skilful, but I was stronger, and nerves didn't play such a part in my performance. I could breathe and think. I still only got a draw, but had proved to myself that the first fight had been no fluke.

Del and I got to Siem Reap from Phnom Penh by fast boat, up the Tonle Sap river. We cruised around the complex of Angkor, searching for what might be the most atmospheric site to view the eclipse from. We started at Ta prom temple, where the giant parasitic tree roots still engulfed parts of the tumbledown structure. It was surreal then in the cool dawn, very quiet, sheltered and seemingly quite private. Just a few bird calls heralded the comfort of early morning in the tropics; dappled sunlight emerging through the leaves, touching and warming the huge stone blocks the ruined complex was made from.

We followed the 'Grand Circuit' to Neak Poen and Preak Khan, which for me evoked a sense of journeying through a mysterious labyrinth to discover some great lost entity. There was no one else there, just us, making our way through the carved stone corridors set amidst thick secondary jungle. The only sounds were birds, and the light at the end of each covered passage was rich and soft. The increasingly eclipsing sun made the experience feel like we were going back in time to the dawn – only the light came from above the trees instead of the horizon, and the temperature became so pleasant everywhere.

We realised we needed open sky of course and so moved on through the giant north gate of Angkor Thom with its causeway bridge and looming, four faced, archway. The road led us to the centre of the ancient city and the Bayon temple. We were there fifteen or twenty minutes before totality, enough time to secure the bike and climb up amongst the hundreds of huge carved images of the same oddly smiling face. This was the place. Angkor Wat would be crowded, but the much smaller, and in my view, kinder stone monuments in the area were not. There were a handful of visitors and the temple's regular hawkers, but the gathering was surprisingly sparse.

The two minutes of celestial homage was awe-inspiring. Birds returned to the trees, everyone went silent and the stars came out. It was hauntingly serene amongst those smooth stone faces with their strange unemotional smiles.

As the first diamond of light emerged from the other side of the halo the noise began, gasps of amazement and excited chatter. I became aware of an unearthly trance-like humming sound emanating from high up on the other side of the temple and followed it. When I rounded a corner, I found it was a couple of backpackers with a didgeridoo and I was a little disappointed, but it was a good sound.

There was a group of Buddhist nuns in pale robes, not the usual orange the monks wear; they were chanting and attempting to stare into the light. It clearly hurt, as they were all blinking while their retinas were being welded to the back of their sockets. I had snatched several quick glances of the diamond ring myself, against good advice. As a consequence of this folly I had suffered mild 'arc-eye' for a couple of days after.

The leader of these nuns, an old woman with a shaven head and an iron faith, sat in front of her flock with eyes wide open. She was leading the chant and, I think, driving out the demon that had devoured the sun. We could see the eclipse reflected in her eyeballs and if she wasn't blind to begin with, she almost certainly was afterwards. The chanting went on for about fifteen minutes until the sun was a good quarter free.

Del and I left Siem Reap the day after, on a speed boat packed to the gunnels with passengers. The pilot was a maniac and hammered it between the submerged trees across the wide Tonle Sap lake, as the fibreglass hull started fracturing. The only thing keeping it from sinking was the speed the he kept up to keep it planing with the bows up out of the water. When we all got off and the hull could rise, I saw that the crack had gone from the passenger door right down to meet the stem below the water line.

Within days, we were working as English teachers at a low budget Phnom Penh school near the Chroy Changvar Bridge. This was an easy enough job, as you didn't need to speak Khmer, or spell, or be able to explain any rules of grammar. English didn't even need to be your first language to get a job in one of the hundreds of budding English schools opening up all over the capital. We got two hours work a day, which just paid for our food, lodgings and shared moto-dop rides to and from.

I met up with a very memorable character called Bert Hoak, who was running the only second-hand bookshop in Cambodia at the time. Bert was from Alaska: a big bloke with thick glasses and a Cuban revolutionary's beard. He was one of the few expats out there who had actually married a Khmer and started a family. We had met in ninety-three at the UN control compound when he was a UNV. Bert was an outspoken and enthusiastic critic of the Cambodian government, and also of the United Nations' contribution to the election process. I heard he had to flee the country in ninety-seven after the coup d'état, as he had put himself on Hun Sen's blacklist. He took his wife and daughter back to Alaska with him, where I understand he became involved in local radio.

Anyway, Bert suggested, as I had a pilot's licence, that I approach an American named Tony Negro. This soldier of fortune ran a company called Cambodia Aerospace and had connections with the Royalist side of the Cambodian military headed by the Prince Ranariddh. The other side of the coalition government were the supposed socialists, controlled by the pro Vietnamese ex Khmer Rouge commander Hun Sen. I don't believe either team had more than a handful of working aircraft of any type at their disposal in those days, so Cambodia Aerospace were providing a useful service.

I went up to the office twice and had long chats with Tony over coffee. I was hoping I could work for the company and get some real experience; they did all sorts of contract work in-country, but also stuff in Burma and the Philippines: anywhere hot, it seemed.

Tony showed me a load of photos of him with various employers, past and present, including the Sultan of Brunei, the Shah of Iran and the Prince himself, here in Phnom Penh. I so much wanted to fly small planes in and out of jungle airstrips, and the money was huge, but he wouldn't take me on as a pilot. What he said to me was 'A man is, like a bucket, you don't know how much he can really take until you fill him up.' He suggested that I might want to familiarise myself with some specific coffee shops in town frequented by Iranians, as they were full of dissident expats and good money could be made taking one or two out.

At that time, Phnom Penh was a haven for little cells of foreign criminals and outlawed political groups, Tamil Tigers,

PKK and some Central African groups who seemed to have no reason to be there. They all kept to themselves, but they were up to no good. Then there were Triads and the deported members of L.A. street gangs, made up of Cambodian child refugees from the eighties. These gangs had names like Big Brother and CBC (Cold blooded Cambodians): robbers, rapists and murderers they were.

Phnom Penh was a sick place. Tony told me I should go away and think about it and come back for another chat when I had made some consideration. I might well have found out what my personal capacity was, but I never went back.

The city was an open book to anyone and anything. Generally, people didn't go out after dark; there were no, streetlights, or real laws that anyone knew about. You didn't know who was carrying a gun or grenade, and no one gave a shit if you were never seen again. It was really easy to become desensitised and many foreigners let themselves silt down to a state where, accustomed to an upside down set of morals, they stopped questioning their own personal boundaries. Cambodia Aerospace disappeared after the coup in ninety-seven and I never heard of Tony Negro again.

Just before Christmas in ninety-five I left Cambodia for a short walkabout. Del had no travelling money, so had to stay on and try to earn his ticket money. I was only planning to be away for three weeks, but due to unplanned circumstances I ended up in New Zealand without any onward money.

I took a qualification for my NZ pilot's licence and got some experience of flying and navigating amongst mountain- ous terrain. I didn't get up in the air again after that for eighteen months. It wasn't until I got back to the UK that I could get my ticket marked up again. I flew a couple of times after that and then just stopped. I think my heart went out of it and it became a chore, instead of a hobby that was never going to turn into a job. Probably just as well, as I would have killed myself three or four times over if I had kept it up.

New Zealand was fantastic, and I have never forgotten those big empty roads, absolutely made for riding. There was quite a motorcycle culture out there too, but it seemed to be either ultra-violent Maori gangs in the North Island or white power thugs down south. It would have been great to have got hold of a big bike down there and done my own thing, but I had left Del back in Asia's lower intestine and owed it to him to get back as soon as I reasonably could.

I took on a couple of low paid manual jobs to put some money back into my belt, then hitched across Australia, island hopping my way to Singapore. From 'the city of lions' I took a flight to Phnom Penh, landing with just $100 left in my pocket to start over again.

I found Del skeletally thin and just about broke too. Cambodia cannibalised itself and anyone who touched it – it was Sodom and Gomorrah. I'd loved the place when I first went there, but then I was wearing rose tinted fake Ray bans. It's always different when you actually live somewhere, but when you have to exist in a degenerate place that hates you, it's bad.

It was May 1996, they had two Prime ministers: Hun Sen, 'second prime minister' and Ranariddh, 'first prime minister.' The elections had sorted nothing and those two were at each other's throats, both were building up their own private body-guard forces and the national army and police were split between whichever party managed to bribe each district commander.

Armed robbery was a daily occurrence anywhere and at any time. I survived one attempt myself, when a couple of soldiers on a bike sped past my moto-dop on the inside, just fifty metres from my guest house gates. It was early evening and I was on my way back from work, having stopped at the local outdoor market for French sticks.

Failing to get my case of school-books from me on the first grab, they stopped further up the deserted unlit dirt road and seemed to be deciding on their next action. Fortunately, I was able to slip right into my place before they made the turn. The next day I bought a meat cleaver just the right size to fit in my case, which I then kept on my lap, with my right hand on the grip the whole time I was travelling on moto-dops through the city, day or night.

I personally witnessed a motorbike snatch at gunpoint, in broad daylight on the busy main road just around the corner from my place. I was walking back from the same Psa Deum kor market one morning and it played out metres from me, outside the laundry shop we used. It wouldn't be the last time guns were aimed or fired over my head that year either.

Guns were everywhere on the street, as were brothels, squashed rats and the ever-increasing presence of paramilitary styled police units. They worked for whoever paid them the most. Phnom Penh had become a really ugly place, filthy, run down and disease ridden. There was never a night when there were not gunshots sounding out. Often, we would hang out on the flat roof-top of our block and watch tracer bullets arc across a black skyline from the AK-47s Russia had flooded Indochina with during the last three decades. Most of the military hardware playing out the last throws of this Vietnam War sideshow was the same basic stuff that had been killing people over there back in the sixties. It was like a living museum of pointless self-harm.

I saw some horrible things; death and depravity, but rarely despair. There were bright moments too, like when a smile straight from the heart would lighten the shadow on mine and keep me there another day.

Del, had become dependent on the locally grown weed, whilst I had been away. This was for sale in the Russian Market at Toul Tom Pong, $5 for a bag the size of your fist. Most nights, after a sorry evening meal, I'd hear Pink Floyd moaning through the walls from Del's cassette player, mercifully broken up by the regular blackouts, during which it was just dogs barking and the occasional sound of a moto-dop travelling slowly in top gear.

I had a couple of mind expanding nights in Del's room, soon after getting back into the country. I never smoked, so Del made me a pot of marijuana Milo. Nothing happened for ages on both occasions and then it hit me like a wave. The first time I did it, I got so paranoid I threatened the landlord with a bottle opener as he stood in our doorway. All Mr Heng had wanted was to warn Del that he had left his bike in the yard and he wanted him to bring it indoors, so it didn't get stolen.

The second and last time I touched the stuff was about a month later and resulted in me overdosing. I spent half the night just lying on the shower room tiles, unable to move, and believing I might actually die. I wasn't right, mind or body, till halfway through the next day and fortunately I didn't have to work.

I could fill a book with accounts of my experiences over

that nine-month period alone, which would enchant, disgust, depress and enlighten, but if you hadn't been there at that time, you would doubt my words. The long and the short of it was that we lived through some of the most unreal times that country has experienced.

I think I adjusted pretty well to being back in Kent when it was all over. I remember going out in the back field where my caravan was and just standing and listening to the peace. It was, so quiet, I could pick up the sound of the motorway three miles away – it was a comforting sound. I didn't go out much once back on home turf, just worked and saved. I found it secure and comfortable, but boring. I missed my teaching job; I had ended up doing seven hours a day at a pretty good school, which was plenty enough for my needs. It got me and Del home, with some money in the bank to boot.

The story wasn't over though, just before we left Cambodia, in late January ninety-seven, I had got myself engaged to the lady I'd been courting for the previous four months and I had promised to return in July or August. Sithekesravottey would have waited a year for me if I'd asked it of her. I did really need to get home and sort stuff out though, for when we would eventually make life good. By the end of May I was ready to try.

# CHAPTER TWENTY-ONE

## Hard goodbyes

My diary entry, dated May 15th 1997 reads:
*Time is creeping up so fast now I'd better get everything finalised.*

**May 16th**
*I spent the whole day sawing the second Ash trunk into two 6'3"*
*timbers for my caravan. Del helped me cart all the timber I had*
*felled in February down from the wood, so I could prepare it for*
*the construction of a super living wagon.*

It had been my plan for many years to build my own home, but I had just been thinking of my own simple needs up till then.

**May 17th**
*Laurent Kabila & his Tutsi rebels have marched into Kinshasa*
*& renamed Zaire 'The Democratic Republic of Congo.' Del & I*
*had a barbecue & wine up evening. I burned my pictures of Yui.*

A few days later Dave Bish phoned me out of the blue, to say he hadn't been drunk for four years and wanted to meet up at the Sellindge Steam Rally over the weekend. Del and I had a stall at the rally, where I was selling mainly mechanical junk and Del was just selling junk.

We'd bought a load of cheap cans of soft drink from Ashford market and doubled the price. On hot days we made a killing. I sold other stuff, like fake Zippo lighters with Vietnam War inscriptions on. Some of the ones I'd bought were gen, but the mark up on repros was far better.

Walking round the sideshows that evening, I met Klumsy Chris. He was down there with the wall of death ride and they weren't bad either. He told me he was taking time out from the Oakmen to do the wall for that summer and travelling with the fairs up and down the country.

Craig Gammon was there at the rally as usual, pissed up with an even drunker mate called Wayne (from Crewe) that he had picked up somewhere. I managed to stop Wayne from getting arrested, but then ended up dragging him through a hawthorn hedge. I can't stand drunks.

A few of the old Sellindge lads came back to the van we had parked up beside our pitch for a two am barbecue, where we all caught up with what was going on in our lives. The steam rally was always a gathering call for the old boys to come home and reconnect.

Dave told us how his marriage wasn't panning out too well and we all compared our individual situations. Matt Godden and Ant Old both seemed happy with their lot, they had both married girls, who were sisters, from the village.

Back in my caravan at the farm and only days away from my flight back to South-East Asia, I prepared to throw my dice. I was still keen on fortune telling and had had this set of dice from my late teens. I had often cast them, prior to an important venture, or decision I needed to take and I reckoned I was pretty good at interpreting the patterns as they fell. They didn't fall as I had hoped; three jacks and two aces indicated an exciting time with rewards too, but no indication of any romantic balance or security at all. I threw again and it was much the same story, only less rewarding. I didn't throw those dice again for another seven years.

My stag night was held at the Mucky Duck on the last day in May. A small contained affair. I had stopped in to see the Vicar on the way into the village and then parked up at Del's caravan round the back of Oldies at Gibbons Brook. We walked across the fields to the pub, where a bunch of Oakmen came to see me off. Martin, Klumsy, Knuckles, Chip and Fat Rob were there – to name a few of the faithful. Matt Godden and Oldie, Dave Bish too, and even Stuey turned up from somewhere. I don't remember where he said he'd been working overseas, but it was somewhere pretty exotic – he had done well for himself.

They all forced me to down a load of Jack Daniels, before mixing up a concoction that Martin called a 'Monkey's armpit.' It was a really good night and when the bikes roared off, job done, Del and I set off back to the Brook.

Instead of going under the motorway bridge, which was almost on top of the pub, then crossing the road, as would make obvious sense; we crossed straight away and headed up into the field. Trouble was, we were then on the wrong side of the motorway.

In a semi incapable state, we did get across that motorway without being mown down and made for the general direction we thought would take us to the Brook. It was quite a journey, involving tripping over mole hills, being bothered by a horse and Del having to search through a pile of his own vomit to get his false teeth back.

We got lost in the woods and had to crawl through banks of stinging nettles, before finally locating the gravel path to Oldies. Me throwing up on Del's carpet in the middle of the night was the cherry on the cake.

Preparing to leave England was becoming a routine. I packed my stuff away and locked up my barn, shaved off my beard and I was on my way. My plan was to spend a month training (with a bit of party life thrown in) at Lanna Muay Thai, culminating in a third entrance to the Thai Boxing ring. After that I wanted to re-visit Laos prior to checking into Phnom Penh. I would pick up my old job and get married in a traditional Khmer ceremony in the autumn. Then it would be a flight back home for a wedding blessing at Monks Horton church.

Things went fine in Chiang Mai, although there were some changes at the old place. Arjan and Andy had parted company over money and trust issues. Moon Garden was history and there was only one other foreigner living and training daily at the camp when I got there.

James West was an extroverted Australian who I had many a laugh with. We lived in the cement and laterite-built villa that had been David's, while the Thais occupied the old wooden terraced huts. We still had use of David's Honda, which got us in and out of the Bar Beer Centre at weekends and we had adopted a couple of the bars there as our hangouts.

There was Daniel, a young Skandi, who arrived a couple of weeks later to train for a fight (he moved into the villa) and Pierro from Italy, who came every year for training and still does. We had first met when I started at Joe's Gym behind Moon Garden in ninety-three. Of the old town crew, Russell and Paul were still around and doing okay it seemed. Marcel was running a different, less interesting guest house and Nuit had found herself a boyfriend and left town.

There were a few memorable moments, like James nearly getting me bitten whilst carrying me on the back of the bike through a neighbourhood full of angry stray dogs. He laughed his head off, while I screamed at him to go faster.

There was also a rainy day we took off training to get Thai massages. We paid up at the desk and were directed up the old wooden stairs. James landed a pretty young thing and I was stuck with a hippo who wasn't going to let me get away when I tried to change my mind. James laughed shamelessly while I had to put up with it. We didn't miss training again.

Fight night came and I was in great shape. I was hailed the winner after knocking my bloke down three times in the first round. Then we partied the night away and I blew all my winnings.

Two days later we were in Daret open air restaurant, as they had a big TV for live sports. We watched in disgust and disbelief as Tyson bit chunks out of Holyfield's ear. Russell gave me some worrying news that night about the situation in Cambodia: it seemed that full blown war was inevitable and imminent.

My last night out in CM was an anti-climax and I left Russell sitting at the only bar that was still open at five am. I was feeling excruciatingly sad at the prospect of giving up the freedom I loved for the next stage in my life. I had what I can only describe as a deeply prophetic dream when I finally got my head down that morning: it involved a crossbow misfiring and then me and a girl I didn't seem to know trying to connect a car to a trailer. I'd have rather dreamed of a white horse galloping across a hillside or anything remotely positive.

That evening, James and I caught the night train to Bangkok, took a risky tuk tuk ride into Kao San road (where James was to meet up with his girlfriend, flying in from Luxembourg) and that was that.

# CHAPTER TWENTY-TWO

## *Metal rain*

On Wednesday, 2nd July 1997, I was on a plane looking down on the quiet peaceful landscape of Western Cambodia. Forests and rivers, then small trails, leading to wider red dirt roads that were bordered by rice plains all dotted with sugar palm trees. More rice fields, Ox carts and the odd Honda moto. The scene got busier towards Phnom Penh, the only real city they had, but it was still quite unobtrusive until the filthy streets came into focus.

The first friendly face I saw as I stepped out from the arrival hall was 'Sony Boy'. I'd known Sony for years; he was one of the original moto-dop riders who plied their trade from the coca cola stall opposite the Capitol Hotel. He had been the baby of the bunch, but quite soon his quick and friendly business rapport, delivered like a stand-up comedian, had elevated him to the top rung in the taxi rank pecking order.

Sony is now a well known and much sought after guide and translator in Cambodia, working for various news agencies and documentary companies, National Geographic to name one. Sony took me to *Bert's Books & Guest House* at the riverside near Wat Phnom, where I checked in, and I had never seen Bert so disillusioned. It seemed like he'd given up. I caught up on what was going down and it was momentous.

The army was totally divided between Hun Sen's Cambodian

People's Party and FUNCINPEC (Front Uni National pour un Cambodge Independent Neutre Pacifique Et Cooperative), which was Ranariddh's lot. They both had their own independent military bases, full of sections of the RCAF (Royal Cambodian Armed Forces) as well as personal bodyguard units and were reasonably evenly matched, or so people thought.

There had been various short violent disputes, over the previous six months, between small groups of drunken soldiers loyal to the opposing sides, but the big one was coming down fast. The catalyst was the Khieu Samphan press conference due to be held that Friday, in two-days-time.

Since around November the previous year, various less hard-line KR factions had become absorbed into whichever government force controlled the area closest to it. In return the KR commanders were awarded officer commissions in the RCAF, gem mining and logging rights, money, whores and an amnesty from prosecution for the war criminals of the killing fields.

Democratic Kampuchea was imploding and there was no more Chinese support. Pol Pot was under house arrest and the bulk of the hard-liners, commanded by Ta Mok, were concentrated in the northern province of Anlong Veng and along the Thai border. The unassailable fortress temple of Preah Vihear, perched on top of the Dangrek escarpment, was surrounded by Thai-controlled, disputed territories and could not be taken from the Cambodian plains below – not with the simple ground weapons the RCAF had. FUNCINPEC commander Nhiek Bun Chhay was courting Kieu Samphan (the nominal political leader of the DK), and at this press conference the decisions that had been made for the future peace of Cambodia were to be announced to the world.

The revelation would almost certainly be that the hard-liners would renounce their position, so that the country and people could be reunited. This would appear as a positive leap into the light, but would also result in a massive loss of power for the CPP and Hun Sen.

Striking a deal with Kieu Samphan that legitimised DK territory, with a standing army intact, would be an opportunity for the Royalist forces to overturn Hun Sen. Then they might actually get more than they bargained for, as no one really knew how much fight the communists had left in them.

The second day back in the country, I went to my old school and asked for my job back, I got it, four hours a day, starting on the Friday. This was the four hours that 'Tall John' was giving up, because he had just landed a reporter's job for the Cambodia Daily. John had worked at that school all the time I was there the previous year. He was six foot something: a Belgian hippy type from Antwerp, born in Leopoldville, Congo. His family were in the diamond trade, he had told me, and he was on a self-imposed exile from Belgium, stating he had been caught trying to smuggle dope in from Amsterdam. He said he'd jumped bail and come to the Kingdom of Cambodia, where he was intent on spending the next decade indulging in his hobbies of drinking, smoking and growing his hair.

John had a place on the huge Russian Mi-8 transport helicopter that FUNCINPEC owned. It was leaving for Preah Vihear before dawn on that Friday.

A helicopter full of journalists did make it up there once, but that one had been dangerously overloaded and came down on its side into a mine field. Miraculously they'd all survived and had been rescued by KR soldiers.

I was jealous of John's scoop and considered trying to blag my way on to the chopper. However, the previous year had taken away a lot of my need for senseless danger and I couldn't get myself blown up before I got married. I took the teaching job instead, starting the very same day.

I went for lunch at the big central market, Psa Thom Thmei. Business was pretty suppressed, there were very few visitors and a lot of the stalls were locked up. Anyone who could afford to, had sent their families abroad, people were scared. Hun Sen was on the warpath and his angry rhetoric was being broadcast round the clock from the radio stations he controlled.

There happened to be a collection of playing cards discarded on the ground in front of the stall that my Cambodian family kept. I noted those which were showing face up and their positions to each other – Queen of hearts, Ace of spades, five of spades, seven of clubs, seven of hearts, five of clubs and eight of hearts. It was all values which were divided between love and war – as I interpreted.

There had already been a small skirmish on the Wednesday night, fifteen kilometres north of the city and I'd heard weapons fire and shouting coming from the Wat Phnom area too.

I had checked out of Bert's and moved in with the family near the Pailin Hotel off Monivong Street, right near the market. Friday night was ominously quiet, only a handful of students had turned up for the lessons that day and mostly they just wanted to talk about the situation. There was not a lot I could reassure them about. The conference had not taken place, as the helicopter had not been cleared for take-off. If it had gone, it's quite likely it would have been shot down before it got clear.

Saturday 5th July started with the market traders turning up, then shutting down mid-morning, none of the gold shops had opened.

We went back to the family flat, which was really a smallish brick and cement building with a corrugated asbestos roof. It was constructed on top of the existing block of flats, as an afterthought, and got really hot in the middle of the day. We had held the engagement ceremony there earlier in the year, and it had the advantage of direct access to the open flat roof where I could look out across the city.

At three pm it started. Boom, boom, boom: big guns, the sound coming from somewhere to the south and west of the city. Ma Houn went straight to the washroom and filled up a plastic barrel with water – she knew what to do – she'd been there before. Sure enough, the power cut out pretty soon and no more water got pumped through that day.

Very soon, all the extended family started arriving at our doorstep, on foot and carrying sacks full of food and some meagre possessions. They had come from the south-west section of town (Teuk L'aork), where the tanks were rolling, and described the mobile heavy machine gunfire they had fled the area from. The sky grew dark and the atmosphere heavy, a monsoon wave was blowing over the country and then it fell to earth, dulling the sounds of battle and chilling the air.

One memorable moment for me was looking down into the narrow alleyway between our block of flats and the opposing one and watching the open drain as it flooded with dirty water from the teeming rain. The sound of a moped grew louder and then there he was, Ravey, my fiancée's younger brother, all caped up in a plastic poncho. He had ridden all afternoon from some logging outpost, where he was working as a forestry officer. Rain was running down his face and he looked like a catfish. I'd never been so pleased to see him; also, I knew he had a 9mm automatic, so that was good.

The silence of dawn the next day was broken by the sound of a lone APC making its way towards our block down the long, ruined street opposite; it was coming from the direction of the river. The streets were empty and so were the roof tops, it seemed like I was on my own up there.

I went in to wash and was halfway through shaving when it started again, much closer to home. This was small arms fire and RPGs. One big shell explosion was so close, it rocked our whole building and the family quickly abandoned our house to take refuge in one of the flats below. I went too, when I'd finished my shave and not before. It was quite hot down there, with about sixteen people crammed onto the tile floor.

The family formed a plan to flee the city, down highway one to the Mekong town of Kien Svay, hoping to join up with other relatives and be away from the city – and if it really came down, that was the road to Vietnam and the shortest way out of the country. They wouldn't believe that where we were was the safest place we could be, for the time being anyway.

Their very real fear, which wasn't an impossibility, was that the KR would take this opportunity to enter the fray under their own name and force the country back into a communist regime. I didn't believe it likely and said that if the British evacuated their citizens, then Vottey could be allowed to accompany me, but we would need to remain at the address I had registered my passport to.

Ma agreed and they all packed supplies and left on foot for

the long trek to Kien Svay (thirty kilometres or so) and we were left strangely alone. Within fifteen minutes Ma had come back, saying she wouldn't leave her only surviving daughter, and then the rest of them came back, saying they wouldn't leave Ma. It was 1975 all over again for the family, or so they feared.

To get us both evacuated, we had to prove we were married, which wasn't quite the case, we needed certificates. Luckily the woman in possession of the marriage certificate stamp lived just down the block. We paid her a visit and $5 each, then walked out with backdated certificates of marriage. Now we just needed the British consulate to come through.

Only the post office, near Wat Phnom and the Hotel Cambodiana, south of the Royal palace, had international telephone connections and they were at opposite ends of the city. A few people had mobile phones, which cost $1000 a piece, but they all jammed in the state of emergency I'm told, anyway we didn't know anybody who owned one.

Fighting raged in three main areas on this day that I could make out: the airport road, Independence Boulevard (near Ranariddh's house), around the French Embassy and the Toul Kok area to the north. I watched from the roof top as a few Jeeps with rocket launchers in the back headed up Monivong Boulevard towards the railway station. Then bugger me! A couple of Honda 90s, ridden by westerners, two-up, going the same way. Tall John was on the back of one, camera in hand and chequered krama scarf flying from his neck, bastard! I was so jealous. He was living it, while I was stuck on a roof top with sacks of rice and dried fish.

By mid-afternoon, the first refugees started coming south down Monivong, poor families pushing wooden carts with their children and everything they had salvaged from their homes. A big column of black smoke was spreading out across the north west of the city from where it was all happening. It turned out that a large section of the FUNCINPEC forces, which had been built up at Nhiek Bun Chhay's fortified compound, called Tang Krasang, was on the move. They were met by Hun Sen's soldiers on the airport road and two tanks were on fire. It seemed like CPP had control of our area, the fighters I saw on the street all wore red cloth strips on their sleeves, or red bandanas.

By the second nightfall, the battle for Tang Krasang had been won and lost and Hun Sen was on every TV channel. Much was made a week or so later of the incredible journey of Nhiek Bun Chhay, who had resurfaced in Thailand. So, the legend went that he had escaped the city by the forces of magic. Once out in the countryside, he had discarded his bullet proof vest when given a magic garment from a wizard he had met. This magic jacket had the power to make him invisible and to deflect bullets.

Whatever *had* happened during that time, the photos of him in Bangkok did seem to show that he had lost some weight. At least he was there directing actions though, unlike Ranariddh, who it turned out had left the country by private plane the day before it all started.

The KR never came to town; they sat it out for months up on the Dangrek Mountains with the remnants of the royalist army. Ranariddh went to Paris and never returned to politics, bit by bit the Khmer Rouge melted away or got pardoned and the whole country opened up to tourism and big business. It took at least ten years before even Phnom Penh started to look like a regular Asian city and it will take twenty more still, for the country to follow.

I rode out on the Monday morning, through a nearly deserted capital city, cruised along the riverside way and saw nothing. I didn't really expect the schools to be open, but went there on time for my first lesson, to prove a point I suppose. It turned out that pretty much all the foreigners who could, had holed up at the Cambodiana and that was where all the news could be gathered.

The next few days were actually the most dangerous, as people started coming out for food and the looting began. Hun Sen's boys drove tanks through the industrial areas like Teuk L'aork and loaded up with stolen motorbikes and anything else they could strap onto them.

There were countless murders during the mopping up operations and robbers with handguns were out on bikes picking up the scraps. Every night there was a curfew and I was pleased that we were right on the top of our building.

Eventually the two of us did make it to Thailand – with no help from the British consulate, despite the fact that all the other embassies had evacuated their nationals. Thailand had sent a Hercules C130 to pick up Thais and thrown out an open invitation to stray westerners, but not Cambodians. I watched that plane do a half circle of the city before coming down at Pochentong airport, knowing that I could be on it if I wanted to. It was an odd feeling.

Anyway, about ten days later we were in the land of the free (that's what Thailand means), but we had to wait two or three weeks for the visa clearance, so that we could come to England as man and wife. We had spent most of our money by that time, as we had to buy one-way tickets at short notice.

We stayed for free at Lanna, and Andy bought my video camera for a reasonable price: they were rare and quite expensive to buy back then, as well as being huge and clumsy.

Right from the start, I knew I wasn't ready for married life. Things had all happened too fast and few of the decisions had been my own.

Going home to England in the middle of the summer wasn't bad though and I started working as an official observer on Channel Swim boats. This kept me away from home for twenty-four-hour stretches, leaving poor Vottey to her own devices in a strange land, while I was out at sea. One day I came back to the caravan and she showed me the burned curtain and other fire damage to our kitchen, caused by her trying to make an Asian stir fry with a pan of hot oil and a tin of tomatoes over a gas flame. I couldn't believe it, and have to say I wasn't as understanding as I could have been. There were a whole host of cultural hang-ups that made themselves apparent quite quickly and seemed unsurpassable, on my part as well as hers.

I was used to living alone, I liked people, but not all the time and I started to resent the erosion of who I thought I was. The beard came back and I dug out my old riding leathers that had sat in a wooden trunk in the barn for two and a half years. They were covered in mildew inside and out. I washed them by hand and hosed them through, then I just put them on wet, and took off down to the Dukes Head on my lime green KH400.

On Sunday 31st August, Del came over and the three of us went up to Lyminge Forest to see the 'Asterix Camp.' Throughout that summer, New Age travellers had been setting up camps and tree houses in the pine forest up on the old Stone

Street ridge that led to Canterbury. This was a popular protest against the clearing of a fair section of the trees from the centre to create a holiday park.

I disliked these kinds of people, but sympathised with parts of their philosophy, and as Westwood was a place that had been favoured by our lot a decade before, we wanted to have a look to see what they were up to.

Nothing I saw helped me to change my opinions on this breed of university dropouts. I couldn't see why they felt the need to deliberately grunge up, priding themselves on remaining unwashed and letting nature sort things out. Well, I love nature and I've noticed that animals with hair generally spend a lot of time cleaning it.

These people hadn't actually managed the woodland like true children of the earth should either. There was lots of plastic sheeting hanging around, discarded bottles and the odd burned out car battery just left by the path.

However, we were invited into their camp and sat and talked with some of them for a while. Entered reasonably casually into the conversation was the acknowledgement that Princess Diana had been killed in a car crash the previous night. I had heard this on the radio in the morning, but it hadn't registered enough emotion for me to give it further thought.

Some regret and disbelief, as well as indifference, was expressed amongst the circle; the event would take a week to build to a state of national mourning.

I was surprised to find even myself experiencing this phenomenon, as I sat with Vottey in near silence for four hours watching the funeral on TV. I wasn't a Diana supporter, but I defy any human being with a heart and soul not to have been moved on Saturday 6th September 1997. It wasn't for the loss of a person we didn't know, but a kind of mass psychic connection for the loss of a perceived spirit of goodness in the world, as well as some communal guilt that we all probably felt.

# CHAPTER TWENTY-THREE

## Back to the jungle

Being a married man gave me an unbelievably claustrophobic feeling that I can't blame on anyone.

The eight years of on and off travelling had meant I'd bypassed developing into an adult in the regular way that most young people had done. You're a different man when you come out of the other side of your twenties, no matter how the pattern is formed. I felt wiser than the people around me, but less able to live in a conventional way and so had fallen behind socially and materialistically. None of the new technological advances meant anything to me; I would not sign up to a personal email account or carry a mobile phone until well into the first decade of the twenty-first century. Also, I still used rolls of 35mm film until 2011, when my last usable camera finally gave up the ghost.

One thing I did get out of the northern temperate climate that I'd been missing out on was snow. Just before Christmas that year we had some and I was able to take my KT250 out into the field and lark about. Riding in virgin snow is not dissimilar to tackling the soft dry sand of the desert. There is a purity to it and it's a wonderful feeling to race out onto an empty white canvas reclaimed by nature. It doesn't hurt too much when you fall off either.

That KT was a good trials bike – with higher than usual

gearing for trials, and a motocross tyre on the rear, there was nowhere I couldn't go. The bike was so light, I could actually lift it up with both arms underneath and load it in and out of my Ford Transit van. Unfortunately, by the next summer, my finances had got so low that I took that bike to the Steam Rally and sold it on.

My stable of bikes got whittled down further when the following year I let the H2 go for a shameful pittance to generate some spending money, only days before I set off for what was supposed to be my last extended trip to South East Asia. I had lived for those feelings for so long, I just wasn't giving up without one last big one.

It wasn't purely selfishness that led to me abandoning my wife for three months in the middle of a UK winter, while I tried to live some of the good times I'd been used to, when I was free to make my own way. It had never been my intention to spend the whole of each and every year in the UK.

I had for the best part of the decade seen myself like I'd seen the swallow tattooed on my left forearm – as a migratory bird, not exactly a nomad, but a man with more than one base. My ideal was to live my life dependant on the seasons and that seemed right at the time.

Vottey had to put in two years of continuous residency to get her position updated to permanent resident and she absolutely refused to leave the country during that time. It was hard on her, but I'd never made any promises I couldn't keep and, although I thought I'd always strived to do the honourable thing, I wasn't going to be captive to anyone or anything.

My philosophy of life has altered somewhat over the years for various reasons, but the freedom to experience life is still one I'm willing to make sacrifices for.

That trip in November began with a shock. I had gone straight to Chiang Mai, with the intention of spending another month training, then fighting again, before winding my way through Laos and eventually picking up my old teaching job in Phnom Penh.

When I got to the boxing camp at the foot of Doi Suthep, there was another spirit house beside David's. Kom had passed away. Although ill for some time, he hadn't gone to hospital until only weeks before the end. Trusting in magic charms and traditional remedies, as was his way, he had been able to go on doing what he loved for so long – training fighters.

Kem and I prayed for Kom's spirit at the miniature wooden house on a pillar and I stayed on for a couple of weeks, but then decided to go without taking another fight. My heart was just not in it, now that my old friend would not be there to live it with me.

I travelled up to Chiang Kong in the Golden triangle region and took the long-tailed speed boat down the Mekong into Laos for an eight-hour trip to the old capital of the *Kingdom of a million elephants*.

The river passed through almost continuous jungle, with steep banks a lot of the way and limestone cliffs either side. Huge boulders and sand banks protruded from the brown water, which the boatman skimmed over at racing speed.

These boats have a high curved bow, flat bottom and a powerful car engine at the back. The propeller is mounted on the end of a long shaft which dips in and out of the top surface of the water at a very shallow angle. The prop shaft is attached directly to the engine, which pivots and swivels on its mounts to give thrust and steerage. These custom styled hot-rod boats have four or five rows of low wooden seats and the shock projected through the hull of the boat, as it bangs relentlessly against the hard surface of the water, is quite severe.

The handful of passengers on this trip were issued with very old and inadequate life jackets that didn't do up, and the helmets were made for people with small round heads – mine was open faced with no real padding and a Perspex visor with a third of it sheared off. In the event of a crash this smack hat, that didn't do up either, would most likely have sliced into my face or neck on impact with the water's surface. I wore it though to keep the sun and spray off me as best as possible.

Luang Prabang was a sleepy little town set on a bend in the river, a nice place to spend two or three days, before flying over the central highlands to the plain of jars in Xieng Khouang province.

This was a fascinating landscape of denuded hills, clearly showing lines of bomb craters from the B-52 drops during America's 'Secret War'. There was a ton of war junk littered around, as well as several thousand huge sandstone jars of unproven origin, spread over such a wide area you needed a jeep to tour it.

The old Russian plane that took me from Phonsavan to the new capital of Vientiane was five years more run down than the ones that were used in Cambodia when I first went there. The ground crew were having trouble with the engine on my wing and I could see that aviation fuel was dripping from its housing. It was spitting black smoke too, but the plane made it to Vientiane.

Just before boarding the plane at Phonsavan, who should I

meet outside the check in shed but Tall John, the hippie drug smuggler turned English teacher/war correspondent. Now he was a French tour guide in 'the land of a million irrelevances'.

John told me he had left Phnom Penh shortly after the coup and gone to work in Chiapas, Mexico, which was the most dangerous place he could have gone to at that time, and he told me that that was why he went there. I liked John, he was, totally irresponsible. We had a meal at a posh French restaurant, which got quite loud and I've never seen him again.

I relaxed for a day or two in the quietest capital city in Asia and took in the sights, before flying on to Phnom Penh and getting my old job back straight away. The place was a lot calmer than it had been; regular people were starting to come out a little in the evenings, those out after midnight would be armed though as often as not. The leather shops did a good trade in custom holsters and gun belts, as wearing a shiny six-shooter to a restaurant was so much cooler than just sticking one of those ugly battered K-54 automatics in a back pocket.

Cambodia has a boxing culture similar to Thailand and I met up with ex-champion boxer Long Salavorn, at the main stadium one Sunday afternoon. I'd seen Salavorn fight at least twice back in ninety-six and took up his offer of training at his club in the Met Police yard. He was easily likable and became my mentor. Well respected by the Khmers, he drew attention as he cruised into the police yard on a Honda Phantom with leather tassels at the grips.

Vorn had learned his trade in the eighties whilst a boy in one of the huge refugee camps on the Thai border. He told me the Thai soldiers used to let him out of the compound to take him to matches, but they kept most of the money he earned, leaving him with a tiny amount to take back to his family.

I couldn't compete with the free-style boxers, who fought weekly at the national stadium, but could hold my own on the western boxing circuit, so that's where I concentrated.

I trained for about a month with real determination. I knew I wouldn't get an easy fight, but there were few other distractions. I really wanted to prove to the stubbornly uncompromising, ethnocentric Khmers that the Barangs (Frenchmen), as they called all Europeans, could earn some respect up there.

The Christmas party, that a bunch of my students invited me to, put paid to the boxing plan. I had the use of a badly maintained poor man's version of the Honda 100. Sanyang (a Taiwanese company) made the copy bikes, but the moto dealers imported substandard reconditioned parts and put them together in filthy dingy yards like the one I was living above in Teuk L'aork. These apparently new bikes could be bought for half the price of a genuine Japanese Honda that had been on the streets for twenty years. The old ones were getting rarer though, so eventually they all got replaced.

Traffic had increased tenfold since the early years and most major roads had been resurfaced. This meant that vehicles went a lot faster, but although there was no longer a need to swerve all over the road to avoid fridge-sized potholes, it was still normal to cut into traffic to get to the opposite lane, or force traffic already on a roundabout to give way to vehicles coming onto it.

There were a bunch of nonsensical rules of the road which I can't believe were written down anywhere. No one knew if there was actually a highway code, but the traffic police survived by collecting bogus fines for things like having your lights on during daylight hours; It wasn't an offence to have no lights at all after dark.

Police waited at junction points, where they would be able to pull as many people over as possible and collect a few hundred Riel, or $1-$2 from each rider. I avoided these checkpoints whenever I saw them (foreigners got fined $5 a stop). I would often U-turn into oncoming traffic and take another route if I sensed they were homing in on me. Once a cop jumped out in front of me, intent on getting some beer money. I swerved and ducked as he swung his light baton at me, missing by inches. I can confidently say that after a month of this death circus, I had developed some excellent defensive riding skills and I was enjoying it.

This Christmas party began early in the morning, miles out in a suburb off the airport road. There was an inexhaustible supply of food and beer and the students, really nice kids they were, all wanted to ensure that I was fully satisfied for the several hours that I was there. Christmas wasn't a national holiday in Cambodia: only rich families and students knew anything about it, but it fell on a non-working day for me all the same.

Halfway through the afternoon, and drunker than I realised, I left the party on the Sanyang, bound for the college to pick up my salary. The road was long and straight and the sun warm. I was just right into it as I sped straight through each inter-section I came to, judging my speed and distance in relation to the traffic crossing my path. I got it right two, three, four times, picking up more and more speed as I got further into the main part of town.

The maximum speed of my bike was around fifty-five miles an hour and I was doing that in jeans, denim jacket, sandals and sunglasses when I got it wrong by a hand's breadth – but that was enough.

I saw the bikes crossing my road from right to left at moderate speeds and started to judge their positions from seventy – fifty – thirty metres and then I was committed. There was this one bike, two up and moving faster than the others. If I'd had a couple more mph, I'd have made it clear: I thought I had.

That bike struck my rear tyre as I shot in front of it. The force was not great, and I held it through the first twitch, the momentum carrying me forward without any noticeable loss of speed. I think I could have ridden it out if I'd had a straight road ahead, but there was a wooden handcart full of fruit, sat beside the kerb fifty yards ahead. I didn't have the distance or steering to get around the cart, or stop, before I hit it.

My rear wheel must have caught up with my front as I barrel rolled it, keeping a hold of the bars all the way. I had this strangely painless sensation of the left grip entering my eye socket, then bang! I heard it more than felt it, as my lower back slammed into the hardwood cart and the bike was on top of me. A second later I got a terrific whack on the back of the head, as the cart toppled off its blocks and tipped forward. It must have been quite a spectacle, fruit all over the road and a Barang trapped between a crashed Sanyang and a fruit cart.

I saw that the other bike was down too – it was back at the intersection and I knew the unwritten law here, that immediate financial compensation was demanded from whoever was not the strongest, at any accident scene. If an agreement was not reached quickly it would turn nasty, but to wait for the police just guaranteed that the payment would be higher, as you had to pay them too. In any case, the foreigner is always in the wrong and ends up paying.

I actually *did* know that I was in the wrong, but I also knew I needed to be in a position to defend myself quickly. I kicked the bike off me and got to my feet, beckoning the two angry looking men over; I just wanted to get the proceedings settled quickly before any police arrived. The two blokes dusting themselves down must have thought I was up for a fight, as they picked up their bike and rode away, leaving me standing in the road bleeding.

People quickly started gathering and someone came out of a shop to give me a pad of cotton wool and a part used tin of Tiger Balm. I felt dazed pulling my bike upright, the steering and foot pegs were buckled, but it went into gear. The fruit cart man pointed angrily to his stock spilt over the road, but I knew he would stack it back up and sell it all the same.

I had to get myself to the college compound, past the aggressive parking ticket woman, and rode straight up the steps of the building to the main foyer; I just didn't have the energy to deal with her or find a parking spot in the yard amongst hundreds of similar looking bikes.

I picked up some pretty shocked expressions as I made my way to the cashier's office to claim my dollars for the previous two weeks work. That was what it was all about and I don't remember the ride back home. I just got myself up the long dark cave of stairways to the top floor and collapsed into my hammock.

Two or three hours later, Ma came back from the market and found me there in quite a bad state, I had been immobile since getting myself up there, like a cat that has crawled home to die. My eye itself was okay, but the cut was opened up across my brow and eyelid. My ribs were bruised, but the pain in the top of my right pelvic bone was so intense on any movement that I was sure I must have chipped it. My hands were scuffed, and I had a fair old bump on the back of my head.

Ma kept saying 'Hospital Jim, hospital,' there was no way I was going to a Cambodian hospital: all the local doctors had bought their certificates just like I bought my marriage cert. I got a mirror, my mini maglite and a bottle of purified water. I washed the cut, which had set itself open, and picked out the eyebrow hairs that were stuck in there, using a wooden toothpick. I had some antiseptic cream and Boots Steristrips brought from home, so I closed it up as best I could and held it there with the strips. I didn't do a bad job actually.

Two days later, despite not being able to sit in a chair, I could walk at a geriatric pace and went back to work for my scheduled lessons. My own students sent me home, saying they would stay in class for the full hour so that the management wouldn't know I'd left, and I could still get paid – what a great bunch they were.

I went to Saigon to sit out the New Year, as I knew there would be some celebrations there in Ho Ch Minh-ville.

I had to do a visa run anyway and I needed a break from the Stone Age. All year there had been disturbing stuff in the media about the end of the world, extreme weather phenomena, tornados in England, asteroid bursts over New Zealand and ice in Hong Kong. It all seemed to be coming together as Nostradamus had predicted. There were even hints of a third world war thing again, as Russia had threatened NATO over the Serbia Kosovo conflict.

The year 2000 was upon us and the new fear was that the

computers were going to kick-start Armageddon. Some of my students had asked my advice on how the Y2K syndrome would affect Cambodia's economy. My advice had been that, as Cambodia was the only country in Asia that didn't use its own currency or have any form of economic management, the computers could do what they liked and the man on the street would survive the way he's always had to. Probably not quite how they wanted to hear it, but I wasn't going to lie.

Well the lights didn't go out and the planes didn't fall from the sky. I rode on the bus to Saigon with my old moto-dop friend Chhonn, who just happened to be waiting at the Capitol stop when I got there. Chhonn was a gentle, intelligent Khmer who knew what was right and wrong. He was early twenties when I'd first met him five years before and used to spend his time between customers, reading books and educating himself. In the real world he would have been a university graduate and done something with it, but he had grown up in a rice field under the Khmer Rouge regime and then spent twenty years working every day to support his poor old mum.

A week later I was back in Phnom Penh and wondering where my life was going, at the age of thirty-three, I should have been at my peak and had a plan well underway. The boxing dream was shelved for this year as I couldn't take a hit to my left eye, but I wasn't ready to go home just then.

Since the end of the war, the previous no-go zones (which was most of the interesting stuff) became available to be redis-covered. As 90% of the roads were practically motocross tracks then, dirt biking took off as a sport option. Small groups of adventurous expats would take off into the 'boong' for week-ends, on Honda XR250s or Asian market versions of the Suzuki

DR. I did my foot in on a Susuki Djebel, coming down Phnom Bokor from the plateau of the ghosts, very eerie place. This is where the French had built a hill station and casino in the 1920s. It was a grand place before Year Zero and the 1970s holocaust swallowed it up.

I had decided to invite my parents to come out with Vottey and visit for a couple of weeks in February, as they had never been to South-East Asia. I gave them the real Cambodia experience, as much as it was safe to, so that they would know that it wasn't just a long holiday for me, but a living ordeal to some degree from day to day. I don't think they could quite believe how people lived and behaved, no one who hadn't been there then would believe it all now.

The only concession I made for them was a trip to the Angkor temples, which neither Vottey, or her ma, had ever visited before. The temples were still, by no means, crowded and the collapse of the KR meant that it was safe to visit some of the famous sites outside the regular circuit. Phnom Kulen was controlled by the same KR soldiers who had been stationed there during the last stages of the war and it showed on their faces, despite the new uniforms.

The area was still heavily mined, so it could not be freely explored. This site would feature in the Angelina Jolie film *Tomb Raider*, with its primeval waterfall scenery channelled over Buddhist imagery carved into the rocks of the river-bed itself.

# BOOK THREE
## Revelation

And they had breast plates, as it
Were breast plates of iron; and the
Sound of their wings *was* as the sound
of chariots of many horses running
to battle.

Chapter IX verse 9

# CHAPTER TWENTY-FOUR

## *New world order*

Once back in England again, I tried various ways to make a living that didn't involve trading in my freedom. Although I was able to live and work and travel, there was never any money left in the kitty.

I had all sorts of schemes I was trying out, but nothing really got moving fast enough to generate any kind of a secure future. The choices I put to myself were to knuckle down and live a conventional life, buy a house and raise a family or give it all up and start anew in some failed African state.

I got the push I needed, stepping into my local shop, me and my wife, late one November evening. We found ourselves in the middle of a robbery.

I didn't make a move: I wasn't armed, unlike the three thugs in balaclavas who had already got what they wanted and were preparing to leave. It hurt though, not at the time, but for a long while after. I hadn't witnessed anyone being abused, and the money belonged to a big corporation, not any individual. So, what was the problem – I'd kept my wife safe and not taken any risks, which was right... eh? Still felt wrong though.

I now know quite a lot about the law and have no doubt that if I had been in a position to use a suitable weapon and move on the robbers, then I would have ended up in prison myself. It makes a mockery of the whole system and it's where our country is going wrong as opposed to the US or Israel, Russia even. People know what is right, but we don't do it.

Two months after the incident, Kent County Constabulary had my application and I was inducted in May 2001. The very same month I got a mortgage for a brand new home being built on the site of Ken Cork's old mower shop in Sellindge; that had been right next door to Kestrels, the old shared house from the eighties and no longer a party den. My life was changed just like that.

I tended the lawn, grew roses round the door and proudly washed the new car on the private block pavement yard at the front. I bought furniture and things that normal people had, and I worked hard at being a good cop. I hated every single day of it.

Six years later I prepared my resignation letter, stating that they had been: *six of the most depressingly negative years of my life.*

OK, there were a few short glimpses of excitement and some laughs, but most of it was just soul-destroying crap. I quote one of my supervisors' comments on my 2006 annual appraisal, which was certainly intended as a negative. It went:

'PC Taylor has his own moral and ethical code and acts on his own feelings and opinions. He either does not consider the force policies and procedures or rejects them.' In my opinion, those are the finest words ever officially laid down against my name, and if that's what my misguided career adventure amounted to, then I'm alright with my side of the bargain.

What the job did give me was the ability to buy a string of brand new motorcycles, each one I was able to change in for the next, about every eighteen months. Firstly, I part exchanged my old green KH400 for a Kawasaki W650, in charcoal and silver.

I chose this machine over the similarly retro New Triumph Bonneville, primarily because the Jap bike had a kick start and the Brit didn't.

I did get fed up with people telling me how nice my new Triumph looked though; I got bored explaining that the Kawasaki derived, more accurately, from its own 1960s ancestor than the new Bonneville did from its Meriden family tree. The bike was nice but unremarkable and I changed it in for a good second-hand Triumph Trophy 900. This had a big blue fairing and panniers covering up most of its unstylish and functional metal parts.

I liked the Trophy and it felt right for my new lifestyle. The three-cylinder engine had a nice feel, but I felt the bike was a bit top-heavy. There was also a recurring electrical fault relating to the side stand sensor and neutral light. The bulb would blow and then the bike didn't know it was in neutral, so the engine would cut out whenever the stand went down. The shop took it back in a couple of times and I think all they did was change the bulb. The third time I took it back I made a big fuss and came out with a brand new Triumph Thunderbird Sport, black and yellow, another 900cc triple.

This was a fast bike, easily running to 120mph plus before having to work for it. I never took it to its limit though, partly I think, due to its height and riding position not quite suiting me. It looked great though, a retro sports bike with a good badge, twin front discs on really good-looking, spoked wheels. The bike had good steel mudguards and side panels, as well as swept up twin exhausts and I liked the black engine, it contrasted with just enough chrome to make the whole thing look special.

The trouble was, I didn't get to ride it much outside of commuting to and from work. The shifts meant that weekends and evenings, when things I wanted to do were going on, were few and far between for me. I didn't much like talking about being a copper when I was out anyway and people you don't see often always ask you what you are up to.

Of the old gang I used to hang with, Del was the only one I still had contact with. I hadn't seen the Oakmen since Klumsy's wedding reception, September 1999. This had been a good do, at the George pub and beer garden in Shalmsford Street, off the A28 between Chilham and Canterbury. It seemed like everyone was there. I had turned up fashionably late and immediately 'doughnutted' my KH on the back lawn. I noticed that a lot of the blokes had become family men with a string of semi-feral, young brats, mostly boys, roaming around with haircuts that looked like their dads had done them with gardening tools in the shed.

We drank well into the small hours, until the main bench table out back just had me, Chip, Martin, Knuckles and White Trash Andy left on it. That was the last I was to see of that lot for many years, in fact they all split up and went their own ways in the first half of that new millennium decade.

On the last snowy day in the beginning of March 2005, I stood at my Father's grave after the funeral ceremony. So many people had come, and the packed church service had done him proud. As most of them were drifting away, I noticed a familiar figure approaching from a respectful distance. It was my old friend Dave Bishopp: I hadn't known he was there, but he had thought to come, and there was no one I was more pleased to see. We talked for some time before walking from the churchyard together.

In midsummer that year, Del and I met up with Dave and old Tony Heaps at a Meat Loaf concert at Leeds Castle. Twenty years previously Dave, Tony and I had gone to see them at Wembley and this reunion served as a bit of a reawakening for us.

It rained on and off all through the show and we took up a place at the top of the bank, 150 yards away from the performance. It didn't matter that we couldn't see who was on the stage; we were having such a good time like the years didn't matter. We saw a couple of other people we knew, including Becky, an old flame of Stuey's. We sang along to all the songs we knew by heart, staying up on the bank until the first chords of *Bat out of Hell* called us down into the crush.

When Dave first suggested we go to the event, I knew I would need to prepare myself. I had been laid up for three months at home with a broken foot after a car crash I was involved in at work. So, spending long evenings in on my own, I'd decided to take up casual drinking, which hadn't been a part of my life since the Mad Mile Club broke up.

I discovered that one bottle of Stella was enough for me and realised that if I was going to be fit to get involved then I'd better start training, otherwise I was never going to last the afternoon out, let alone be 'Mad Jim' again.

I hadn't drunk heavily since joining the police and realised that I had my work cut out there, so over the couple of months prior to the event I prepared the ground. I started by having a bottle or two every evening as a rule, moving up to three or four as my tolerance built up. It all paid off on the day.

Dave and Del swore they would get bikes again and we

would reclaim the pubs. It wasn't long before we were planning a motorcycle trip to Scotland (Dave's idea): he had always wanted to go to John o'Groats, see Loch Ness and experience 'Scotch mist'.

Well, it took those two another eight months or so to get sorted out with their bikes, Del went for a new Triumph Speedmaster, a really good looking semi-custom cruiser with the Bonneville 865cc air cooled engine. It handled like shit, but I have to admit he looked good on it.

Dave looked to eBay ads and finally got himself a 1980s Kawasaki EN 454LTD, a midrange twin, or half a Z900 as Dave put it. It was black, with kind of banana handlebars and the sort of king and queen seat only available on those early 1980s factory custom jobs. Dave put his own touch to it with a Maltese cross rear light, plus hand painted silver flames on the tank and side panels.

It was a funny looking thing, too short for its own good and belt drive like a Harley. The small fat rear wheel brought it pretty low to the ground. I don't know how he got it round corners; I tried it out once and nearly threw a tank slap. He was proud of that bike and in a way, I suppose, he should have been. He'd missed out on so much since he left the gang and he hadn't got too far in life to show for it either. His bad leg had stiffened up more and he walked with a noticeable effort.

Meanwhile, I had decided on a radical upgrade for this highland road trip, as a prelude to conquering the world on two wheels.

When we met up to trawl the local pubs that first spring evening in 2006, I dominated this odd spectacle on a ridiculously high, bright orange KTM 640 Adventure, a Paris Dakar style desert enduro racer. I saw this daring and unconventional single-cylinder model, by a non-mainstream Austrian company, as the ultimate in all round capability. It came with a rugged indestructible frame that doubled as the engine oil cooler, electric and kick start, plus easy serviceable big carb. All fed by a huge 28 litre plastic tank that could take it 250 miles between fuel stops. The whole thing fronted up with a twin headlight you could see into space with, surrounded by a well sculpted quarter fairing with a fly screen that actually did the job it looked like it should.

I loved that bike from the start to the end, despite its several major flaws. These did technically outweigh its good points to be honest, and although it was often said that this bike could take you round the world and handle anything it came across, yes it probably could, but not without a backup team armed with all the specific tools and replacement parts.

I have compiled the following list of negative points regarding KTM's 640 Adventure:

I gave up trying to change a front tyre with hand levers: there was no way the aluminium rim would have come through the operation unscathed.

The sealed gel battery had to be at full power every time to turn the engine fast enough to fire it through its four high-compression strokes. This was a tough calling.

I don't remember being able to start the bike using its long kick start lever more than a couple of times throughout – I just didn't have the weight or leverage.

If the engine didn't get used in four or five days, it wouldn't start without draining the carb to draw in fresh petrol.

There was no way the bike could be bump started – the rear

wheel just locked in first and second gears, and none of my mates could run fast enough to push it in third, how was that going to work in the desert!

Changing the oil (which had to be done every 3000 miles) was a two-hour laboratory operation, involving various new filters and O rings. If not done right, an air lock in the frame could lead to disaster.

Bleeding the hydraulic clutch system required two people and a pump or siphoning set up. It needed doing about every 1500 miles.

The worst thing was the wiring system, made up of minutely thin electrical wires throughout. The super-vibrations pulsing through the frame wore the insulation through, wherever wires touched and rubbed (even against each other) and fractured the circuits in places you couldn't even guess.

The motor used and leaked oil at an advanced rate, meaning that after the first few thousand miles the chain had become self-lubricating. That was quite useful actually, but it meant I would always have to bring a couple of litres of a specific grade of very thin engine oil with me on any decent length trip.

The Metzeler tyres were good, but wore out so quickly that my trips were limited to about 3500 miles on new tyres alone, which calculated into two weeks of hard riding: just enough for a European circuit then back home for a major overhaul.

I did like the carrying ability – robust plastic suitcase panniers which were sealed against water and dust were decked out very wide and away from the heat of the exhaust silencer. I had to run on an illegal, small number plate, because the first standard plastic one had melted. Then, when I put an aluminium backing plate onto the next one, the heat transfer melted the rear mudguard.

The top of the panniers formed a ridged platform for loading my gear onto and, being quick release, I could unlock one or another from the frame to use as camping stools.

The main obvious problem, was that the bike was so high off the ground that the optional side stand wasn't safe unless the angle was just right. The frame didn't allow the side stand and centre stand to be fitted at the same time and the centre stand was essential for the servicing operation.

When I first got on the bike I could only just touch the ground with my tip toes: to safely hold it upright at traffic lights I had to twist half off the saddle to get a foot firmly on the road or make sure I stopped by a curb.

I quickly set about modifying my new bike. Firstly I loosened the bolts holding the front fork tubes in their yokes to allow the steering head to slide down a couple of inches. Then I unstapled the vinyl seat covering to expose the dense foam beam. I cut out a quite well shaped saddle and re-stapled the vinyl. I then bought some after-market mono-shock links to replace the originals as part of the rear suspension arrangement. This gave me an extra one and a half inches in overall drop without compromising the suspension capabilities – not forgetting that I then had to cut an inch off the bottom of the side stand.

Finally, I reduced the loading on the rear gas shock to better represent my weight. The result was a groundbreaking super endurance tour bike I could handle, that would haul all my gear for 230 miles on a motorway, then rough it in the hills before setting up camp.

I'd tested it out initially along parts of the Pilgrims Way in Kent and then the Ridgeway track from Goring Gap to the Marlborough Downs. It was over geared for those types of trails, not unexpectedly, as it had been developed for the open desert.

I came a cropper up there twice, both times with the bike upside down on the steep banks. Retrieving it and getting to the bottom safely used up all my energy: it was hard enough to pick up off a flat road, let alone a hundred-yards-deep bank too steep to walk up. Apart from the mirror brackets, which were ridiculously weak, the bike did in fact prove to be practically indestructible – just how it looked.

Once we all had our bikes up and running, we set about deciding which local watering hole was to be our place. The Drum Inn at Stanford North won out. The location was perfect, quiet and away from everything else, but just 200 yards from a fast road and a blast through the wide sweeping lanes.

The Drum, has also been the long term meeting place for the local vintage motorcycling fraternity on a Tuesday evening. We had several meetings there to plan our trip to bonny Scotland; such was the enthusiasm that Del's dad, Brian, went out and bought a big Kawasaki VN cruiser and joined the gang. Brian had been a rocker in the sixties, prior to doing his twenty years in the army, but this was the first bike he'd had since selling his 400 Superdream, to me, back in 1988.

# CHAPTER TWENTY-FIVE

## Return to paradise

Mid July brought on a heat wave and the fellowship agreed to meet up for 8 am on a sunny Saturday morning by Phil's tree. The photos show it on our faces – we were never happier than we were on that trip and we never will be again.

It was already warm that morning, as we admired the view from the Farthing and cracked a beer for Phil. We took some photos, then, full of optimism, set the engines running to wind off down Hempton Hill and through the village, picking up Brian at the A20 junction.

It turned out to be a baking hot day and spirits were high as we stopped at the Dartford toll. There was a bit of confusion and Dave only just missed getting pole axed by the barrier, because he tailgated another bike.

In the middle of the tunnel, Del pulled his trick of cutting his ignition, then flipping the switch to cause an exhaust explosion that resonated deep under the Thames. I'd have been quite concerned if I hadn't known what it was.

Several hours, and a few coffee stops later, we were in the north of England and it was still just as hot. Our first planned destination was the Lake District in Cumbria. The Harbottles had some relations up that way and we got to camp out on their back lawn in a big trading tent they had put up for the occasion.

Brian got bitten by a horse fly as soon as we got there and

during the night, I deflated Dave's airbed for a laugh. He had brought so much stuff, wrapped up in bin liners and piled high against his sissy bar. It was all secured with a collection of bungee cords. It did look a funny sight and must have made the steering lighter than it should have been. It didn't take long for him to start ditching stuff he didn't need, just to lighten the load.

That first day at the lakes was great. The terrain was like a mini Scotland. We went into Keswick and did some shopping, then off around Derwent Water and over Honister Pass. I had taken the lead by this time, as I knew my way around a bit and the others were happy to trail.

The first time I pulled in for a photo stop was at the foot of the pass and I didn't give a lot of warning, if any actually. I saw the others skidding to a halt in my mirror and Dave's front wheel couldn't hold on the loose surface. He went down with the bike, breaking his left-hand mirror. I probably would have seen red, but he was fine about it: he hadn't tasted freedom since before he first split from the gang and got himself hitched.

Sixteen or seventeen years of marital bliss with three kids thrown in; that's a heavy commitment under any circumstances and there never was a man more committed to the ideal than Dave the Goober. All that weight just seemed to have washed right over him and he'd left it behind in Ashford. It was the old Dave back again, not very lively, but twice as happy. Looking through a collection of photos with his old mum Brenda, sometime later, she said she hadn't seen him really laugh like that since we were kids. We laughed a lot on that trip.

I lost my right-hand mirror on the stretch of motorway between Carlisle and Glasgow. The repair I'd made on the snapped bracket lug from my first off-road spill just couldn't take the vibrations any longer – I saw it wobble, then it was gone before I had a chance to make a grab for it. Still, we were in Scotland and the sun was shining, some things you've just got to let go.

At the end of a long hot day of snaking roads, deep glens and a standoff with a highland bull, we rolled into the west coast town of Oban. Just out of town, and south along the coast road, we found a perfect spot to use as our base. A camping site with a holiday feel to it and a small hill in the centre, where we would spend each evening for the next three to four days, watching the sunset over the islands in the bay, drinking warm beer, while being bitten by midges and laughing our heads off.

There were only two rainy days during that holiday: one was the day we booked for a boat trip. The other passengers on the small launch looked pretty miserable by halfway through the day, but we were having a good laugh despite the drizzle. On a boat in full riding gear, crash hats too, drinking coffee and chatting with the girl who ran the tour. Brian was in his element, stripped to his vest and talking boats and magnets to the skipper in the wheelhouse. I even caught a mackerel off the Garvellach Rocks to cook for my supper.

On the last day at Oban, Del and I took off down the Kintyre peninsular, all the way to the Mull, that's about 250 miles all in. High above the lighthouse it was just possible to see Rathlin Island, just off the Antrim coast of Northern Ireland. The ride out was interesting with a few stops, but we had to ride hard back to Oban.

We met up with the others at the harbour, ate fish and chips, fed the seagulls, bought beer and took a slow ride back along the coast, crash helmets on our arms and each with a head full of our own dreams.

Dave thought we should mark our trip with some kind of commemorative tattoo, but the rest of us weren't that keen. We went for identical silver rings instead, with Celtic knot work design to seal our fellowship.

Eventually, we had to move on, and it was a long haul to Fort William, then right through the Great Glen to Inverness. We should have stopped there for the day, but decided to push on, up the east coast. The further north we got, the more the weather closed in and we didn't even realise that we had the cliff edge just there on our right arm the whole way up.

Dave got his Scotch mist alright: it was a solid wet fog, totally impenetrable and we could only judge eachother's positions by our bike lights. Some of those bends were so steep and tight, Dave was complaining he was grounding out. I believed it too, as I had to lean so deep into the corners that my panniers were almost down on the tar.

We got to John o'Groats in fog so thick, we had no idea where the sun was going down. A few buildings could just be made out from the roadside as we passed them and there seemed no point in looking for the sea. We decided to check into a guesthouse that had a bar and restaurant and there was nothing else to do but get down there and start drinking.

I think it might have been the last pub on the Land's End to John O'Groats trail. Quite a night anyway, we partied with some locals from the Dounreay atomic power station. It started out good natured, but by gone midnight it had degenerated into a pretty raucous battle of stereotypical insults from all sides with 'see you Jimmy' hats and bog brushes being wielded recklessly. I think I turned in about 2 am with the room swimming around me.

The following day, the fog had miraculously lifted and it was high summer again. We posed for pictures at the famous signpost and took an easy ride to the Castle of Mey. I remember the flowers in the meadows and the herd of Aberdeen Angus cattle roaming the seashore in the castle grounds. I just thought Scotland is a great place, and it is, when the sun shines and the wind eases off to a light breeze, just enough to keep the midges at bay.

The ride back down the same coastal road was a revelation. We were moving through rolling countryside with gentle cliffs to our left and a glimmering sea out there. Various ruined castles and brochs on isolated headlands showed up the history of this part of Britain. Inland there was nothing but an open wasteland, a reminder of the clearances a century ago. Stone ruins of crofts and tumbled dry stone walls, heather and grouse the only crop. There was not a tree in sight – a lonely place I thought.

That night we made it to Carrbridge on the edge of the central highlands. There was a live band playing Celtic folk music in the local pub. Brian didn't like it, as it reminded him of his times in Northern Ireland and I think we all detected a bit of a republican element within the group's style; the locals weren't welcoming either. Although the music was good enough, the vibe had us a bit on edge and it wasn't the right place to be getting drunk in.

Next morning, Dave and I sat drinking tea after breakfast and watched the red squirrels in the garden of our B&B. We waited for the Harbottles to rumble up from their digs just around the corner and we were off.

The Cairngorm Massif is vast with few inroads. We made it up to the ski lifts, then back down to a wide round glacial lake where Del and I took a canoe out for an hour, while Dave and Brian sat on the shore eating ice creams and smoking. Those two got on pretty well together, considering the age gap. Brian liked someone to listen to his army stories and Dave was in no rush, always happy to talk about anything really. He always had been a bit of an old man at heart, down the Swan in his moccasins on a Wednesday night to play darts with the old boys, while making half a mild last forty minutes.

The vastness of the region took us aback I think, and we stopped several times while making our way around it. At one stop I noticed petrol draining from the undercarriage of my bike, one section of rubber hose had worked its way off a fuel tap. I was lucky not to have lost my whole tank load on the ride. Another thing I noticed at that time was my engine oil was disappearing; I had to chuck in all the spare oil I had brought (which wasn't enough), then buy another litre at the next garage. I only topped up to the minimum to get me home, as it wasn't the grade I wanted. I later learned that it was accepted by KTM riders, that these machines burned oil through their valves and you should never be without spare oil on any trip.

Brian's bike developed a fault with its immobiliser system, which slowed our progress south through the Cheviot Hills: we had to make several forced stops by the roadside later that day. This all made for a long day and we didn't get to Scots Corner till near to sunset. It was dusk when we mercifully rolled into the driveway of a rather odd bed and breakfast place close to the Catcleugh Reservoir in midge valley. We were back in England, but just short of where we had planned to get to and still north of the wall.

The last stop on the trip, other than for petrol, was at the village of Harbottle (Del's namesake), with its ruined castle and little museum. Nice place on a nice day (apart from the horse flies) – I'm sure it's pretty bleak up there in winter though. The ride back to Ashford from Harbottle was long, hard and uneventful. We should have made another stop somewhere, but the closer you get to home, the keener you always are to just get there. Anyway, we had left all the great roads and scenery behind us out of reach and it just became a run for home. Dave pared off at junction nine and we stepped up to a ton on the short final section. A cruise down the mad mile and it was all done.

Back in the workshop, the KTM got the new tyres and the fresh oil it needed, and I was pleased to be able to refit the side stand. The fact that I had lowered the bike by several ways without shortening the centre stand had meant that, loaded up, it was almost impossible for me to raise it onto the stand on my own. In Scotland I had needed the others to come and help me whenever we stopped for any reason. Getting onto the beast with the luggage high on the back of the seat had been hard too. I really needed some assistance to keep her balanced, while I manoeuvred my right leg up and over. For later trips I had it sorted out, being more used to the feel of the thing and having cut an inch off my side stand. It made the solo mounting technique achievable.

The KTM was never an around the world bike; for that you need something like a 1990s Honda 750 Africa twin or even a pre-electronic ignition Royal Enfield Bullet – and all the time in the world.

# CHAPTER TWENTY-SIX

## *Blue moon rising*

During the summer of 2007 I had my first midlife crisis: everyone over forty is entitled to one. Crippled by a massive mortgage, I felt trapped in a job I hated, with no time to do the things I should always be doing: messing around on the farm, 'mechanicing' and building a relationship with my little daughter Rebecca, who was coming up for two years old.

She had sandy hair like mine once was, all wispy, so it picked up the sunlight. She would come out into the garage with me and poke around with a screwdriver that I let her call her own, whilst I was putting my dad's Super Rocket back together after a comprehensive overhaul. It was never long before she would fall asleep on a mat beside the bikes, while I got on with the job.

I also wanted very much to travel again and planned on ditching the police uniform once the house was sold, taking off as a family to the other side of the world, where we could appreciate the freedom to grow outside the rat race. It all happened, but it wasn't the dream I had envisaged.

The house sold about six months before the property crash, so things started out well. Travelling didn't work out for us as a family, so when we got back from Asia we settled back in at the farm. I did realise a dream from my youth though, by finding and buying a 1976 Kawasaki Z900-A4, in metallic dark green. It was a US import, so no rust, and had been upgraded with stainless spokes and a stainless four-silencer exhaust system. It was like a right-of-passage for me, to own this iconic machine once in my life, even if I didn't keep it long.

Del had taken me up to Essex to view the bike and I rode it home after paying the man £4,300. Not many years later, the value of these bikes had started to skyrocket, but I'd already passed it on to Del, pretty damn cheap, as a favour, before I noticed the trend.

In truth, it was a little heavy for me and the handling was not as I had imagined. With the KHs I'd felt natural, they were an extension of my own frame; they went where I moved without effort on my part – this statement is contrary to what most people (who had probably never owned one) seem to believe. The Z never really felt a part of me; it felt a bit like I was guiding a cruise missile when I rolled out of the petrol station, for that first ride home on the A11, to show it the road.

There was no mistaking the noise and smell of a big four-cylinder Jap bike and I liked it well enough, despite a bit of oil seepage that I never was able to properly sort out. It was mechanically sound, but some clever person who had installed an alarm and immobiliser had also created an electrical short somewhere and the battery would run down quickly, needing to be charged every few weeks. The kick start was surprisingly usable though, so if it wouldn't go on the button, then a couple or three kicks would always do the job.

The KTM took a back seat that summer; I used the Z whenever the weather was fine and always liked to take it out on our pub rides. I'd thrash it on the straights, but it was hard work cornering and the exhausts grounded well before the tyres got near their edge.

Into that autumn Dave seemed pretty down, complaining about money, his boring dead-end job, and all the stresses of home life. Kids playing up, wife being a bitch (although he still loved her more than life itself) and the increasing pain he was always in because of his leg. He was taking a fair amount of pain killers, quite strong stuff, but I didn't realise he was on anti-depressants as well. He began to talk about his perceived hopelessness and then switch to go on about plans as to how things were all going to come up right. He'd had a good summer actually, broken out of the rut and gone out doing all the things he'd wanted to do for years – but he'd stopped laughing.

On Sunday 29th October, I got a call from Sharon in the early evening, asking if I'd seen Dave at all. She had called Del too and Chip, apparently. It had been raining most of the day and the dark was setting in as Del and I went out and around to some of Dave's favourite haunts: the pubs we used, Farthing Common and even Westwood, where we used to go for a smoke as teenagers on hot summer's nights after the pubs closed.

We had drawn a blank, so I phoned Sharon. Within minutes, she was telling me a police car had just stopped outside their place. She talked me through it, as I heard the kids reporting that the police had come to the door, then she asked that I speak to them. It was a Detective Sergeant I knew from the job, a decent bloke, who told me they had found Dave in his car, up a quiet road outside town on the way to the hills. He had shot himself with his old 12 bore.

They waited for us to get to the Ashford address, where we talked with the family until Dave's brothers, Robert and Colin, got there.

Dave had left home about eleven in the morning after preparing a roast dinner for the family. Once it was in the oven, he'd told them he was popping out in the car. He'd parked up in Bockham Lane, put his music on and ended it all. We had missed all the signs and warnings and let him down when it really mattered.

A suicide note had been found in the car, naming the songs he wanted for his funeral and stating that he wanted me, Del and Chip to take his ashes up to Mount Snowdon for the last run.

I didn't go back to work that year. I hadn't planned on being there after November in any case, but now we had to do the right thing for Dave. Robert planted a hastily made wooden cross beneath a small oak tree in the field entrance where the car had been found. It was quite a nice spot when the sun came out, with the autumn leaf colour and the sound of pheasants calling.

Some days later I went to the chapel of rest, where Dave was laid out in his coffin. He was dressed in denims and wearing a Harley Davidson belt buckle. They had done a good job, as despite the method he'd used, it *was* Dave's face I saw. He didn't look as if he had found peace and I didn't stay long.

Del and I went to Sharon's house to meet up with Chip and we planned the funeral to be held at Charing crematorium.

This was the first time I had seen Chip since Chris's wedding, although I did know he and Dave had stayed in regular contact. The thing was, Chip had joined a hardcore, outlaw biker club after the Oakmen disbanded. Some stuff I didn't really ask too much about had gone bad and they'd called it a day. Some of the more serious members had been absorbed into the new

Outlaws MC making waves in the area. Chip said there was a lot of commitment demanded of members, but it was the best thing he had ever done.

Earlier that summer, Dave had filled me in on the news and about a party for Chip's 40th that was being held up at their clubhouse. I had wanted to go, but the word had come back that I wasn't welcome. Chip later told me that he had put it to the club, but some members had said 'We don't want no fucking coppers round here.' I could understand that, as the clubhouse, up at a farm not far from Kestrels, had already been raided by police teams not long after the gang moved their colours into the area. Well, the club were going to do the roadblocks for the funeral cortege, and I would meet them then and we would see who was who.

The big day arrived, and when Del and I got to number 50 Twelve Acres, Chip was already there in the house and he had Fat Rob with him. There was a roar of V-twin engines and Chip said 'They're here' … So, we went outside. More and more people were starting to arrive, a good many on bikes, including Guy, and Dave's old mate 'Johnny Hifi', or 'Snowbeast' as we used to call him at school.

I don't think Dave could have imagined that his passing would be honoured in the way it was on that chill November morning under a clear blue sky. It was the last time I rode the Z900 that year, but what a ride.

The Harley combination that carried the box arrived and we all lined up behind it. Del and I carried Dave's eldest kids Zak and Stacy, immediately behind the funeral bike, with Brian making up the fellowship close behind us. Chip was with the outriders and the rest of the bikes followed, at walking pace to start with to the end of the street.

Onto Hythe Road and into town we rumbled. At the entrance of Henwood (the industrial estate where Dave had worked) stood his colleagues to witness the ride by and show their respects. All the time there was the growl of big engines coming from the sides, overtaking again and again to get back to the front and force all traffic to give way... It was tremendous.

We stopped before the crematorium on the A20 to remove our helmets, then we rode slowly up the driveway, bikes parking up to left and right of us like an honour guard. There were a lot of people there, many who I hadn't seen since we were young.

Del, Chip, Rob and I shouldered the box and then the awful, slow drumbeat began. Ozzy Ozborne, *See You on the Other Side*. It boomed out from the sepulchre – heavy, drawing us in up the stone steps and into the building, where every seat was full. We set Dave down and each patted the box, before being ushered to seats by the front and I don't remember the walk away: it was like a dream. I couldn't look at anyone's face, but I could hear people taking deep breaths all around me.

In addition to the songs Dave had chosen, the family had slipped in two simple hymns, *Lord of the Dance* and *All Things Bright and Beautiful*. I stood to sing and recognised Mark Thomas, one of my old friends from primary school – he was right there at the front. So, we sang like we had thirty years before, when life was simple, and all things seemed good.

Dave went into the great beyond to the accompaniment of *Goodbye Blue sky* from Pink Floyd's *The Wall* album: certainly not a happy song, but it was surprisingly calming.

We walked out into the sunshine to the unbearably morose utopian lyrics of Ozzy's *I Just Want You*. It was such cruel irony:

*There are no unlockable doors; there are no unwinnable wars,*
*There are no unrightable wrongs or unsingable songs.*

I went out and bought those albums with the songs Dave chose soon after and I played them over a few times, full of intense feeling, but with a kind of absolution from it all at the same time.

A funeral can create a kind of death and rebirth type of experience. When you put a loved one into the ground you are creating a permanent resting place, where their bones become a part of the land and there is a comfort in that feeling, but no instant release. The pain lessens over time, but it's a long time.

When you commit a companion to the fire, you send them to a freedom without boundaries. I'm no longer sure what I believe in, but I felt that day, as we walked out into the garden, that the unbearable pain Dave must have felt in his soul had just lifted and his happy face was shining all around with the sun's rays.

Filing out of the building, I found myself shoulder to shoulder with Will Missing, one of the original five. He was dressed very uncharacteristically in a black suit, certainly the only suit he owned – we were all in denim and leather. A lot of water had passed under the bridge and I wasn't sure I knew that person anymore.

Will had split when we were just out of our teens. He'd just cut himself out and made no contact with any of us for years. Will's brain revolves around the agricultural calendar and whatever female he's getting what he wants from. I don't think he ever loved another human being, truly. He told me his wife

Sarah had left him a few years back and that he didn't see any of his children. Sarah was there, at the funeral and the wake with her two teenaged girls. I spoke with them, but Will kept his distance. She looked okay on her Harley Davidson cruiser; it was nice to see that people hadn't changed too much.

Mickey and Keithy Bryant were there, Alan Massey and Matt Godden too. Colin Cadell, one of Dave's oldest mates and Wilf Missing, as well as some of the girls from the old village days. I was pleased to see Sue Tibbles standing right at the end of the line of flowers.

Sue and Colin Tibbles still lived in Greenfields where Dave had grown up and we'd all been round their house at some stage as teenagers. Like the Bishopp's place, it had been a bit of a gathering pad and Greenfields wouldn't have been the same without either family.

The ride back down the A20 was fast and exciting; Zak and Stacy had gone back with family members, so Del and I were able to race a bunch of modern sports bikes back to Ashford. We stopped at the Bockham Lane site for the laying of flowers, before making it on to the Drum for the wake.

I didn't see one person who wasn't happy during the time we spent there that day, out in the gardens, milling around the bikes or on the brick terrace. The pub did us proud and I personally thanked the team who had done the road work. Chip later told me that I was welcome any time at their clubhouse and it didn't matter that I had been 'Old Bill', as I no longer was. I said I had never been 'Old Bill': I'd just put that uniform on and got paid. There was a little bit more to it than that, but… I have to say it felt good to be accepted as a man again – I never had been accepted as a cop.

I'd certainly done nothing out there to dispel my maverick reputation, and was once reprimanded for single-handedly resolving a 'firearms incident'. I'd got myself some more black marks for reacting strongly against the release, without charge, of a sex offender, and also for refusing to process an illegal immigrant, amongst a long list of misdemeanours. However, when I rode my Royal Enfield through the locker room, blipping the throttle in the ground floor stairwell of Ashford police station, nothing was ever said, which disappointed me a little.

The wake moved indoors after most of the bikes had left. It was mostly close friends of Dave and the Bishopp family who were gathered around the fireplace late into the evening. Finally, we called it, and Del and I saluted the day by tipping our last pint glasses over our own heads. I wanted to ride home and thought I could, but Brian stopped me, so the Z900 remained there, up on the high ground, as if observing a solitary vigil.

# CHAPTER TWENTY-SEVEN

## *Silver mountains*

As I was due to go off round the world, just a few weeks after I got the invite from Chip's lot. I didn't actually make it to any of their club events until the following year. It wasn't really for me though, I prefer small gatherings of close friends, and although the club members were friendly enough, it was all quite closely governed by a strict set of rules. No member could really be an individual. I like the spirit of a brotherhood, but these big clubs are too regimented for my style. Also, to them, a brother is a brother regardless; well, I've always had an opinion on that.

The May Day weekend was chosen as the date for our ride to Snowdonia. The three of us rode the route that had been taken two decades before and Dave's urn rode on the back of Chip's 1200 Sportster – he would have liked that. It was a good ride up, cold but bright. My KTM had let me down the day before we left and its battery wouldn't take charge enough to turn it over on the vital morning, despite the charger indicating full. I couldn't start it with a kick either.

Del had had problems too, his Speedmaster had been in and out of the shop for weeks and in the end, they had provided him with a 2300cc Triumph Rocket III for the trip. I just jumped on the back of that when we all met up at the cross, ready for the off. Rob Bishopp and Zak were there to meet us and they drove up to Snowdon on a different route with all the tents and gear. We set up camp at the foot of the mountain that had meant more to Dave than I think anyone had imagined. He had climbed it on a school trip before the accident that left him with a broken hip joint. We had been there on our first bike trip twenty years earlier and Dave and Sharon had had their first holiday in Snowdonia after getting married. It did seem right that his ashes should end up there.

We got a good day for the climb, and having done it twice before and seen nothing from the top, it was a revelation to get a 360 degree view, from the highest mountain in England and Wales. We began from the south side, a lesser used starting point, but it gave us the mountain almost to ourselves.

We stopped short of the summit on a grassy space, with the shelter of great rocks at our backs. It was like a narrow, raised, lawn with views either side of the ridge. Amazingly, a seagull appeared, standing on a rock at the far edge of the lawn. We all felt like the bird had chosen the spot for us and we decided there was no better place. It was a private spot: an arrow shot from the summit, and a pleasant place to sit.

At our end of the lawn rose a huge splinter of rock, standing upright like a spear head out of the soft grass. We chose that as Dave's rock, drank a bottle of Old Speckled Hen each and poured the last one down the stone. We each took a handful of the ashes, said some words and cast them. Then Del shook the rest of the urn out into the wind.

That wasn't the end of the story, as there were to be other gatherings organised in Dave's honour over the next couple of years. We met at the oak tree in Bockham Lane on the first anniversary and set in a permanent memorial, a cross which I had carpentered from old oak; I made the joint fit so tight that no fixings were needed. We shared a beer at the spot, before retiring to the Drum for thoughtful conversation.

The Halloween party we held in the wood was a wilder affair, with a six-foot hexagon we had made from young ash withies all lit up as a backdrop. A tape recording of all Dave's favourite heavy metal records resonated around the clearing, as we celebrated the darker side of eulogy.

There was fire and ritual, helped along by a stack of old boat flares and orange signal smoke. It was a howling rainy night, but no one used the tarpaulin shelter I had thrown up. When the conventional rockets, their explosions lost in the fast moving clouds, failed to represent the God of Hellfire, we took to ramming the sticks into the soft mud, so that they were trapped and exploded on the ground, filling the clearing like cluster bombs of white phosphorous.

Matt started chucking anything that hadn't gone off into the bonfire. This was mostly twenty-year-old parachute flares that launched from tubes, so when they did go, the aluminium cylinders shot out through the trees at low angles in any direction they fancied, sending us all diving for cover. Soaked by beer and rain and with the hellfire spent, everything went on the fire. That included my shelter, Del's tape player and Dave's six-foot hexagon to finish the proceedings and send it all off.

We said goodbye to one original, but reforming the old gang served to bring little Willy back into the circle. Still the same old Will, just without the small frame and boyish looks. He was still a semi-feral sociopath with his own uncompromising views on society.

Old habits don't die either. Since our re-acquaintance Will

has passed through a string of cheap shitty cars ready for the scrap heap, equalling his list of needy females he always seems to come across, none of which he has kept longer than any of his cars. On the bike front he's been a bit choosier, keeping and maintaining these metal rides into their second year for some of them.

Being that Will's life is still directed by the farming seasons and he is tied to the land, he is almost totally unobtainable from July to October, so he missed the next bike trip that came along.

Del had been going on for years about returning to the Dam Busters region of northern Germany, where the Harbottles had spent happy years when Brian was stationed out there in the early eighties.

It was the first week of July 2008 and three bikes set off through the Channel Tunnel to Europe. For this trip only, we broke the 'No Bitches' rule and Del took Karen (his wife) along for the ride. After getting lost in Brussels and then riding halfway back to Oostende by mistake, we corrected ourselves and made it to the pine woods east of the Rhine.

Del and I rode the same bikes as on the Scotland tour, but Brian had upgraded to a VN 900 in red, that oddly enough also developed an immobiliser fault too. In the end we had to cut the chip out and straight wired the system back to standard, whilst hauled up on the side of a busy main road through the French Alps.

A few days were spent in northern Germany, camping by the Biggesee reservoir, before heading down into the Moselle valley, where we visited a castle, indulged in a wine tasting evening in an ancient cellar and dined out on wild boar and venison.

We all got ridiculously drunk, then signed up to have crates of Moselle wine sent back home. I still like a Spätburgunder to this day.

The next stop was the Black Forest, just north of the Swiss border. We couldn't find a camp site, but a local man called Volker offered us the use of his isolated wooden cabin for free. We were a bit wary after he had led us out there. The whole scene smacked of one of those nasty films, where an unsuspecting party of young thrill seekers gets lured to a cabin in the woods for a night of horror.

First, this little dead-end road took us across a rushing mountain stream, then it deteriorated into a gravely hairpin that the cruisers only just got up, and there it was. A strange lonely shack on three levels at the edge of an escarpment. The dense woodland rose high above it and the thick undergrowth below was part covering an abandoned saloon car. We joked that it had likely belonged to the last hapless group of trippers who had come along this way.

Volker unlocked the door and left us to it, saying he would be back in the morning to meet us before we left and to lock up behind us.

As the pleasant leafy glade started to darken, with the surrounding hills cutting out the sun, we took a recce of the place. It was quite funny really, exploring each room and joking about the last poor souls who might have stayed there. By the time we made our way into the basement, down the creaking steps, we had succeeded in unnerving each other just a little. It was built into the escarpment and the windows had bars on them. On the walls was a collection of dusty woodworking tools and a bench with a vice dominated the floor space. It really did resemble, with a bit of imagination and self-induced paranoia, a nice little torture chamber.

We sat outside, eating, drinking and chatting around our campfire till late, then retired to the individual rooms we had chosen for ourselves upstairs. As Volker had taken the key, we couldn't actually lock the door and didn't feel particularly comfortable about that. We raided the torture chamber and selected a chopper and some metal bars as bedside companions. The bikes were chained together and I tied a trip line from them, leading under the door to a chair. We stood a collection of beer bottles around on the floor immediately inside the door, to act as an alarm if anyone were to open it. We also checked that all the windows were secure.

The next morning, we were all still alive and the alarm system unbreached. The sun was shining, and the bikes were out there. We laughed about the whole thing and were happy that we hadn't found a regular camp site after all. Volker was a good man and turned up at the given time to lock up; I gave him a bottle of Kräuterlikor I had got from the Biggesee as a thank you.

Del and I revisited the cabin, the following year, but were unable to find Volker. We had our fire and slept on the porch. I left some Cuban cigars that time as a gratuity.

That next day started fine and we worked our way through the forest to Lake Constance, where we set up at a decent camp site. The water was blue and deep, right from the start-point and we all went for a swim. Sitting on the restaurant porch, we watched the huge black cloud move along from the east like a curtain and the rain followed in its wake. That was it for the next three days and nights.

We never saw a thing through Austria or into Lichtenstein; there we found a quiet little site just off the main road and above the raging brown water of the Rhine. It was not very wide there, but swollen with tree trunks, washed down from the Alps and fast flowing.

Each morning we got out of the tents hoping to see a mountain, but it was just cloud and rain the whole time. I refused to move on into Switzerland unless we could actually see what we were riding through. The mood took a downward swing and we were all pretty fed up. Only *my* simple tent didn't leak, which I have to admit amused me somewhat. Brian discovered, on the first morning there, that his tent did leak and had part filled one of the new fur lined boots he had bought just the day before. On the third evening, the poor bloke had run out of wine and resorted to whiskey; we had all had about enough by then.

Mercifully, on the third morning, it wasn't raining and the clouds were white, hanging tantalisingly onto most of the mountain peaks. We could see the Alps at last, there was snow high up on the jagged ridges and that was good enough.

Switzerland was uniquely interesting, right from when we crossed the Rhine Bridge. The landscape was so big and fresh and each town we passed through was displaying regional heraldic banners, giving it a medieval tournament atmosphere. We stopped at the town of Chur and realised how expensive food and drink was. We were living on a diet of coffee, chips and beer but I cut out the beer straight away when I saw the price tag.

It was hot the whole rest of the trip, except for just one night. We had crossed two high Alpine passes, the Oberalp and

Furka, to get across from the head of the Rhine valley to the Rhone. We were deep in the middle of the mountains, with high snow-caps all around restricting the low sunlight from reaching our tents. The river we camped beside was mountain cold, the colour of copper sulphate. That was a pretty chilly night, remaining fresh right into mid-morning.

There were a lot of bikes on that main trans-Alp road: different groups of sports bikes, adventure tourers and custom cruisers. Each country we went through seemed to have a different method of acknowledging a fellow biker. The Swiss way of pointing with a free hand didn't make for the safest cornering and a lot of the time, instead of showing the sign, I just kept my eyes on the bends. We stopped at the viewpoints, but there was no doubting we were riding through some of the most awesome backdrops anywhere in the world.

We spent a second night in Switzerland, at Martigny in the south west, a big wide valley where the Rhone makes a turn to the north. In the morning we took the machines up into the snow again and over the Grande St Bernard Pass, south into Italy. The pass was so high we got breathless from the altitude walking around the Col at the rest point.

Into Italy we went, and a night in the Valle de Aosta, then up and over the Col du Petit St-Bernard. A snow drift had filled a bend of the original road that was firm enough to walk on, despite looking to be ten to twenty feet thick at its height. I took a run up on the KTM and made it up the slope and half way round, before bogging down to the wheel spindles, proving that no matter how good the bike potentially was, it couldn't go just anywhere off the road – not on the same tyres that made it such fun leaning around those beautiful smooth hair-pin bends. Once over the top, we rode down dozens of steep wide zigzags into France and the heat of the Savoie.

The rest of the day was just hot and hard, with stops to sort out Brian's electrics and a lot more map reading than we'd had to do so far. It was sunset before we started looking for a place to stay and saw nothing, we were heading north-west and away from Lake Geneva and had resigned ourselves to riding through the night, so stopped for a meal in some small town on the way.

Del has a limited list of acceptable meals in his head and won't stray far from it, but the menu was all in French and the staff didn't speak any English. He went for what he thought read salmon with tartar sauce. Brian and Karen indicated something that was being served to another table, but I confidently ordered the tatare de boeuf and was complimented on my choice by the waitress.

When Del's meal arrived, it was a big bowl of raw minced salmon flesh, with some token salad article and lemon sections on the side. He won't eat vegetables and I laughed at the bowl of raw fish he had committed himself to, because I knew he would hate it.

There was no tartar sauce on Del's dish and that prompted Brian to start telling an army story of when he was in North Africa and the squadies had ordered steak at a French restaurant. It had come in the form of big, fat, raw, minced meat patties and they had all sent it back to be cooked into burgers. I was studying the menu at the time when I heard him say 'They, eat it raw, it was called steak tartare.' My mind ticked over a little and I knew that was what I had just ordered.

I called the waitress back to try and get myself out of the ordeal, but she just assured me the tartare de boeuf was nearly ready. I sat and waited while they all laughed.

When it did arrive, it was in a sunken bowl, huge, and a lurid pink colour. It was minced so fine it looked like a blancmange. To add insult to injury, a raw egg had been cracked over the top of it and the only side salad I got was a few cold pale slices of watermelon, which tasted like they had been stored beside the meat in the fridge.

I did my best and actually managed to load about two thirds of it into my throat. I had to stop because it felt like it wasn't going down any further. I could feel it cold and thick, up level with my chest. That was a meal to remember. When we did actually come across a campsite about midnight and set ourselves up, I could still feel it sitting there, not wanting to finish the journey down.

We were up and out early the next morning, for once I was packed, seated and on the starting line before the others. Del decided to roll back onto the road without looking and hit me broadside. I went over with the bike as it fell bar end to pannier in the middle of the road. Del and Brian had had their rants and sulks earlier in the trip, this was my turn and I think I might have woken a few campers.

There was just one other stop on the road back to Calais, somewhere close to the Somme. It was still hot, and the corn fields were flush with scarlet poppy flowers. I pressed one in a book I was carrying and brought it back home with me. That last day we took it easy, meandering along the gentler road networks of Northern France and breaking out to the coast at Le Touquet for chips and moules marinières.

The last sunset came at Wissant Beach, where we stopped amongst the dunes. The plan had been to camp out there and finish the trip in a way to remember, but the sight of England across the Channel influenced the general consensus. I would have quite happily put my tent up once more and spent a few hours around a driftwood fire with a beer in my hand, talking away into the night about the lives we planned to live. I was out voted though, and we got a late ferry back to Dover, which was stupid for so many reasons.

# CHAPTER TWENTY-EIGHT

## *New horizons*

I didn't see much of the Harbottles for the rest of the summer, Will was harvesting and the Fellowship seemed to be on a hold. I was resurrecting my travelling spirit and had just got back from a trip to Cuba, in time for the Halloween party in the rain.

The Drum changed hands later that year and the new people got a baptism of fire when we used the place for our Christmas party. There was the usual gang, plus Shane and Heidi over from Germany and Triton back from Australia. Matt Godden, as usual, was the worst of us, pulling off plastic baubles from the decorations and chucking them at us.

Beers flew, furniture was abused, and Will won the yard of ale competition, where we used a dusty old copper horn picked off the fireplace as a funnel. That pub was pretty good, and we soon built up a respectful relationship with the new management who seemed to see us as the evening's entertainment whenever we were in.

The following year we booked Henry's Rock Band as a tribute night for Dave. All the gang were there, and it soon got messy. Del and I got up and did a pogo rendition of *500 miles* and I managed to crack my head on a low beam. I felt the blood running down my face, but refused to stop, till the end of the song.

Will threw up on the floor in front of the band and we just carried on, while Mick (the landlord) went around our feet with a mop. It was a great night, we filled half the pub with our lot, and Zak was there to the end wearing Dave's leather jacket; everything just seemed right.

In mid May 2009, Del and I set out together from Dover, intent on crossing the Alps and making it down to the Med. From there we wanted to follow the Côte d'Azure to the Pyrenees and on into Spain. All this we did and more – with stops at Triberg, the Walensee, and Lake Como, before hitting Liguria and finally finding some sun.

Along the Mediterranean coast we camped just outside Monaco, then on to St. Tropez, where we unwittingly gate-crashed the Harley Davidson festival and proved ourselves the craziest party goers there. We put the grizzled Harley crowd to shame, while throwing it all out to this great folk-rock band called Quill, oddly enough from Wolverhampton. It was like I had been growing my hair for eighteen months just to let it fly for that one night.

Next stop was Aigues-Mortes in the swampy Camargue region, thick with mosquitoes and gypsies. We stayed one night down there and then pushed on over the mountains, making it over the pass into Andorra as the sun was setting.

The following day was a long one, the roads in the Pyrenees were magnificent and I may never get tired of riding them. The climate on the Spanish side is hotter and dryer than the French side and the contrast in scenery is huge. All along that rugged stretch, between the two seas, we kept coming across places that made it feel like we were journeying between different worlds. You can't do justice to it in the two or three days it takes to make it coast to coast.

Our second night south of the snow caps was at the small town of Broto, where an icy blue river ran straight through. The place was about two thirds of the way along the route and we decided to hole up there, after catching the beginning of a deluge. The main drag was all hotels, coffee bars and gift shops, but the old town, centred around the big square-towered church, had a lot of rustic character.

We followed the Rio Gallego north up into the hills, having passed through some real Tolkienesque scenery, of deep gorges, broken stone bridges and abandoned villages that blended in with the landscape. The high pass of Frontera del Portalet still had snow drifts beside the road. It was cold but bright as we looked down into France.

A steady meandering descent followed, through twenty or thirty miles of heavenly countryside in the full blow of spring, taking us out of the valleys and onto the L'Adour basin region of the Pyrénées-Atlantiques. The country didn't seem to change much for a couple of days really after that. It was pleasant enough and the roads were fine, but the excitement and adventure had been left behind. The rest of the ride was unremarkable, given the distance covered *and* we kept off the motorway toll roads too.

There was one last urgent dash up the Cherbourg peninsular, getting us to the port just before the ferry left for Portsmouth. We got there in the early evening and were soon greeted by noisy traffic and wet roads. Not the best way to end such a great ride. Home and in bed by midnight though.

Later that summer, I bought myself a little Suzuki DRZ400, a light trail bike really, with a very small tank. It was fun for a while and I even took it on the ferry to Spain the following year. Del was still on his Triumph and we had planned an extensive trip around the Iberian Peninsula to finish off the job we'd started.

The KTM had let me down again, the day before the off. I'd done an extra trip to Maidstone, as a last thing, just to pick up a new battery. On the motorway stretch back to Ashford, something started going wrong and I knew it was top end. It turned out that the needle roller bearing on the overhead valve cam had disintegrated and the bike would be out of action for a month or so: KTM parts travel from Austria slower than you could actually walk the distance.

I lost no time in securing the orange beast in the yard at Ashford police station, got myself home and rapidly serviced and kitted out the Suzuki. There was no back rack on it and no pannier options, but I did manage to strap on a spare Triumph tank bag, and I left behind most of the gear I had already packed. I was there though, on time to meet Del the next morning and we made the Portsmouth ferry OK.

That trip was enough to stretch the limits of a DRZ 400. It did everything I asked of it and handled a restructured tour of just the north east parts of Spain.

The bike had a little tank, a short memory gel battery and no kick start to back it up. Checking and topping up the oil each morning was a little complicated and needed to be exact, as it didn't hold much in its frame reservoir. It was good for sixty miles an hour, but not in a strong wind. Sports style cornering was not to be considered under any circumstances, but it was light, nifty and reliable. I could park it anywhere and play around off road if I wanted.

We made the most of that trip, even though early May was definitely not the time to be in that region. It was freezing cold, day and night and the further we got into the central plains, the colder it became.

Sixty miles an hour is a great way to see the Spanish countryside though; we passed through so many fascinating places we just wouldn't have come across if I'd been on a bigger bike. I got to play around in the Irati National Park that straddles the border with France in a deep river valley shared by both countries. We went down into it below the snow line and I had a go at fording small river tributaries along the Irati itself.

I would have tried the main river crossing and attempted to make it up the valley to the French roads, but Del couldn't follow me on a cruiser, so we turned back up and over the mountain again, looking for any border crossings where the passes were clear of snow.

We tried two more passes and even rode under the arc of snow that was being thrown up by a giant snow blower. We thought we were in luck, as the road had been cleared and went on for a mile or so more, but then the clean road stopped right at the border and the French side hadn't been touched. The machine operators must have thought we were idiots and, if they had seen the snowball fight we were having ten minutes later, they would have known we were.

We turned our bikes south down the Valle del Roncal with the snowy Pyrénées in our rear-view mirrors. We rode on down through the rocky canyon valley of the Rio Esca into a dry, warm spaghetti western type landscape. It all changes so quickly as you move on down, from cold forested hills on the snow line, to wastelands of gorse and scrub oak that suddenly drop into canyon lands, leading out to plains of swaying barley and the long blue body of water called Embalse de Yesa that stretches ten kilometres east to west.

We had been through the Picos mountains in Cantabria and down to the edge of Portugal in rain and sleet. Then into the cold wind of the central plains to Segovia and up into the Basque lands of the Western Pyrénées. It didn't need a big bike to find adventure, just a ship to take us there and pick us up afterwards. The great thing about motorcycling in Spain is that most of the time you have the land to yourself. The real Spain is nothing like the popular image and the only way to see it is on a motorbike.

Before I sold that DRZ, I needed to sort out the chain: every other link seemed to have fused to its neighbour, so it had a serrated look to it. That came off and I boiled it in grease which did the trick. Then there was the rear tyre I'd worn out. It didn't seem justifiable to fit an actual new one, as I wasn't going to change the front. I found an old competition trials tyre that had been up in the stable loft for twenty years, gathering dust and bird's nests. It was a soft compound tyre but worked all right.

Once my KTM was up and running again, I had one last need of it. I have to say the 640 proved one of my most unreliable bikes but, when it ran it was unstoppable and so easy to forget all the negative points, I'd forgive all of it.

The final trip I used it for was back down to Spain on the ferry to Santander that September. I rode for two days right across the dusty heartlands of the peninsular. I kept off the mountains and broke out for the Med at a place called Blanes in Cataluña. I had to go there to meet up with several groups of historical re-enactors for a Romans and Barbarians weekend on the sands.

My group had travelled down from Kent with a van load of swords, shields and chainmail. We met up there at Blanes and, after the battles were fought, we just loaded my bike into the van and drove it all back.

I'd just started to love that bike again and had plotted with Stuart about shipping it over to Tasmania, where he had emigrated to. It turned out he had bought the same machine out there and we were going to do the Gunbarrel Highway across the Northern Territories outback. It never happened and we both sold our bikes before the year was out.

I had thought that I'd finished with my experiences as an officer of the law, which was my plan. However, after a year and a half of travel and motorcycles, I'd used up most of my hard-earned disposable income and I just couldn't be bothered to go out and get a job – so I went back to the station.

I ended up doing another six years and I hated that uniform more every day I put it on. I fell out with every supervisor they threw at me and had finally burned all my bridges by the summer of 2015.

The exit date I shook hands on was 12th October, fourteen years to the day from the date of my 2001 passing out parade. My most ridiculously laughable gripe with the top brass had been when, one festive season, they'd served me with notice that I was subject to an internal investigation by the Professional Standards Department: 'gross misconduct.' The crime was that I had brought into the station, and sold to a fellow officer, a Christmas turkey, without first obtaining an additional business clearance from on high.

2010 was the year that I saw in the local paper that Guy

from the Oakmen had taken on the Plough public house in Brabourne. I had met him on occasions over the last few years, but when I saw the notice that he was finally getting married to his 'Ol' Lady', and the reception was at the pub, I had to go along.

The Plough turned into another local pub for us to start frequenting; although it hadn't actually become a biker's pub, they did have regular bands and Guy's old mates, the 75 Club, got down there a bit. Del and I went on a run with them to the Margate Meltdown one May. It's a good bike festival, held each year on the Whitsun bank holiday Monday.

Getting there was half the fun, riding in formation at the back of the pack, I was flat out and flat down, on the tank of my new Royal Enfield 500T, trying not to fall too far behind the Harley riders on the Thanet way.

We hadn't been to a mass biker's event like that for close on two decades and found it odd that it seemed acceptable for bikers to dress like skinheads, while 'scooterists' sported leather jackets and greasy hair. The old ways of pledging allegiance didn't seem to matter anymore, and denim cut-offs were nowhere to be seen.

Everywhere I went that summer, people were telling me what a beautiful bike the 500T was, and she was, with her rounded silver tank on a neat little black frame, aluminium mudguards, trials seat and a long swept up chrome exhaust silencer – Just not fit for a lot of the stuff I wanted to be doing.

The 500cc fuel injected engine with catalytic converter was R.E.'s most advanced evolvement of the sixty-year-old Bullet model, but it still had the guts and sound of a lawn mower: a nice lawn mower, mind you. When I got the bike new, it came with an application form to join the R.E. Owners Club, which stated it was open to anyone owning cycles or lawn mowers of the marque.

It did feel great on a nice day, popping along the lanes and whirring through town. Gear changes were infrequent, and it just carried itself along on the wound-up energy it produced. Being the trials spec. version, there was no luggage carrying capacity and although it ran on miles per litre rather than litres per mile, it was not a 'getting you somewhere' machine. It was also far too pretty to actually get dirty, so I never even used it off road, other than in the snow a couple of times the first winter I had it.

I left the trialing to the couple of old competition bikes Dad and I had kept hold of, the 1976 orange Ossa TR250 and its 1980s competitor, a blue Bultaco Sherpa 350. Both bikes had been road registered and we used to ride them the couple of miles up the lane to Coombe Wood, which still gets used once or twice a year for trials competitions. I entered the Ossa in the classic section a couple of years back and it was very well received. It was the only classic there that was in its original, un-restored, condition and so quite a rarity. I didn't get anywhere, but having not practised for years, I think I did well to finish most of the courses. I was absolutely exhausted, but the bike held its own.

# CHAPTER TWENTY-NINE

## Riding out the future

In September 2012 I went into Laguna Motorcycles in Ashford, to look at the new KTM 990 Adventure. It was the last year of manufacture before they changed everything and then it would no longer be right to call it a fully off-road machine. In practice, the 990 was rarely taken off the road by its owners, but with the right tyres it was more than capable. I didn't think I'd get on with it and, despite having said I would not buy another KTM (or even another new bike), I went out and did just that.

The striking colours helped to sell it: deep blue body and KTM emblazoned across the tank in white, all decked out with bright orange crash bars. The unbreakable suspension and businesslike wheels couldn't go unnoticed, but, overwhelmingly, it was the certainty that this bike was made for chewing through Moroccan dirt that tipped the scales. For years I'd dreamed of such a trip and thought if I didn't buy that bike right then, I may never get to Dakar. I may not anyway, but now I know that I can if I want it enough.

The '990' final edition, was the last of the boldly styled KTM desert racers. It was surprisingly more manageable than my previous 640. I could get the balls of both feet down without the need for any modifications, although it was still tall. The bike came with a side stand as well as a centre stand, symmetrical silencers that did not melt the mudguard, a better light set up, more efficient fly screen, less noise and vibration from the V-twin engine and of course it was faster than the 640 with, believe it or not, slightly better fuel economy.

The Pirelli Scorpion tyres are duel-purpose, but gave plenty of control when I took the bike up onto the Ridgeway track to see what it was made of. It will lean into a roundabout too, until I'm shaving rubber off the toe of my boot, and those are all of its very good points.

Taking for granted the massive carrying capacity of the bike and the sure fact that it was so comfortable to sit on, hour after hour, on long trips, there are some heavy negatives too. If you fill both tanks full and leave it on the side stand, then petrol will be draining from the overflow before you get back from paying. If you adjust your chain to the correct tension before you set out on a short ride then that is perfect – but if you ride for an hour in Mediterranean temperatures, you'd better have spanners handy 'cos it will inexplicably tightened right up.

The short memory of the gel battery is annoying; the clever and expensive maintenance charger the shop sold me won't bring it back once it has lost its starting power. If there is a steep enough hill nearby with a tarmac surface and you have a heavy pal to give a running start, then the bike itself can do the recharging, but you'd be buggered out in the desert.

The first puncture I got, I tried levers, a club hammer and then even using the bike's own side stand, leaning the weight into the side of the tyre, but I couldn't break the bead from the rim without risking damage to either or both, so that was another trip back into Laguna.

The worst thing was that, soon after I got it, its electrical system immobilised itself. It took KTM UK six or seven months to identify the fault and put it right. I didn't mind as much as I should have, as Laguna supplied me with a string of courtesy bikes to put miles on. This included the £18000 Ducati 1198 Panigale: an awesome machine.

It turned out that the KTM ignition key has a chip in it and the key was not properly machined to be a constant perfect fit, so stopped recognising the ignition block as its own. Bill from the workshop told me that technically my bike should never have worked when it left the factory.

One thing they didn't mention in the sales room was that the KTM 990 drinks a litre of a specific grade of engine oil, made in Switzerland, for every thousand miles you travel. But when all's said and done it is an incredible machine, as long as you have a back-up plan. It will cover vast distances at a high cruising speed over a variety of surfaces, hauling as much as you need to carry – but when you break down you've had it.

I've been riding out long distances for quite some years now, eating up the miles with one or two companions, or out there alone just seeing how far I can get from our island, with it all still being fun. There's a lot of Europe to cover and endless places to discover. Then there are the old favourites I find myself back at, Triberg in the Black Forest, L'Scala in Cataluña: the kind of places where you get the feeling that you're home for a few days, and it doesn't matter what's happening tomorrow. They say 'Never look back'; well I do, but I don't stay put long enough to stop me looking forward as well. Africa is still out there.

I had been throwing small parties again, for the faithful, each year before Del went off to Australia. Big bonfires, dangerous fireworks, some fighting, laughing and a variety of obscure barbecued animals thrown in, mostly shot by myself. They were small gatherings at first and no one even questioned why there was no music. There was noise alright, but it was mostly all about reminiscing on times gone by.

Then one day I happened across Knuckles, walking through Ashford with a guitar on his back, he was on his way to the Beaver Inn for a music session. We chatted for a bit and he pointed out where Martin's house was, just up the road, 'That one with the black door.'

I'd bumped into White Trash Andy, at a bike auto jumble earlier the same year and was still in touch with Chip and Fat Rob, so I called them all down for a barbecue, as I'd say. It was a good night, Knuckles didn't show, but Martin turned up and brought along Allen Lewis from the good old days.

Allen was a decent bloke, used to ride a Z750 when Guy had the Castle; I think Guy bought it off him for customising actually. I remember the first time I met Al; he was telling me that you could make wine out of anything, including stinging nettles and teabags.

For that party I had built a huge pyramid from maybe two hundred wooden fruit boxes on the top of a forty-foot earth mound I'd built in the back field. The idea was that if people turned up late, they would be guided in by a beacon that could be seen for miles around.

Knuckles stepped away from the bike scene years ago, but it would be nice to get him over some day, playing some Dylan type guitar ballads, I think that's his style.

Along came 2014, the Chinese astrological Year of the Horse, the sign I was born under. This year was when it all came together for me, inside as well as out there on the road. The summer started off with Al's 50<sup>th</sup> birthday party at Ashford rugby club.

There must have been two hundred people there: so many old faces, people I'd not seen for decades, and some I had come across here and there over the last thirty years. Trog, Jez, Klumsy to name a few.

There were other faces I knew, that had been a part of the whole scene all along and still were. It was the sort of society where a nickname was all you needed, mine had been 'Mad Jim'. There had been no need to enquire about people's full names or even their real ones; anyway, I suppose I had thought the crowd would always be there.

Some faces were unmistakable, despite the hair loss and wrinkles, some seemed little changed. It was euphoric and sad at the same time. I loved this so much, but mourned the loss of a carefree youth, and the blinkered values we'd all shared. The band played *Radar Love*, while we sprawled on the decking outside in the orange twilight haze of smoke and alcohol, talking about anything and nothing.

Weeks later I was on board another ferry bound for Santander. I'd set off with Will and Derek along the south coast, camping on the edge of Dartmoor, before dropping down into Plymouth to catch our sailing.

There were thrills and spills along the way and one or two tantrums. Del smashed a tea set, tripping over on his face in a crowded café garden in Devon. In Spain I set fire to my pants while making a cup of tea, as well as riding down a storm drain attempting to escape from a lady of the road. I lost my dignity and ended up hopelessly trapped in a concrete culvert full of mud and broken glass, whilst getting no sympathy from my companions.

Will half drowned himself trying out cable wakeboarding at a lake in France; he'd had a go despite the fact he'd never actually learned to swim.

The party came to an end in Switzerland, when Will's clutch cable snapped and, despite a pretty reasonable repair, he didn't want to risk the Susten pass.

I wouldn't give it up though. We did originally plan to meet up in Germany once I'd cleared the mountains, but it wasn't to be and I ended up riding north on my own, while they turned straight for Calais.

That ride through the Black Forest on a warm June afternoon was the best bit. The road was good and smooth, and the bends were perfectly engineered. Keeping my own pace, I could use the KTM the way it wanted to run. The dappled sunlight, the green forest and the sound and feel of the 1000cc V-twin engine eating into the twists and turns. It was just so good.

I made it up to Longuyan that night, just short of the Belgian line around sunset, turned into a stubble field, set my tent up behind a hedge and I was done.

I got out on the road bright and early for the remaining five-hour haul along to Calais, keeping off the motorway till the end. That road across rolling green countryside is a great one, mostly straight, with repeating fast stretches of up to a mile a piece, broken by blind summits like the swells of the ocean.

I don't mind the short crossing back to Dover; there are plenty of ferries going most of the time and it's quite satisfying to be looking towards the White Cliffs at the end of a 3,000-mile jaunt across Europe. I don't ever want to stop doing it.

I love the freedom of riding out on my own, but I still need the camaraderie of those first best friends. We need to get out together, every once in a while, to keep the old times close, or memories fade and people forget what it was that made us feel so alive. You can never get that same bond as with those first few friends you had, when you stood side by side and dared the rest of the world to meet you head on.

# CHAPTER THIRTY

## *Unexpected pleasures*

B ikers are comrades out on the road, and that's what makes it remarkable. I have met so many out there, complete strangers who you never forget, one or two who surprise you as well.

Down there on the ferry deck, loaded up and preparing to ride out on a new trip into northern Spain at Bilbao, I noticed a pretty large grizzly looking bloke securing his luggage on a 2300cc Triumph Rocket 3. He was sporting all the warning signs to show us his allegiance with 'the Big Red Machine' AKA the Hells Angels MC. The man was riding solo and I ignored his presence, a few bikes ahead of mine in the queue. I keep myself to myself: just not interested in that stuff anymore.

This was October 2015, just a week after my final departure from Kent Police. People think police officers all retire with nice pensions and smug grins; well I like to think I sacked myself, by resignation to the fact that the service wouldn't allow me to make a difference, not in any way I deemed to be worth the money they paid me.

Anyway, I would ride off the boat, full of my own plans and be heading south for the African coast; it was sort of like a release from the 'open prison' environment I'd had myself trapped in all those years. People also tend to think that a warrant card must be a handy thing to be carrying around, but to me it had been more like an ankle tag, or a loyalty card where responsibility runs only one way; no one imagines it to be a form of ownership, but that was my experience of it all.

Coming out of the port and skirting Bilbao, the road system is quite intense and you have to keep a string of directions in your head because the only places you can safely stop and look at a map are at the toll tunnels, if you're at the wrong one then it's too late already. I was going east and south and at every toll stop I would either pass the Triumph or he would pass me – and we would ignore each other. I kept seeing that bike in my rear-view mirror and then it would roar past me whenever I stopped to check the map. Then half an hour later I would catch up somehow and he'd still be on my road!

Finally, about sixty miles in, I thought we'd taken different routes, but then I heard the big Triumph and he pulled up alongside me at a traffic light, leaned over and said,

'Where *are* you going?' I think the bloke was as suspicious as I was.

It was late in the afternoon and had started to rain a little, it would have been odd not to share a bit of road knowledge as we were clearly set on the same route; he was going to meet the coast at Valencia and so was I. I said I would maybe drop off at a stop I knew outside Soria, as I didn't want to miss the experience by riding through all that great countryside in the dark.

We both needed petrol so happened across each other again at the first station we then came to. He was okay, despite the red and white colours he was wearing – I knew what he was, but he knew nothing about me as we rode on together.

A turn off from the N111 led us into the small municipality called Garray, where I knew there were some places to stay. We drew a blank at all but one hotel and the thing was, there was only one room available. I wouldn't normally want to share a hotel room with a complete stranger from a psychopathic biker gang – but there we were... And he had this huge holdall bag strapped to the back of his bike that he was very protective over; whatever it contained was valuable, I knew, it weighed a ton and it wasn't camping gear.

In the real Spain, outside the British tourist resorts (which is most of the country), you can't get to order dinner before 9pm. There was nothing for it but to head for the hotel bar. After about half an hour I thought 'Fuck it' and volunteered that I'd been a copper. I didn't tell him I'd known friends in the Outlaws MC as well though – the two clubs being bitter enemies and sworn to kill one another whenever required to.

We'd ridden together and were now drinking together in a foreign land, just two English bikers, nothing more. I didn't ask John what was in that bag, not that I wasn't curious though, and I still am.

I will say that for a veteran 1%er, my new comrade obviously had a cosy side to him, despite the threatening image. John checked in with his 'Ol' lady' back in Manchester, morning noon and night. I never phoned home once the whole trip away. I don't know what that says about either of us but that's just me.

The ride south the next day was great fun; passing through some real cowboy country with scrubby hills, cactuses and plenty of vultures. John knew the route and we kept off the big roads, passing by dusty places like Calatayud, Daroca and Calamocha. Somewhere along that route I saw the vultures circling low and dropping to a patch of scrub by the side of the road ahead. John was riding ahead of me and one of those things (it was the size of a turkey) came up, off from its meal and flew straight into the path of the Triumph. John swerved and ducked, I'd thought it was going to take him out, but he made it through okay.

At Teruel we stopped for some lunch at a roadside place, where a bottle of rioja came as part of the meal, despite the countries strict drink-driving laws. It's a great country away from the coast, I've stopped at petrol stations out there that serve beer on tap!

John put me up at the villa complex he was building when we got down to the Costa Blanca and we went out for dinner at an English place where he knew the crowd. It was funny when some old East-London lag came to join us for the after-dinner conversation, and after bragging a bit about how he was making his money he turned to me and said,

'You ain't old bill, are you?'

'Yes, I was last week', I said, and we fell about laughing.

Dénia was nice enough but I didn't hang around the next day. I was gone – off on my own journey. I won't forget that couple of days though, and what I'd got from John was a little bit of unexpected humanity from somewhere I wasn't anticipating.

On my way back up from Gibraltar, heading for the British winter, I met a couple of 'adventure bikers' on BMWs while I waited to board my ferry. Mick and Al had just come from the Bardenas Reales, a genuine bit of desert in Navarra Province. I don't know how I'd kept missing that place; I'd bypassed the area several times while riding Northern Spain over the years.

I met Mick a year later, at the National Motorcycle Museum

outside Birmingham, and ended up buying a load of Yamaha XT660 extras, that would turn my newly acquired Ténéré into a machine better fitted to do a desert trail.

# CONCLUSIONS

The story hasn't ended yet, and I won't let it.

In 2018 Kawasaki brought out the Z900RS, a retro modern version of the original 1970s superbike. I came close to buying one and haven't ruled it out yet – the Café version is really appealing and, for my money, beats Triumph's own retro entry: the new 1200cc Thruxton R. I watched the Kwak demolish all competitors at the Café Cup, held at the end of that year at Lydden near Dover. Charlie Boorman was riding the Thruxton, he did alright I thought, but the picture I wanted in the pits after the race was bright green with a white stripe.

2019 brought together the Mad Max 40th anniversary meeting at Maryborough racetrack in Victoria State Australia… I just had to go.

It was a bit of an odd do, just a one-day event with, mostly replica, cars and bikes from the films, lots of people in costume too. Maryborough is outside Clunes where the original film was made – there and on those long sweeping roads surrounded by dry farmlands and emptiness.

I knew that a great friend of mine, and old Ashford girl, Susan Parker, was living close to Melbourne – although I hadn't seen her since the early nineties. We drove out to the racetrack and camped at the event. It was a 40-degree-heat-wave, and everyone was in black T-shirts! A small can of ice-cold Victoria Bitter cost $7-$9 and we were on it for ten hours – while the V8 engines throbbed and roared out on the track. Wasteland warriors partied in the dust and the Great Humongous goaded the free world to ruin.

I even got to meet Jim Goose. A few of the original actors and stuntmen were there and a pair of them drove a pursuit special through two empty caravans, to replicate a scene from the first film.

I had, at first, wanted to turn up to the event on a Kawasaki Z900, and I brought my riding gear for that purpose. Sue hadn't been on a bike for an age and didn't have any stuff anyway, as it happened the three-hour-drive was just what we needed, to catch up on how each of us had been striding through life since we'd both left Sellindge behind.

I couldn't be there on that coast without riding the Great Ocean Road before I left the country, so I hired a Harley Sportster 1200 and went out and did it. I had never owned, or even ridden a Harley before. Although it wasn't my kind of bike, I did find it fun for a couple of days. The first day was blistering heat, then cloud and drizzle set in; South Australia has a weird old climate.

I had a couple of spare days, before flying on, and happened across a skydive centre while taking a walk along St Kilda bay. It was pretty much on the toss of a coin, as I said to myself, I'd do it if there was a free space that same day. Twenty minutes later I was being kitted out with the jump suit and we were off to the airstrip.

I hadn't been up in a Cesna since my flying days, more than twenty years gone, but it felt okay making the spiral climb to fifteen thousand feet.

When it came to my time there was not a lot to think on really. I didn't look down, the Ruskie strapped to my back just tipped us both out and the force of the air took over. I do believe that was one of the greatest things I've ever done

– terrifying because I had no control over what was happening – and I don't particularly want to do it again either.

When I got back to Kent, the opportunity came to buy, from another ex-cop, a proper old rat bike. It was a 1970s Z: a four-cylinder 750 engine, fitted into a modified Z650 frame. It runs, but there's work to do on it.

Emu Creek Bridge, an hour outside Melbourne, is the place where, in the film, Max catches up with Johnny the boy and it all ends in a fireball. It was a hard place to find, even once I got to the vicinity. As it happened some luck fell into place and I got led to the turn-off by a friendly Aussie, driving a new Ford Falcon. It was as much as the Sportster could do to keep him in sight as he was leaving me for dust.

When I came over the brow and looked down onto that bit of tarmac which snakes across the low-profile bridge, it surprised me a little. It was so obviously that same image from the film, the place hadn't changed in forty years and it was just as deserted…It was perfect.

*When the metal is hot and the engine is hungry*
*And we're all about to see the light…*

*Bat Out Of Hell,* by Meat Loaf

## THE END

If you have enjoyed this book, then you will love its
companion volume:

## WHEELS OF STEEL

– a rollercoaster ride of adventures by road and by rail –

## PROLOGUE

Chip was taking us out to the Bull in Bethersden; he was
driving the car he had just bought that day. Music – one
of Tony's tapes went into the cassette player and it ate it, the
dashboard started smoking and there was a scramble to pick
the thing out and chuck it through the open window.

The Bull was a nice country pub – you'd think by the look
of it; picnic tables and window boxes. It probably *was* on a
Sunday afternoon, but on a Friday night that summer it was
the newest and greatest biker hang out. Anyone into the nomad
scene would get down there at some point; it was mobility and
the ability to not give a fuck. The town was for pretty boys and
tarts in 'ra ra' skirts, but we ruled the lanes and the out of the
way places; in worn out jeans and army shirts.

On the way back we took a short cut through a farm yard
where Chip ploughed through the edge of a muck heap, just for
a laugh, sending fresh manure into the air as well as ramming it
through the front grill – the fan throwing it all over the engine
so we got the hit coming through the air vents. We ended up
in an open field, racing around after rabbits in the headlights,
doors ajar and everyone ready to jump out and catch their

own if we got close enough. Of course, we never got close to anything, but we did manage to get ourselves stuck. With everyone out there pushing and Chip screaming the engine, burning deep ruts, in the soft turf to get us back up the slope, we were going to make it. Then the engine cut out.

Lifting the bonnet in the dark we could see one contributing factor; the exhaust manifold was glowing bright orange and our hunk of metal needed a break.

The engine wouldn't turn on the key, so there was nothing for it but to push the thing back down the hill and hope we could bump it into life before the farmer or the cops arrived. The motor popped and burbled and then took on some life, and three leather clad rejects ran along behind, not daring to stop 'til we got it around and up to the gate. We were half ruined by the time we slouched back into the vehicle, sweating like apes, and Chip was the only one still laughing as he turned round to us and said: *I think it's about time I was getting a new car.*